University of Stirling Library, FK9 4LA
Tel: 01786 467220

LONG LOAN

Please **RETURN** or **RENEW**
no later than the date on the receipt
Subject to recall if requested

THE MOTIVATIONAL IMPACT OF NICOTINE AND ITS ROLE IN TOBACCO USE

The Nebraska Symposium on Motivation
Series Editor: **Debra A. Hope,** *University of Nebraska, Lincoln, Nebraska*

MOTIVATIONAL ASPECTS OF PREJUDICE AND RACISM
Edited by Cynthia Willis-Esqueda

THE MOTIVATIONAL IMPACT OF NICOTINE AND ITS ROLE
IN TOBACCO USE
Edited by Rick A. Bevins and Anthony R. Caggiula

THE MOTIVATIONAL IMPACT OF NICOTINE AND ITS ROLE IN TOBACCO USE

Edited by

Rick A. Bevins
Department of Psychology,
University of Nebraska-Lincoln

and

Anthony R. Caggiula
Department of Psychology,
University of Pittsburgh

Basement

Editors:

Rick A. Bevins
Department of Psychology
University of Nebraska
Lincoln, NE
USA
rbevins1@unl.edu

Anthony R. Caggiula
Department of Psychology
University of Pittsburgh, PA,
USA
tonypsy@pitt.edu

ISBN: 978-0-387-78748-0   e-ISBN: 978-0-387-78749-7
DOI: 10.1007/978-0-387-78748-0

Library of Congress Control Number: 2008937207

Preface

The volume editors for this 55th volume of the Nebraska Symposium on Motivation are Rick Bevins and Tony Caggiula. The volume editors coordinated the symposium that lead to this volume including selecting and inviting the contributors and coordinating all aspects of editing. My thanks go to the Rick and Tony and to our contributors for excellent presentations and chapters.

This Symposium series is supported by funds provided by the Chancellor of the University of Nebraska-Lincoln, Harvey Perlman, and by funds given in memory of Professor Harry K. Wolfe to the University of Nebraska Foundation by the late Professor Cora L. Friedline. We are extremely grateful for the Chancellor's generous support to the Symposium series and for the University of Nebraska Foundation's support via the Friedline bequest. This symposium volume, like those in the recent past, is dedicated to the memory of Professor Wolfe, who brought psychology to the University of Nebraska. After studying with Professor Wilhelm Wundt, Professor Wolfe returned to his native state, to establish the first undergraduate laboratory in psychology in the nation. As a student at Nebraska, Professor Friedline studied psychology under Professor Wolfe.

Lincoln, Nebraska   Debra A. Hope

Contributors

Michael T. Bardo
Department of Psychology, University of Kentucky, Lexington, KY 40536-0082, USA, mbardo@uky.edu

Rick A. Bevins
Department of Psychology, 238 Burnett Hall, University of Nebraska-Lincoln, Lincoln, NE 68588-0308, USA, rbevins1@unl.edu

Darlene H. Brunzell
Department of Pharmacology & Toxicology, Robert Blackwell Smith Building, Virginia Commonwealth University Richmond, Virginia 23298-0613, USA

Anthony R. Caggiula
Department of Psychology, University of Pittsburgh, Pittsburgh, PA 15260, USA, Tonypsy@pitt.edu

Nadia Chaudhri
Ernest Gallo Clinic and Research Center, University of California, San Francisco, San Francisco, CA

Peter A. Crooks
Department of Pharmaceutical Sciences, College of Pharmacy, University of Kentucky, Lexington, KY 40536-0082, USA

John A. Dani
Department of Neuroscience, Menninger Department of Psychiatry and Behavioral Sciences, Baylor College of Medicine, Houston, Texas 77030, USA, jdani@cns.bcm.edu

Eric C. Donny
Department of Psychology, University of Pittsburgh, Pittsburgh, PA 15260, USA

Linda P. Dwoskin
Department of Pharmaceutical Sciences, College of Pharmacy, University of Kentucky, Lexington, KY 40536-0082, USA, ldwoskin@email.uky.edu

Katherine C. Goedeker
Department of Psychological Sciences, Purdue University, West Lafayette,
IN 47907 USA

B. Matthew Joyce
Department of Pharmaceutical Sciences, College of Pharmacy, University
of Kentucky, Lexington, KY 40536-0082, USA

Xiu Liu
Department of Psychology, University of Pittsburgh, Pittsburgh, PA 15260, USA

Athina Markou
Department of Psychiatry, School of Medicine, University of California, San Diego,
La Jolla, CA 92093-0603, USA, amarkou@ucsd.edu

Nichole M. Neugebauer
Department of Psychology, University of Kentucky, Lexington, KY 40536-0082,
USA

Matthew I. Palmatier
Department of Psychology, Kansas State University, 492 Bluemont Hall,
Manhattan, Kansas 66506-5302, USA

Neil E. Paterson
Department of Psychiatry, School of Medicine, University of California, San Diego,
La Jolla, CA 92093-0603, USA

Kenneth A. Perkins
Western Psychiatric Institute & Clinic, University of Pittsburgh School of Medicine,
Pittsburgh, PA 15213, USA, perkinska@upmc.edu

Marina R. Picciotto
Department of Psychiatry, Yale University School of Medicine, New Haven,
CT 06508, USA, Marina.Picciotto@Yale.edu

Marharyta Pivavarchyk
Department of Pharmaceutical Sciences, College of Pharmacy, University
of Kentucky, Lexington, KY 40536-0082, USA

Andon N. Placzek
Department of Neuroscience, Menninger Department of Psychiatry and Behavioral
Sciences, Baylor College of Medicine, Houston, Texas 77030, USA

Jed E. Rose
Center for Nicotine and Smoking Cessation Research, Duke University Medical
Center, Durham, NC 27705, USA, rose0003@mc.duke.edu

Paul Schnur
National Institute on Drug Abuse, National Institutes of Health, Department
of Health and Human Services, Bethesda, MD 20892, Bethesda, MD 20892, USA

Alan F. Sved
Department of Neuroscience, University of Pittsburgh, Pittsburgh, PA 15260, USA

Stephen T. Tiffany
Department of Psychology, University at Buffalo, the State University of New York, Buffalo, NY 14260-4110, USA, stiffany@buffalo.edu

Mathew W. Warthen
Department of Psychology, University of Utah, Salt Lake City, UT84112, USA

Zhenfa Zhang
Department of Pharmaceutical Sciences, College of Pharmacy, University of Kentucky, Lexington, KY 40536-0082, USA

Guangrong Zheng
Department of Pharmaceutical Sciences, College of Pharmacy, University of Kentucky, Lexington, KY 40536-0082, USA

Contents

Chapter 1
Nicotine, Tobacco Use, and the 55th Nebraska Symposium on Motivation

Rick A. Bevins and Anthony R. Caggiula

Tobacco use is a worldwide health problem. As stated by Mackay and Ericksen (2002), "No other consumer product is as dangerous, or kills as many people. Tobacco kills more than AIDS, legal drugs, illegal drugs, road accidents, murder, and suicide combined" (p. 36). Imagine the lives saved, and the amount of pain, emotional suffering, and fiscal burden alleviated, if we could devise approaches that helped current tobacco users quit or remain abstinent, and prevented new smokers from emerging. Although these idealistic goals are worth pursuing, improving cessation rates by only a small fraction or making small gains in preventing people from experimenting with tobacco, would nevertheless translate into significant improvement in the health and well-being of countless thousands worldwide as well as financial savings to employers, government institutions, and the heath care system. Even such small, incremental steps require a concerted and co-ordinated effort by basic scientists, clinical researchers and practitioners, and policy makers to discover the basis of tobacco dependence and apply that knowledge to the imple- mentation of prevention policies and smoking cessation aids. This year's Nebraska Symposium on Motivation was devoted to research on nicotine, which is believed to form the basis of tobacco use and dependence.

For over 50 years, The Nebraska Symposium on Motivation has provided a forum for discussing the concept of motivation and its application in understanding behavior (Benjamin & Jones, 1979; Bevins & Bardo, 2004). Although researchers and theorists who have participated in the symposium over the years have disagreed about the meaning and potential usefulness of this construct (e.g., Birch, 1961; Gallistel, 1975; Schneirla, 1959), one conclusion that emerges from this scientific dialog is that at least some of the processes captured within the definition of this construct are likely to mediate key aspects of behavior.

In the area of drug addiction and dependence, there appears to be an increase in use of motivation and related constructs (e.g., incentive processes, cravings, drug seeking, etc.,). For the 50th Nebraska Symposium on Motivation, Bevins and Bardo

R.A. Bevins
Department of Psychology, 238 Burnett Hall, University of Nebraska-Lincoln, Lincoln, NE 68588-0308, USA
e-mail: rbevins1@unl.edu

R.A. Bevins, A.R. Caggiula (eds.), *The Motivational Impact of Nicotine and its Role in Tobacco Use*, DOI: 10.1007/978-0-387-78748-0_1, © Springer Science+Business Media, LLC 2009

(2004) did a search on Medline that spanned from 1998 to 2002. The search used the term "motivation" with the word "alcohol," "nicotine," "amphetamine," "heroin," and "cocaine," and found 729 hits. We repeated this simple search for January 2003 to July 2007 and found 1,247 hits. Notably, we re-conducted the 1998 to 2002 search for just "motivation" and "nicotine" and found 141 hits. In the subsequent 5 year window (up to July 2007) this number nearly doubled to 263. An increase was also seen for the co-occurrence of "motivation" and "smoking" (426 to 682) and for "motivation" and "tobacco" (170 to 343). This pattern indicates a need to critically discuss motivation as an explanatory construct, while empirically defining the processes underlying this construct in a manner that avoids tautologies.

For The 55th Nebraska Symposium on Motivation, we gathered leading scientific experts on nicotine dependence and tobacco use on the University of Nebraska-Lincoln campus. The diversity of their expertise (see list of contributors) reflects our bias that effective strategies for decreasing tobacco use and preventing initiation will require a translational approach in which genetic, neurobiological, individual, and cultural factors motivating tobacco use and nicotine dependence are considered. At the symposium, the exchange of empirical and theoretical ideas and the discussion of these ideas were richer and more extensive than we could have imagined. We thank the contributors and all those who attended the symposium. Further, we hope that the collection of chapters in the 55th Volume of the Nebraska Symposium on Motivation will continue to stimulate this exchange of ideas and discussion among its readers. Only through open communication and scientific testing of ideas that emerge from this conversation we will be able to eventually eliminate the number one preventable cause of premature death—tobacco use and nicotine dependence.

Acknowledgments The Nebraska Symposium on Motivation is supported largely by funds donated in memory of Professor Harry K. Wolfe to the University of Nebraska Foundation by the late Professor Cora L. Friedline. We are grateful to the late Professor Friedline for this bequest and to the University of Nebraska Foundation for continued financial support for the symposium. Additional support comes from the Chancellor Harvey Perlman and the senior administrators of the University of Nebraska-Lincoln. We also thank Claudia Price-Decker for her continued effort in co-ordinating every aspect of the symposium. The quality and impact of the symposium, and in turn this Volume, would be severely diminished without her tireless work and unparalleled eye for detail. Finally, we thank Matthew Palmatier and the Labbies in the Behavioral Neuropharmacology Laboratory at UNL for all their help.

References

Benjamin, L. T., & Jones, M. R. (1979). From motivational theory to social cognitive development: Twenty-five years of the Nebraska Symposium. In R. A. Dienstbier (Ed.), *Nebraska Symposium on Motivation, 1978* (pp. ix–xix). Lincoln NE: University of Nebraska Press.

Bevins, R. A., & Bardo, M. T. (2004). Introduction: Motivation, drug abuse, and 50 years of theoretical and empirical inquiry. In R. A. Bevins & M. T. Bardo (Eds.), *Motivational Factors in the Etiology of Drug Abuse, Volume 50 of the Nebraska Symposium on Motivation* (pp. ix–xv). Lincoln NE: University of Nebraska Press.

Birch, D. (1961). A motivational interpretation of extinction. In M. R. Jones (Ed.), *Nebraska Symposium on Motivation, 1961* (pp. 179–197). Lincoln NE: University of Nebraska Press.

Gallistel, C. R. (1975). Motivation as a central organizing process: The psychophysical approach to it functional and neurophysiological analysis. In J. K. Cole & T. B. Sonderegger (Eds.), *Nebraska Symposium on Motivation, 1974* (pp. 183–250). Lincoln NE: University of Nebraska Press.

Mackay, J., & Eriksen, M. (2002). *Tobacco Atlas*. Geneva Switzerland: World Health Organization.

Schneirla, T. C. (1959). An evolutionary and developmental theory of biphasic processes underlying approach and withdrawal. In M. R. Jones, (Ed.), *Nebraska Symposium on Motivation, 1959* (pp. 1–42). Lincoln NE: University of Nebraska Press.

Chapter 2
Synaptic Plasticity Within Midbrain Dopamine Centers Contributes to Nicotine Addiction

Andon N. Placzek and John A. Dani

Introduction to the Health Problem

Approximately one-third of the world's adult population uses tobacco, making nicotine addiction a major worldwide health problem. The majority of smokers begin during adolescence, and for those that continue to smoke die from a smoking-related disease (WHO, 1997). In the developing world, smoking-related deaths are on the rise (Peto et al., 1996) and the illness caused by smoking is estimated to be the largest cause of premature deaths in developed nations (Peto, Lopez, Boreham, Thun, & Heath, 1992).

As the primary addictive substance in tobacco smoke (Karan, Dani, & Benowitz, 2003), nicotine has been shown to produce drug-seeking behavior in animals (Corrigall, 1999; Corrigall & Coen, 1989; Di Chiara, 2000; Stolerman & Shoaib, 1991). Nicotine is also known to have effects similar to other addictive drugs, including reinforcement of self-administration, increased locomotor activity (Bevins, Eurek, & Besheer, 2005), enhanced reward from intracranial stimulation, and reinforcement of place preference (Clarke, 1990, 1991; Corrigall, 1999; Dani & De Biasi, 2001; Dani & Harris, 2005; Dani & Heinemann, 1996; Dani, Ji, & Zhou, 2001; Di Chiara, 2000; Mansvelder & McGehee, 2002; Stolerman & Jarvis, 1995; Stolerman & Shoaib, 1991). Like other commonly abused drugs, a withdrawal syndrome is caused by nicotine cessation, which can be relieved by nicotine replacement (Stolerman & Jarvis, 1995). In humans, only about one in five attempts to quit smoking are successful and success usually only after repeated attempts (Balfour, Wright, Benwell, & Birrell, 2000).

J.A. Dani
Department of Neuroscience, Menninger Department of Psychiatry and Behavioral Sciences, Baylor College of Medicine, Houston, Texas 77030, USA
e-mail: jdani@cns.bcm.edu

R.A. Bevins, A.R. Caggiula (eds.), *The Motivational Impact of Nicotine and its Role in Tobacco Use*, DOI: 10.1007/978-0-387-78748-0_2, © Springer Science+Business Media, LLC 2009

Midbrain Dopaminergic Systems

The cellular and molecular processes that are targeted by addictive drugs have a normal adaptive function in the brain that is now beginning to be understood in greater detail. Midbrain dopaminergic systems are involved in the reinforcement of behaviors linked to salient environmental stimuli. Our understanding of the nature of dopamine (DA) signaling has evolved from that of a mediator of the experience of reward, to a reinforcer of rewarding behavior (Berke & Hyman, 2000; Di Chiara, 2000; Schultz, Dayan, & Montague, 1997). The concentrations of DA in the nucleus accumbens (NAc) do not scale directly with reward, but rather the DA signal is associated with novelty or gives an indication of deviation of environmental stimuli from the organism's expectations. Dopamine is thus thought to contribute to the associative learning of survival-related behaviors as an internal representation of environmental saliency develops (Schultz et al., 1997).

As the addiction process progresses, addictive drugs act upon the dopaminergic systems to reinforce actions and environmental cues associated with drug-taking (Balfour et al., 2000; Corrigall, Franklin, Coen, & Clarke, 1992; Dani & Bertrand, 2007; Dani & De Biasi, 2001; Dani & Harris, 2005; Dani et al., 2001; Di Chiara, 2000; Karan et al., 2003; Nestler, 1993; Nisell, Nomikos, & Svensson, 1994; Pontieri, Tanda, Orzi, & Di Chiara, 1996; Spanagel & Weiss, 1999; Wonnacott, Drasdo, Sanderson, & Rowell, 1990) Either the administration of DA antagonists or lesioning of the DA neurons or their target cells in the NAc has been shown to reduce nicotine self-administration, indicating the significance of these systems in nicotine addiction (Corrigall, 1999; Corrigall & Coen, 1989; Corrigall, Coen, & Adamson, 1994; Corrigall et al., 1992; Di Chiara, 2000). Nicotine is known to directly stimulate midbrain DA neurons by activating nicotinic acetylcholine receptors (nAChRs; Calabresi, Lacey, & North, 1989; Clarke, Schwartz, Paul, Pert, & Pert, 1985; Dani et al., 2001; Grenhoff & Johnson, 1996; Mansvelder & McGehee, 2002; Picciotto et al., 1998; Pidoplichko, DeBiasi, Williams, & Dani, 1997; Pidoplichko et al., 2004; Wooltorton, Pidoplichko, Broide, & Dani, 2003) and stimulate the prolonged release of DA in the NAc of rats (Fig. 2.1; Clarke, 1991; Nisell et al., 1994; Pidoplichko et al., 2004; Pontieri et al., 1996). In addition to its direct effects on midbrain DA neurons, nicotine can also act on presynaptic targets to regulate DA signaling in striatal regions such as the NAc (Jones, Bolam, & Wonnacott, 2001; Wonnacott, Kaiser, Mogg, Soliakov, & Jones, 2000; Zhou, Liang, & Dani, 2001). Compared to acute exposures to addictive drugs, chronically administered addictive substances produce adaptations that reflect what are presumably homeostatic responses to sustained exposure to the drug (Berke & Hyman, 2000; Dani & Harris, 2005; Watkins, Koob, & Markou, 2000). In the case of nicotine, chronic exposure causes an increase in the number of nAChRs, probably a result of prolonged receptor desensitization (Buisson & Bertrand, 2001).

The behavioral phenomena of drug tolerance and dependence are, in part, explained by the cellular and molecular changes caused by the addictive drug. By contrast, these changes are not sufficient to account for cravings that can persist long after an addict has ceased to self-administer a particular drug. In these cases,

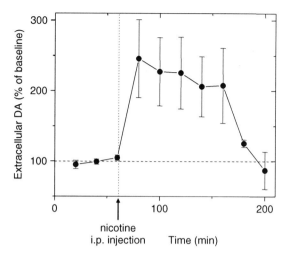

Fig. 2.1 In vivo microdialysis indicates that nicotine boosts the dopamine (DA) concentration in the nucleus accumbens (NAc) shell for more than one hour. Samples were taken every 20 min from a wake freely moving rat ($n = 3$) before and after i.p. injection of 0.6 mg/kg nicotine. Separate injections of saline did not produce a DA signal above baseline [Reproduced and adapted from Pidoplichko et al., (2004)]

contextual cues that permeate the experience of drug users contribute to the likelihood of future drug cravings and possibly relapse even after long periods of abstinence. The salient features of the drug user's environment that are repeatedly paired with drug experience are eventually able to motivate drug use on their own (Balfour et al., 2000; Berke & Hyman, 2000; Dani & Harris, 2005; Dani et al., 2001; Di Chiara, 2000). Addictive drugs are able to initiate and modulate normal synaptic mechanisms, such as those that result in synaptic plasticity and as a result previously neutral stimuli are associated with the rewarding aspects of drug abuse.

Action of Nicotine at Nicotinic Receptors in the Midbrain

The collective evidence describing the effects of nicotine on the midbrain DA systems can be summarized in this oversimplified way: nicotine acts upon midbrain DA neurons and increases DA levels in the NAc resulting in the reinforcement of drug use. This end result is an important contributor to the establishment of addictive behavior. Either DA antagonists delivered to, or lesions of the NAc have been shown to reduce nicotine self-administration, indicating a blunting of the rewarding effects of nicotine (Corrigall, 1999).

Nicotine has been known for some time to stimulate neurons of the ventral midbrain (Calabresi et al., 1989; Clarke et al., 1985; Dani et al., 2001; Grenhoff & Johnson, 1996; Mansvelder & McGehee, 2002; Picciotto et al., 1998; Pidoplichko et al., 1997; Pidoplichko et al., 2004; Wooltorton et al., 2003), and to increase DA release from those neurons which project to the NAc (Fig. 2.1; Clarke, 1991; Nisell et al., 1994; Pidoplichko et al., 2004; Pontieri et al., 1996). The act of smoking a cigarette delivers approximately 50–500 nM nicotine to the brain over the course of seconds to minutes (Benowitz, Porchet, & Jacob, 1989; Gourlay & Benowitz, 1997; Henningfield, Stapleton, Benowitz, Grayson, & London, 1993; Karan et al., 2003). Low concentrations of nicotine persist in the brain for several hours.

In a midbrain slice preparation, bath-applied nicotine at 100 nM causes a depolarizing (activating) current in ventral tegmental area (VTA) DA neurons (Fig. 2.2) mediated initially by the direct activation of nAChRs (Pidoplichko et al., 1997). Despite this initial activating effect, this same concentration of nicotine (well within the range of what a smoker would experience) also produces profound nAChR desensitization as evidenced by reduced responsiveness to subsequent agonist application. The nAChR desensitization is revealed by brief puffer applications of acetylcholine (ACh at 1 mM for 30 ms, downward arrows in Fig. 2.2). Prior to nicotine application, ACh produces a current of roughly 50 pA (Fig. 2.2), but after the 3-min bath application of 100 nM nicotine, the current evoked by ACh is almost completely gone (Pidoplichko et al., 1997; Wooltorton et al., 2003). Even though the DA signal measured by microdialysis in the NAc shell is relatively long-lived (Fig. 2.1), the nAChRs on DA neurons are largely desensitized within a relatively short time (Fig. 2.2). In order to explain the long-lasting DA signal in the NAc produced by nicotine, it is necessary to consider how nicotine can affect the afferent projections to the VTA DA neurons (Dani et al., 2001; Mansvelder, Keath, & McGehee, 2002; Mansvelder & McGehee, 2000, 2002; Pidoplichko et al., 2004; Wooltorton et al., 2003).

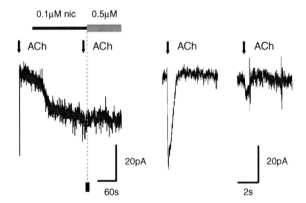

Fig. 2.2 Nicotine, at the concentration experienced by smokers, activates and desensitizes nicotinic acetylcholine receptors (nAChRs). (*Left*) Bath application of 0.1 µM nicotine activated a 17pA current. After 3 min in 0.1 µM nicotine, application of another 0.5 µM activated very little additional current, reflecting receptor desensitization. The *solid rectangle* marks the average size of the current that would have been activated by 0.5 µM nicotine if there had been no desensitization. ACh pressure injections (1 mM, 30 ms, *downward arrows*) were applied before (*left*) and near the end (*right*) of the 0.1 µM nicotine. Those ACh-induced currents are shown on an expanded time scale (*far right*) to illustrate the extent of desensitization. (Reproduced and adapted from Pidoplichko et al., (1997))

In addition to its direct action at DA neurons, nicotine also produces modulatory affects via nAChRs at presynaptic, preterminal, and non-synaptic locations. Neuronal nAChRs are pentameric ligand-gated ion channels that can be assembled from a combination of subunits arising from a relatively large number of gene products, including subunits $\alpha 2- \alpha 10$ and $\beta 2- \beta 4$. Thus, a vast array of functionally different combinations of nAChR subunits can result (Dani & Bertrand, 2007; Jones, Sudweeks, & Yakel, 1999; McGehee & Role, 1995; Role & Berg, 1996; Wonnacott, 1997; Wooltorton et al., 2003). The majority of heteromeric neuronal nAChRs are produced by the combination of five alpha subunits ($\alpha 2- \alpha 6$) and three beta subunits ($\beta 2- \beta 4$). The other major neuronal nAChR subtype contains the $\alpha 7$ subunit ($\alpha 7^*$ nAChRs), which has rapid activation and desensitization kinetics, and is selectively blocked by α-bungarotoxin (α-BTX) or methyllycaconitine (MLA; Alkondon, Pereira, Wonnacott, & Albuquerque, 1992; Castro & Albuquerque, 1995; Gray, Rajan, Radcliffe, Yakehiro, & Dani, 1996). While relatively high agonist concentrations (e.g., 500 μM ACh or nicotine) will cause a rapid desensitization of $\alpha 7^*$ nAChRs, a low affinity for nicotine means that these receptors are able to maintain a steady-state activation in the presence of low concentrations of nicotine, such as those delivered by cigarette smoke (Pidoplichko et al., 2004; Quick & Lester, 2002; Wooltorton et al., 2003).

The DA neurons of the midbrain primarily express nAChRs with relatively slow kinetics and a sensitivity to inhibition by dihydro- β-erythroidine (DHβE; Klink, de Kerchove d'Exaerde, Zoli, & Changeux, 2001; Picciotto et al., 1998; Pidoplichko et al., 1997; Wooltorton et al., 2003) indicating that the predominant nAChR subtype is composed of $\beta 2$-containing ($\beta 2^*$) nAChRs. These $\beta 2$ subunits co-assemble with other nicotinic receptor subunits, specifically $\alpha 4$, $\alpha 6$, and $\alpha 3$ (Charpantier, Barneoud, Moser, Besnard, & Sgard, 1998; Goldner, Dineley, & Patrick, 1997; Klink et al., 2001; Le Novere, Zoli, & Changeux, 1996; Wada, McKinnon, Heinemann, Patrick, & Swanson, 1990; Wada et al., 1989), a conclusion that is supported by studies using $\beta 2$-subunit knockout mice in which midbrain DA neurons have significantly diminished nicotinic receptor-mediated currents (Picciotto et al., 1998; Wooltorton et al., 2003). Although the $\beta 2^*$ nAChRs compose the main nicotinic receptor subtype in midbrain DA neurons, the $\beta 2$-null mice do show a relatively small, MLA-sensitive current with rapid kinetics, indicating a minor amount of $\alpha 7^*$ nAChR expression (Wooltorton et al., 2003).

Nicotine Influences Over Midbrain Synaptic Function

Nicotine, at concentrations approximating those experienced by cigarette smokers, modulates excitatory afferent signaling to midbrain DA neurons. The effect is presynaptic, as evidenced by the fact that nicotine application increases the frequency (but not the amplitude) of spontaneous excitatory postsynaptic currents (sEPSCs; Dani et al., 2001; Mansvelder et al., 2002; Mansvelder & McGehee, 2000, 2002; Pidoplichko et al., 2004). This effect on sEPSC frequency persists during the entire 25-min nicotine delivery period, indicating a lack of significant presynaptic receptor desensitization (Pidoplichko et al., 2004). In addition to enhancing spontaneous excitatory synaptic events, nicotine is also able to increase the amplitude of evoked EPSCs on DA neurons. The nicotine-induced increase in either spontaneous or evoked excitatory currents persists even after nicotine is removed from the bath solution, suggesting the induction of long-term potentiation (Dani et al., 2001; Ji, Lape, & Dani, 2001; Mansvelder et al., 2002; Mansvelder & McGehee, 2000, 2002; Pidoplichko et al., 2004). Similar presynaptic effects mediated by nAChRs have also been demonstrated in other important brain regions, such as the hippocampus (Albuquerque, Pereira, Alkondon, Schrattenholz, & Maelicke, 1997; Dani et al., 2001; Ge & Dani, 2005; Gray et al., 1996; Guo, Tredway, & Chiappinelli, 1998; Ji et al., 2001; Jones et al., 1999; Li, Rainnie, McCarley, & Greene, 1998; McGehee, Heath, Gelber, Devay, & Role, 1995; McGehee & Role, 1995; Radcliffe & Dani, 1998; Radcliffe, Fisher, Gray, & Dani, 1999; Role & Berg, 1996; Wonnacott, 1997). This type of long-lived enhancement of excitatory synaptic transmission onto DA neurons is similar in many respects to the synaptic plasticity that has been linked to learning and memory (Martin, Grimwood, & Morris, 2000).

Nicotine-induced excitation of DA neurons gradually decreases due to desensitization of the predominant β2* nAChR subtypes. However, concurrent nicotine-mediated modulation of afferent synaptic activity permits continued excitation, prolonging the microdialysis DA signal measured in NAc (Fig. 2.1; Clarke, 1991; Corrigall et al., 1992; Dani & De Biasi, 2001; Di Chiara, 1999, 2000; Di Chiara & Imperato, 1988; Imperato, Mulas, & Di Chiara, 1986; Pidoplichko et al., 2004; Pontieri et al., 1996). In summary, smoking a cigarette provides an initial dose of nicotine that activates postsynaptic β2* nAChRs on DA neurons and presynaptic α7* nAChRs located on the excitatory, glutamatergic terminals that project onto the DA neurons (Fig. 2.3). However, the β2* nAChRs significantly desensitize after the initial activation, but the α7* nAChR are not significantly desensitized while a smoker uses a cigarette (Dani et al., 2001; Pidoplichko et al., 2004; Wooltorton et al., 2003). Since α7*-type nAChRs are highly calcium permeable, they often have the combined effect of mediating a direct calcium influx besides causing calcium increase indirectly via voltage-gated calcium channels and via release from intracellular Ca^{2+} stores (Dani et al., 2001; Gray et al., 1996; Ji et al., 2001; Mansvelder et al., 2002; Mansvelder & McGehee, 2000, 2002; McGehee et al., 1995; McGehee & Role, 1995; Radcliffe & Dani, 1998; Rathouz, Vijayaraghavan, & Berg, 1996; Seguela, Wadiche, Dineley-Miller, Dani, & Patrick, 1993). Thus, activation of presynaptic α7* nAChRs results in increased calcium levels in glutamatergic presynaptic terminals, facilitating glutamate release and subsequent synaptic excitation of DA neurons, despite desensitization of the postsynaptic β2* nAChRs expressed by the DA neurons (Fig. 2.3).

According to contemporary models, long-term potentiation (LTP) occurs when activity at presynaptic excitatory inputs coincides with a postsynaptic depolarization to permit calcium influx via NMDA-type glutamate receptors (NMDARs). After nicotine initially excites VTA DA neurons increasing their action potential firing rate, postsynaptic activity is coupled with a nicotine-induced increase in presynaptic glutamatergic afferent excitation. It is this combination of presynaptic and

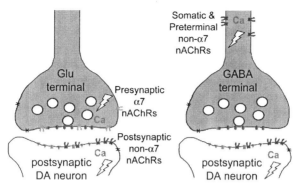

Fig. 2.3 The major sites of influence by nicotinic acetylcholine receptors (nAChR) subtypes at glutamatergic (Glu) and GABAergic synapses onto rodent ventral tegmental area (VTA) dopamine (DA) neurons. Activation of nAChRs induces a local depolarization indicated by *lightning bolts*. This activity may also initiate direct and indirect Ca^{2+} signals. The Ca^{2+} signals can influence subsequent Ca^{2+} release from intracellular stores and initiate intracellular cascades. The size of the Ca^{2+} signals will depend on many factors, including the subtypes of nAChRs that are present and activation versus desensitization by agonists and modulators. The diagram is simplified to show only the major subtypes at each location, however minority subtypes can also be present. Nicotine, as obtained from cigarette smoke, will briefly activate, then begin to significantly desensitize the non-α7 (usually β2*) nAChRs located on DA and GABA neurons. The α7* nAChRs will be activated to some extent, but will not be strongly desensitized by physiological concentrations of nicotine. Thus, the increased excitatory drive via presynaptic α7* nAChR on glutamatergic terminals coupled with the short-lasting increase in DA neuron firing caused by nicotine's direct action creates the coincidence of presynaptic and postsynaptic activity that favors the initiation of synaptic plasticity, such as short-term and long-term potentiation. Thus, multiple synaptic events contribute to the prolonged increased firing by DA neurons [Reproduced and adapted from Pidoplichko et al. (2004)]

postsynaptic coincidence that facilitates the formation of LTP (Dani et al., 2001; Ji et al., 2001; Mansvelder et al., 2002; Mansvelder & McGehee, 2000, 2002; Pidoplichko et al., 2004).

In contrast to the sustained enhancement of excitatory afferent transmission onto VTA DA neurons, nicotine has a qualitatively different effect on the inhibitory, GABAergic inputs. Nicotinic receptor activation at somatic or preterminal sites is known to produce local membrane depolarization sufficient to cause or facilitate action potential firing. In this way, bath application of nicotine may initially increase action potential firing in GABAergic neurons. However, because of the specific subtypes of nicotinic receptors expressed in these inhibitory neurons (primarily the β2* subtype, Fig. 2.3), sustained exposure to bath-applied nicotine causes nAChR desensitization (Dani et al., 2001; Mansvelder et al., 2002; Pidoplichko et al., 2004). This ultimately results in a reduction in the local inhibitory tone, the third part of the synaptic events that further increases the likelihood of nicotine producing LTP in this dopaminergic center.

Thus, the synaptic changes that are brought about by nicotine are very similar to the normal kinds of synaptic plasticity that are thought to contribute to learning and memory: Increased presynaptic calcium concentrations that facilitat excitatory synaptic transmission coupled with an initially strong postsynaptic response, leads to both short-term and long-term potentiation. Nicotine inserts itself into these normally adaptive pathways, favoring potentiation of synaptic activity related to drug-associated behaviors that are ultimately detrimental to the organism. Nicotine is able to misdirect very basic synaptic mechanisms that normally function in the learning and memory process.

References

Albuquerque, E. X., Pereira, E. F., Alkondon, M., Schrattenholz, A., & Maelicke, A. (1997). Nicotinic acetylcholine receptors on hippocampal neurons: Distribution on the neuronal surface and modulation of receptor activity. *Journal of Receptor and Signal Transduction Research, 17*(1–3), 243–266.

Alkondon, M., Pereira, E. F., Wonnacott, S., & Albuquerque, E. X. (1992). Blockade of nicotinic currents in hippocampal neurons defines methyllycaconitine as a potent and specific receptor antagonist. *Molecular Pharmacology, 41*(4), 802–808.

Balfour, D. J., Wright, A. E., Benwell, M. E., & Birrell, C. E. (2000). The putative role of extra-synaptic mesolimbic dopamine in the neurobiology of nicotine dependence. *Behavioural Brain Research, 113*(1–2), 73–83.

Benowitz, N. L., Porchet, H., & Jacob, P., 3rd. (1989). Nicotine dependence and tolerance in man: pharmacokinetic and pharmacodynamic investigations. *Progress in Brain Research, 79,* 279–287.

Berke, J. D., & Hyman, S. E. (2000). Addiction, dopamine, and the molecular mechanisms of memory. *Neuron, 25*(3), 515–532.

Bevins, R. A., Eurek, S., & Besheer, J. (2005). Timing of conditioned responding in a nicotine locomotor conditioning preparation: Manipulations of the temporal arrangement between context cues and drug administration. *Behavioural Brain Research, 159*(1), 135–143.

Buisson, B., & Bertrand, D. (2001). Chronic exposure to nicotine upregulates the human (alpha)4 (beta)2 nicotinic acetylcholine receptor function. *The Journal of Neuroscience, 21*(6), 1819–1829.

Calabresi, P., Lacey, M. G., & North, R. A. (1989). Nicotinic excitation of rat ventral tegmental neurones in vitro studied by intracellular recording. *British Journal of Pharmacology, 98*(1), 135–140.

Castro, N. G., & Albuquerque, E. X. (1995). alpha-Bungarotoxin-sensitive hippocampal nicotinic receptor channel has a high calcium permeability. *Biophysical Journal, 68*(2), 516–524.

Charpantier, E., Barneoud, P., Moser, P., Besnard, F., & Sgard, F. (1998). Nicotinic acetylcholine subunit mRNA expression in dopaminergic neurons of the rat substantia nigra and ventral tegmental area. *Neuroreport, 9*(13), 3097–3101.

Clarke, P. B. (1990). Mesolimbic dopamine activation – the key to nicotine reinforcement? *Ciba Foundation Symposium, 152,* 153–162; discussion 162–158.

Clarke, P. B. (1991). Nicotinic receptor blockade therapy and smoking cessation. *British Journal of Addiction, 86*(5), 501–505.

Clarke, P. B., Schwartz, R. D., Paul, S. M., Pert, C. B., & Pert, A. (1985). Nicotinic binding in rat brain: autoradiographic comparison of [3H]acetylcholine, [3H]nicotine, and [125I]-alpha-bungarotoxin. *The Journal of Neuroscience, 5*(5), 1307–1315.

Corrigall, W. A. (1999). Nicotine self-administration in animals as a dependence model. *Nicotine Tobaco Research, 1*(1), 11–20.

Corrigall, W. A., & Coen, K. M. (1989). Nicotine maintains robust self-administration in rats on a limited-access schedule. *Psychopharmacology (Berl), 99*(4), 473–478.

Corrigall, W. A., Coen, K. M., & Adamson, K. L. (1994). Self-administered nicotine activates the mesolimbic dopamine system through the ventral tegmental area. *Brain Research, 653*(1–2), 278–284.

Corrigall, W. A., Franklin, K. B., Coen, K. M., & Clarke, P. B. (1992). The mesolimbic dopaminergic system is implicated in the reinforcing effects of nicotine. *Psychopharmacology (Berl), 107*(2–3), 285–289.

Dani, J. A., & Bertrand, D. (2007). Nicotinic acetylcholine receptors and nicotinic cholinergic mechanisms of the central nervous system. *Annual Review of Pharmacology and Toxicology, 47*, 699–729.

Dani, J. A., & De Biasi, M. (2001). Cellular mechanisms of nicotine addiction. *Pharmacology, Biochemistry, and Behavior, 70*(4), 439–446.

Dani, J. A., & Harris, R. A. (2005). Nicotine addiction and comorbidity with alcohol abuse and mental illness. *Nature Neuroscience, 8*(11), 1465–1470.

Dani, J. A., & Heinemann, S. (1996). Molecular and cellular aspects of nicotine abuse. *Neuron, 16*(5), 905–908.

Dani, J. A., Ji, D., & Zhou, F. M. (2001). Synaptic plasticity and nicotine addiction. *Neuron, 31*(3), 349–352.

Di Chiara, G. (1999). Drug addiction as dopamine-dependent associative learning disorder. *European Journal of Pharmacology, 375*(1–3), 13–30.

Di Chiara, G. (2000). Role of dopamine in the behavioural actions of nicotine related to addiction. *European Journal of Pharmacology, 393*(1–3), 295–314.

Di Chiara, G., & Imperato, A. (1988). Drugs abused by humans preferentially increase synaptic dopamine concentrations in the mesolimbic system of freely moving rats. *Proceedings of the National Academy of Science of the United States of America, 85*(14), 5274–5278.

Ge, S., & Dani, J. A. (2005). Nicotinic acetylcholine receptors at glutamate synapses facilitate long-term depression or potentiation. *The Journal of Neuroscience, 25*(26), 6084–6091.

Goldner, F. M., Dineley, K. T., & Patrick, J. W. (1997). Immunohistochemical localization of the nicotinic acetylcholine receptor subunit alpha6 to dopaminergic neurons in the substantia nigra and ventral tegmental area. *Neuroreport, 8*(12), 2739–2742.

Gourlay, S. G., & Benowitz, N. L. (1997). Arteriovenous differences in plasma concentration of nicotine and catecholamines and related cardiovascular effects after smoking, nicotine nasal spray, and intravenous nicotine. *Clinical Pharmacology and Therapeutics, 62*(4), 453–463.

Gray, R., Rajan, A. S., Radcliffe, K. A., Yakehiro, M., & Dani, J. A. (1996). Hippocampal synaptic transmission enhanced by low concentrations of nicotine. *Nature, 383*(6602), 713–716.

Grenhoff, J., & Johnson, S. W. (1996). Sulfonylureas enhance GABAA synaptic potentials in rat midbrain dopamine neurones. *Acta Physiologica Scandinavica, 156*(2), 147–148.

Guo, J. Z., Tredway, T. L., & Chiappinelli, V. A. (1998). Glutamate and GABA release are enhanced by different subtypes of presynaptic nicotinic receptors in the lateral geniculate nucleus. *The Journal of Neuroscience, 18*(6), 1963–1969.

Henningfield, J. E., Stapleton, J. M., Benowitz, N. L., Grayson, R. F., & London, E. D. (1993). Higher levels of nicotine in arterial than in venous blood after cigarette smoking. *Drug and Alcohol Dependence, 33*(1), 23–29.

Imperato, A., Mulas, A., & Di Chiara, G. (1986). Nicotine preferentially stimulates dopamine release in the limbic system of freely moving rats. *European Journal of Pharmacology, 132* (2–3), 337–338.

Ji, D., Lape, R., & Dani, J. A. (2001). Timing and location of nicotinic activity enhances or depresses hippocampal synaptic plasticity. *Neuron, 31*(1), 131–141.

Jones, I. W., Bolam, J. P., & Wonnacott, S. (2001). Presynaptic localisation of the nicotinic acetylcholine receptor beta2 subunit immunoreactivity in rat nigrostriatal dopaminergic neurones. *The Journal of Comparative Neurology, 439*(2), 235–247.

Jones, S., Sudweeks, S., & Yakel, J. L. (1999). Nicotinic receptors in the brain: correlating physiology with function. *Trends in Neurosciences, 22*(12), 555–561.

Karan, L., Dani, J. A., & Benowitz, N. (2003). The Pharmacology of Nicotine and Tobacco. . In *Principles of Addiction Medicine* (pp. 225–248): American Society of Addiction Medicine.

Klink, R., de Kerchove d'Exaerde, A., Zoli, M., & Changeux, J. P. (2001). Molecular and physiological diversity of nicotinic acetylcholine receptors in the midbrain dopaminergic nuclei. *The Journal of Neuroscience, 21*(5), 1452–1463.

Le Novere, N., Zoli, M., & Changeux, J. P. (1996). Neuronal nicotinic receptor alpha 6 subunit mRNA is selectively concentrated in catecholaminergic nuclei of the rat brain. *European Journal of Neuroscience, 8*(11), 2428–2439.

Li, X., Rainnie, D. G., McCarley, R. W., & Greene, R. W. (1998). Presynaptic nicotinic receptors facilitate monoaminergic transmission. *The Journal of Neuroscience, 18*(5), 1904–1912.

Mansvelder, H. D., Keath, J. R., & McGehee, D. S. (2002). Synaptic mechanisms underlie nicotine-induced excitability of brain reward areas. *Neuron, 33*(6), 905–919.

Mansvelder, H. D., & McGehee, D. S. (2000). Long-term potentiation of excitatory inputs to brain reward areas by nicotine. *Neuron, 27*(2), 349–357.

Mansvelder, H. D., & McGehee, D. S. (2002). Cellular and synaptic mechanisms of nicotine addiction. *The Journal of Neurobiology, 53*(4), 606–617.

Martin, S. J., Grimwood, P. D., & Morris, R. G. (2000). Synaptic plasticity and memory: an evaluation of the hypothesis. *Annual Review of Neuroscience, 23*, 649–711.

McGehee, D. S., Heath, M. J., Gelber, S., Devay, P., & Role, L. W. (1995). Nicotine enhancement of fast excitatory synaptic transmission in CNS by presynaptic receptors. *Science, 269*(5231), 1692–1696.

McGehee, D. S., & Role, L. W. (1995). Physiological diversity of nicotinic acetylcholine receptors expressed by vertebrate neurons. *Annual Review Physiology, 57*, 521–546.

Nestler, E. J. (1993). Cellular responses to chronic treatment with drugs of abuse. *Critical Reviews in Neurobiology, 7*(1), 23–39.

Nisell, M., Nomikos, G. G., & Svensson, T. H. (1994). Infusion of nicotine in the ventral tegmental area or the nucleus accumbens of the rat differentially affects accumbal dopamine release. *Pharmacology & Toxicology, 75*(6), 348–352.

Peto, R., Lopez, A. D., Boreham, J., Thun, M., & Heath, C., Jr. (1992). Mortality from tobacco in developed countries: indirect estimation from national vital statistics. *Lancet, 339*(8804), 1268–1278.

Peto, R., Lopez, A. D., Boreham, J., Thun, M., Heath, C., Jr., & Doll, R. (1996). Mortality from smoking worldwide. *British Medical Bulletin, 52*(1), 12–21.

Picciotto, M. R., Zoli, M., Rimondini, R., Lena, C., Marubio, L. M., Pich, E. M., et al. (1998). Acetylcholine receptors containing the beta2 subunit are involved in the reinforcing properties of nicotine. *Nature, 391*(6663), 173–177.

Pidoplichko, V. I., DeBiasi, M., Williams, J. T., & Dani, J. A. (1997). Nicotine activates and desensitizes midbrain dopamine neurons. *Nature, 390*(6658), 401–404.

Pidoplichko, V. I., Noguchi, J., Areola, O. O., Liang, Y., Peterson, J., Zhang, T., et al. (2004). Nicotinic cholinergic synaptic mechanisms in the ventral tegmental area contribute to nicotine addiction. *Learning & Memory, 11*(1), 60–69.

Pontieri, F. E., Tanda, G., Orzi, F., & Di Chiara, G. (1996). Effects of nicotine on the nucleus accumbens and similarity to those of addictive drugs. *Nature, 382*(6588), 255–257.

Quick, M. W., & Lester, R. A. (2002). Desensitization of neuronal nicotinic receptors. *The Journal of Neurobiology, 53*(4), 457–478.

Radcliffe, K. A., & Dani, J. A. (1998). Nicotinic stimulation produces multiple forms of increased glutamatergic synaptic transmission. *The Journal of Neuroscience, 18*(18), 7075–7083.

Radcliffe, K. A., Fisher, J. L., Gray, R., & Dani, J. A. (1999). Nicotinic modulation of glutamate and GABA synaptic transmission of hippocampal neurons. *Annals of the New York Academy of Sciences, 868*, 591–610.

Rathouz, M. M., Vijayaraghavan, S., & Berg, D. K. (1996). Elevation of intracellular calcium levels in neurons by nicotinic acetylcholine receptors. *Molecular Neurobiology, 12*(2), 117–131.

Role, L. W., & Berg, D. K. (1996). Nicotinic receptors in the development and modulation of CNS synapses. *Neuron, 16*(6), 1077–1085.

Schultz, W., Dayan, P., & Montague, P. R. (1997). A neural substrate of prediction and reward. *Science, 275*(5306), 1593–1599.

Seguela, P., Wadiche, J., Dineley-Miller, K., Dani, J. A., & Patrick, J. W. (1993). Molecular cloning, functional properties, and distribution of rat brain alpha 7: a nicotinic cation channel highly permeable to calcium. *The Journal of Neuroscience, 13*(2), 596–604.

Spanagel, R., & Weiss, F. (1999). The dopamine hypothesis of reward: past and current status. *Trends in Neurosciences, 22*(11), 521–527.

Stolerman, I. P., & Jarvis, M. J. (1995). The scientific case that nicotine is addictive. *Psychopharmacology (Berl), 117*(1), 2–10; discussion 14–20.

Stolerman, I. P., & Shoaib, M. (1991). The neurobiology of tobacco addiction. *Trends in Pharmacological Sciences, 12*(12), 467–473.

Wada, E., McKinnon, D., Heinemann, S., Patrick, J., & Swanson, L. W. (1990). The distribution of mRNA encoded by a new member of the neuronal nicotinic acetylcholine receptor gene family (alpha 5) in the rat central nervous system. *Brain Research, 526*(1), 45–53.

Wada, E., Wada, K., Boulter, J., Deneris, E., Heinemann, S., Patrick, J., et al. (1989). Distribution of alpha 2, alpha 3, alpha 4, and beta 2 neuronal nicotinic receptor subunit mRNAs in the central nervous system: a hybridization histochemical study in the rat. *The Journal of Comprative Neurology, 284*(2), 314–335.

Watkins, S. S., Koob, G. F., & Markou, A. (2000). Neural mechanisms underlying nicotine addiction: acute positive reinforcement and withdrawal. *Nicotine Tobacco Research, 2*(1), 19–37.

WHO. (1997). Tobacco or health, a global status report. *World Health Organization,* 495.

Wonnacott, S. (1997). Presynaptic nicotinic ACh receptors. *Trends in Neurosciences, 20*(2), 92–98.

Wonnacott, S., Drasdo, A., Sanderson, E., & Rowell, P. (1990). Presynaptic nicotinic receptors and the modulation of transmitter release. *Ciba Foundation Symposium, 152,* 87–101; discussion 102–105.

Wonnacott, S., Kaiser, S., Mogg, A., Soliakov, L., & Jones, I. W. (2000). Presynaptic nicotinic receptors modulating dopamine release in the rat striatum. *European Journal of Pharmacology, 393*(1–3), 51–58.

Wooltorton, J. R., Pidoplichko, V. I., Broide, R. S., & Dani, J. A. (2003). Differential desensitization and distribution of nicotinic acetylcholine receptor subtypes in midbrain dopamine areas. *The Journal of Neuroscience, 23*(8), 3176–3185.

Zhou, F. M., Liang, Y., & Dani, J. A. (2001). Endogenous nicotinic cholinergic activity regulates dopamine release in the striatum. *Nature Neuroscience, 4*(12), 1224–1229.

Chapter 3
Molecular Mechanisms Underlying the Motivational Effects of Nicotine

Darlene H. Brunzell and Marina R. Picciotto

Introduction

Cues and Nicotine Dependence

Nicotine reinforcement is important for the initiation of smoking behavior. In addition, incentive motivation, or the ability of environmental cues to drive behavior, may play a predominant role in maintenance of tobacco use and relapse to smoking (Robinson & Berridge, 1993). It is interesting that sensory cues provided by tobacco smoke result in increased pleasure in smokers smoking denicotinized cigarettes (Perkins et al., 2001; Rose & Behm, 2004) and the success of behavioral therapies that devalue cigarettes is dependent on providing the flavor that matches smokers' regular brands (Rose & Behm, 2004). Smoking-associated cues that induce craving activate brain areas associated with liking nicotine (Brody et al., 2002; Due, Huettel, Hall, & Rubin, 2002; Franklin et al., 2007). Together these studies suggest that smoking-associated cues can gain control over the areas of the brain that stimulate reward derived from nicotine, and such cues can be manipulated to aid in smoking cessation.

Animal studies also suggest that cues play a prominent role in nicotine dependence. In the absence of cues, rats self-administer nicotine at a steady rate, limiting their intake to approximately ten infusions per hour (Caggiula et al., 2002a). Nicotine appears to be a weak reinforcer on its own; however, simultaneous presentation of a cue with the same dose of nicotine greatly increases self-administration (Caggiula et al., 2001, 2002a,b). Environmental cues previously paired with nicotine can support self-administration behavior in the absence of nicotine reward for weeks after removal of the nicotine reinforcer (Caggiula et al., 2002a; Cohen, Perrault,

M.R. Picciotto
Department of Psychiatry, Yale University School of Medicine, 34 Park Street, New Haven, CT 06508, USA
e-mail: Marina.Picciotto@Yale.edu

R.A. Bevins, A.R. Caggiula (eds.), *The Motivational Impact of Nicotine and its Role in Tobacco Use*, DOI: 10.1007/978-0-387-78748-0_3, © Springer Science+Business Media, LLC 2009

Griebel, & Soubrie, 2005). Not only do smoking-associated cues promote the maintenance of smoking behaviors, but these cues can also promote relapse to smoking (Shiffman, Paty, Gnys, Kassel, & Hickcox, 1996; Waters, Shiffman, Bradley, & Mogg, 2003). Indeed, a nicotine-associated cue is a more efficient primer than the drug itself in reinstating nicotine self-administration in an animal model of relapse (Lesage, Burroughs, Dufek, Keyler, & Pentel, 2004). By virtue of being paired with nicotine, cues gain incentive salience value (Robinson & Berridge, 1993): they become conditioned reinforcers capable of eliciting self-administration behavior on their own and they become triggers that lead to craving for the drug with which they were paired (Tiffany & Drobes, 1990).

Prior Chronic Nicotine Exposure Enhances Conditioned Reinforcement

Although nicotine can act as an unconditioned stimulus driving drug intake, it is also the case that nicotine, acting through nicotinic acetylcholine receptors containing the $\beta 2$ subunit ($\beta 2^*$ nAChRs), increases the ability to make associations between rewards and novel cues in rats and mice (i.e., conditioned reinforcement) even several weeks after withdrawal of nicotine (Brunzell et al., 2006; Olausson, Jentsch, & Taylor, 2003, 2004a,b). Nicotine also facilitates the association of cues with reward by acting as an occasion setter, that is, a cue that can set the stage for associative learning (Palmatier, Peterson, Wilkinson, & Bevins, 2004). Thus, it seems possible that nicotine can increase the salience of environmental cues, which in turn increase the drive to seek nicotine, resulting in a vicious cycle that is likely to drive both smoking behavior and relapse after smoking cessation (Fig. 3.1).

The nicotine dosing regimens that lead to enhanced conditioned reinforcement have also been shown to result in locomotor sensitization, changes in intracellular signaling, upregulation of nicotine binding and increased mesolimbic dopamine turnover (Brunzell & Picciotto, 2004; Gaddnas, Pietila, & Ahtee, 2000; King, Caldarone, & Picciotto, 2004; Sparks & Pauly, 1999). As has been shown for other drugs of abuse, sensitization of brain dopamine-(DA) systems might regulate nicotine-associated conditioned reward (Robbins & Everitt, 2002; Robinson & Berridge, 1993; Taylor & Robbins, 1984). The ability of nicotine to promote conditioned reinforcement is blocked by systemic administration of the nicotinic antagonist mecamylamine (Olausson et al., 2004a). Further, studies using knockout mice (animals genetically engineered to lack specific proteins) suggest that the ability of prior chronic nicotine exposure to enhance conditioned reinforcement as well as nicotine-mediated enhancement of context conditioning is mediated through nicotinic acetylcholine receptors containing the $\beta 2$ subunit ($\beta 2^*$ nAChRs, where * indicates other nAChR subunits; Brunzell et al., 2006; Davis & Gould, 2006; Davis & Gould, 2007).

There is an apparent dissociation between the role that $\beta 2^*$nAChRs play in nicotine-associated enhancement of conditioned reward and conditioned reward at baseline. Genetically-engineered mice lacking the $\beta 2$ nAChR subunit ($\beta 2$KO mice)

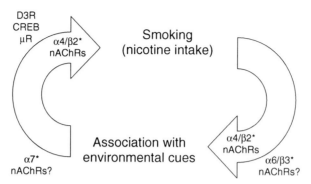

Fig 3.1 Nicotine drives associations with environmental cues that, in turn, drive nicotine intake. Exposure to environmental cues paired with nicotine self-administration greatly increases nicotine intake. Conversely, exposure to nicotine increases the ability of cues to drive responding for rewarding stimuli (conditioned reinforcement). It is clear that α4/β2* nicotinic acetylcholine receptors (nAChRs) are important for both nicotine reinforcement and for the ability of nicotine to increase conditioned reinforcement. Other nAChR subtypes, including α6/β3* and α7* nAChRs may also contribute to these processes. D3 type dopamine receptors (D3R), μ-opioid receptors (μR), and the transcription factor cyclic AMP responsive element binding protein (CREB) can contribute to the ability of nicotine-paired cues to drive behavior. Targeting these molecular processes could result in novel treatments for smoking cessation

have a tendency towards enhanced responding for a cue previously paired with a primary reward when compared with wild-type mice. This suggests that β2* nAChRs modulate conditioned reinforcement at baseline (Brunzell et al., 2006). It is known that baseline conditioned reinforcement and psychostimulant-mediated enhancement of conditioned reinforcement are controlled by DA projections to the nucleus accumbens (NAc) core and shell, respectively (Robbins & Everitt, 2002) and recent data suggest that baseline contextual fear conditioning and nicotine-dependent enhancement of contextual fear are modulated by different nAChRs (Davis & Gould, 2006). It is therefore possible that baseline conditioned reinforcement and nicotine-mediated enhancement of conditioned reinforcement are regulated by nAChRs in different neuronal populations, or that long-term desensitization and activation of nAChRs is important for the ability of nicotine to increase conditioned reinforcement.

Desensitization of nAChRs May Underlie the Ability of Nicotine to Enhance Cue Salience

While it is clear that activation of nAChRs can depolarize and increase the firing rate of DA neurons acutely (Grenhoff, Aston-Jones, & Svensson, 1986; Klink, de Kerchove d'Exaerde, Zoli, & Changeux, 2001; Picciotto et al., 1998; Svensson, Grenhoff, & Engberg, 1990), electrophysiological studies show that continuous nicotine exposure, as might be seen in smokers who have significant blood levels of nicotine throughout the day, results in desensitization of midbrain nAChRs

(Pidoplichko, DeBiasi, Williams, & Dani, 1997). Further, in striatal synaptosomes, lower doses of nicotine are required for desensitization than for activation of nAChRs as measured by nicotine-dependent DA release (Grady, Marks, Wonnacott, & Collins, 1992; Grady, Marks, & Collins, 1994; Rowell & Duggan, 1998; Rowell & Hillebrand, 1994). The progressive desensitization of nAChRs may explain why smokers generally report that the first cigarette of the day is the most pleasurable (Russell, 1989).

In positron emission tomography (PET), a form of imaging using radio-labeled compounds to identify numbers and types of receptors in living human brain, a ligand recognizing $\beta 2^*$ nAChRs has been used to show that very low levels of nicotine are sufficient to displace the majority of nAChR binding in human brain (Brody et al., 2006). This observation may be due to the fact that the high affinity nicotinic binding sites visualized using these ligands represent the subset of nAChRs that are already desensitized, or more liable to desensitize, and therefore in an allosteric state that binds nicotinic ligands more tightly (Changeux, Devillers-Thiery, & Chemouilli, 1984). Another possibility is that smokers take in nicotine both to initially activate and then to inactivate their nAChRs. Electrochemical studies using cyclic voltammetry suggest that desensitization and inactivation of nAChRs in the NAc may be a mechanism that tunes DA neurons (Rice & Cragg, 2004; Zhang & Sulzer, 2004). Nicotine or a nicotinic antagonist result in similar effects on this tuning process suggesting that desensitization is the critical molecular event (Rice & Cragg, 2004; Zhang & Sulzer, 2004). Desensitization of $\beta 2^*$ nAChRs decreases DA release when the DA neurons are firing tonically, but enhances DA release when DA neurons are in a phasic state (Rice & Cragg, 2004), as one would expect during the presentation of a reward (Schultz, 2002). As environmental cues gain more control over behavior following repeated presentation of cues with a primary reinforcer, there is a transition from phasic activity of DA neurons in response to the primary reinforcer, to phasic activity in response to the cue (Schultz, 2002). Thus, desensitization of nAChRs may enhance the response to environmental cues paired with smoking and make them more salient.

Brain Areas Important for Nicotine's Effects on Cue Responding

It is clear that nAChRs in the ventral tegmental area (VTA) are critical for behaviors related to nicotine addiction (Corrigall, Coen, & Adamson, 1994; Maskos et al., 2005). The terminals of VTA neurons project to the NAc, but significant projections also go from the VTA to other brain regions implicated in responding for drug-paired cues including the hippocampus, prefrontal cortex (PFC), and amygdala (Jentsch & Taylor, 1999; Robbins & Everitt, 2002). The PET studies in human subjects show that DA is released in the NAc following cigarette smoking (Brody et al., 2004) and animal studies have shown that both systemic and VTA administration of nicotine result in increased extracellular DA levels in the NAc (Benwell & Balfour, 1992; Di Chiara & Imperato, 1988; Ferrari, Le Novere, Picciotto, Changeux, & Zoli, 2002). The VTA, NAc, amygdala, and PFC are activated in human imaging studies in response to craving and presentation of cigarette-associated cues (Brody et al., 2002; Due et al., 2002) even in the absence of nicotine withdrawal (Franklin et al., 2007), suggesting that these brain areas regulate incentive salience of cues for smoking. Interestingly, cigarette cues also activate the insular cortex (Franklin et al., 2007) which when lesioned, abolishes the desire to smoke without any symptoms of craving (Naqvi, Rudrauf, Damasio, & Bechara, 2007).

Animal imaging studies show that acute administration of nicotine or the $\beta2^*$ nAChR agonist 5IA-85380 activate the PFC and the basolateral amygdala (Gozzi et al., 2005), brain areas known to have glutamatergic inputs to the NAc and to be necessary for expression of conditioned reinforcement (Robbins & Everitt, 2002). Psychostimulant-mediated enhancement of conditioned reinforcement is dependent on DA release in the NAc shell (Cador, Taylor, & Robbins, 1991; Taylor & Robbins, 1986) where both $\alpha4/\beta2^*$ nAChRs and $\alpha6/\beta2/\beta3^*$ nAChRs are found on DA terminals, and is regulated by the central nucleus of the amygdala and the subiculum (Robbins & Everitt, 2002) where $\alpha4/\beta2^*$ nAChRs predominate (Cui et al., 2003; Pauly, Marks, Gross, & Collins, 1991).

Contextual cues paired with nicotine administration result in immediate early gene activation of the NAc, amygdala, hippocampus, and PFC (Kelley, 2006; Schiltz, Kelley, & Landry, 2005, 2007; Schochet, Kelley, & Landry, 2005; Schroeder, Binzak, & Kelley, 2001) suggesting that changes in both neuronal activity and gene expression in these mesolimbic structures are likely to be involved in behavioral responses to nicotine-associated conditioned reinforcers. The DA projection areas also receive glutamate stimulation and it is likely that these neurotransmitters are important for encoding the salience of drug-paired cues since coordinate input of these two neurotransmitters onto NAc neurons is thought to be essential for both drug reinforcement and response to natural rewards (Kelley, 2004; Robbins & Everitt, 2002).

The role of glutamate signaling in nicotine reward has been demonstrated pharmacologically using antagonists of metabotropic glutamate receptor subtype 5 (mGluR5) which decrease fixed ratio self-administration, progressive ratio responding and cue-induced reinstatement of nicotine (Bespalov et al., 2005; Paterson & Markou, 2005; Paterson, Semenova, Gasparini, & Markou, 2003). With respect to the DA system, the DA D3 receptors are upregulated in the NAc shell following repeated nicotine exposure, and blocking this class of DA receptors decreases both the locomotor response resulting from exposure to a nicotine-paired context and nicotine conditioned place preference (Le Foll, Diaz, & Sokoloff, 2003; Le Foll, Schwartz, & Sokoloff, 2003; Le Foll, Sokoloff, Stark, & Goldberg, 2005). Thus, both glutamate and DA signaling are likely to be important for the control of nicotine-paired cues over behavior.

Role of DA in Nicotine-Mediated Behaviors

The mesocorticolimbic DA system is thought to regulate various behaviors that contribute to incentive motivation for drugs of abuse (for detailed review see

Jentsch & Taylor, 1999; Robbins & Everitt, 2002; Robinson & Berridge, 2001). Like other drugs of abuse, nicotine regulates mesolimbic DA release and is thought to act in part via this mechanism to control behaviors associated with nicotine addiction (Di Chiara & Imperato, 1988). DA receptor activity is necessary for nicotine self-administration (Corrigall, Franklin, Coen, & Clarke, 1992), conditioned place preference (Shoaib, Stolerman, & Kumar, 1994), locomotor activation (Benwell & Balfour, 1992; Di Chiara & Imperato, 1988; King et al., 2004) and conditioned locomotor activation (Bevins, Besheer, & Pickett, 2001; Palmatier & Bevins, 2002); all of these behaviors are sensitive to manipulation of cues. Blockade of nAChRs in the VTA (Corrigall et al., 1994; Laviolette & van der Kooy, 2003) or lesions of DA neurons (Corrigall et al., 1992) reduce nicotine self-administration and conditioned place preference. β2* nAChRs on dopaminergic cell bodies increase their firing rate (Klink et al., 2001; Picciotto et al., 1998; Sorenson, Shiroyama, & Kitai, 1998; Wu et al., 2004), and in addition presynaptic nAChRs in both the VTA and NAc can modulate DA release (Mansvelder, Keath, & McGehee, 2002; Pidoplichko et al., 2004; Salminen et al., 2004; Wooltorton, Pidoplichko, Broide, & Dani, 2003) and regulate DA transporter activity (Middleton, Cass, & Dwoskin, 2004).

nAChR Subtypes Involved in Modulating the DA System

Studies of knockout mice lacking individual nicotinic receptor subunits have shown that α4/β2* nAChRs are critical for nicotine-elicited increases in DA release, DA-dependent locomotor activation, nicotine conditioned place preference and nicotine self-administration (King et al., 2004; Marubio et al., 2003; Picciotto et al., 1998; Walters, Brown, Changeux, Martin, & Damaj, 2006). Correspondingly, knockin mice with α4* nAChRs that are hypersensitive to nicotine show nicotine conditioned place preference at a very low dose of nicotine (Tapper et al., 2004). It would be interesting to determine whether these mice show increased incentive salience as well. Both nicotine-mediated DA release and local self-administration of nicotine into the VTA can be rescued by lentiviral-mediated expression of the β2 subunit in the VTA of β2KO mice (Maskos et al., 2005). These studies in genetically modified mice are in accord with pharmacological studies showing that rats will self-administer a selective α4/β2* agonist, 5IA-85380 (Liu et al., 2003) and that VTA administration of antagonists of α4/β2* nAChRs decrease nicotine self-administration (Corrigall et al., 1992; Grottick et al., 2000).

    Another nAChR that may be important for nicotine reward is the α6/β3* nAChR subtype. An antisense oligonucleotide against the α6 nAChR subunit blocks nicotine-dependent locomotor activation in rats (le Novere et al., 1999). α6/β2/β3* nAChRs are located on DA terminals and contribute to nicotine-stimulated DA to release (Champtiaux et al., 2003; Salminen et al., 2004), and thus could contribute behaviors mediated through NAc DA signaling, including conditioned reinforcement and psychostimulant-mediated enhancement of conditioned reinforcement. Upregulation of α6/β2/β3* nAChRs in the NAc could be responsible for the ability of nicotine to enhance conditioned reinforcement (Parker et al., 2004); however, several studies suggest that these nAChRs are downregulated in the NAc following chronic nicotine exposure (Lai et al., 2005; McCallum et al., 2006; Mugnaini et al., 2006), so sensitization at the level of $\alpha6/\beta2/\beta3*$ nAChRs may not underlie lasting effects of nicotine on behavior, such as enhancement of conditioned reinforcement. $\alpha6/\beta2/\beta3*$ nAChRs are also located on DA cell bodies in the VTA (Klink et al., 2001). As α-conotoxin-MII sensitive (i.e. $\alpha6/\beta2/\beta3*$ nAChRs) and insensitive $\beta2*$ nAChRs respond similarly to DHβE and 5IA-85350 (Kulak, Sum, Musachio, McIntosh, & Quik, 2002; Mogg et al., 2002; Salminen et al., 2004), it is possible that $\alpha6/\beta2/\beta3*$ nAChRs are required for nicotine self-administration (Corrigall et al., 1994; Liu et al., 2003). In fact, a single nucleotide polymorphism in the $\beta3$ subunit is linked to tobacco dependence in smokers (Bierut et al., 2007).

Although $\alpha7*$ nAChRs are important for synaptic plasticity following nicotine exposure in the VTA (Mansvelder et al., 2002; Pidoplichko et al., 1997) it is still not clear what role these nAChRs play in nicotine reward. Local VTA administration of methyllycaconitine (MLA), an antagonist which was thought to be selective for $\alpha7*$ nAChRs, blocks nicotine conditioned place preference (Laviolette & van der Kooy, 2003) and high doses of MLA attenuate nicotine self-administration in rats (Markou & Paterson, 2001). Although these studies suggest that $\alpha7$ nAChRs might contribute to nicotine reward, $\alpha7$ knockout mice show normal nicotine place preference across a range of doses (Walters et al., 2006). Since MLA competes with α-conotoxin-MII binding at doses that are behaviorally effective (Grady et al., 2001; Salminen et al., 2005), it is possible that antagonism of $\alpha6*$ nAChRs might be responsible for MLA-dependent attenuation of nicotine reward.

Intracellular Signaling Downstream of nAChRs

The ability of nicotine to change synaptic strength of mesolimbic DA neurons (Mansvelder et al., 2002; Pidoplichko et al., 1997; Rice & Cragg, 2004; Zhang & Sulzer, 2004) is likely to be critical for the long-lasting changes in behavior that result from repeated nicotine administration. Long-term changes in synaptic transmission result from activation of intracellular signaling cascades (Greengard, 2001). A number of intracellular signaling pathways are known to be critical for synaptic plasticity and to contribute to learning and memory (for detailed review see Silva, Kogan, Frankland, & Kida, 1998; Sweatt, 2004). Among those signaling molecules regulated by nicotine are extracellular-regulated protein kinase (ERK) and cyclic AMP responsive element binding protein (CREB; Brunzell, Russell, & Picciotto, 2003; Pandey, Roy, Xu, & Mittal, 2001; Valjent, Pages, Herve, Girault, & Caboche, 2004; Walters, Cleck, Kuo, & Blendy, 2005). *In vitro* studies show that ERK is activated following nicotine exposure and is necessary for nicotine-dependent activation of CREB (Chang & Berg, 2001; Dineley et al., 2001; Nakayama, Numakawa, Ikeuchi, & Hatanaka, 2001). *In vivo*, nicotine has region- and treatment-dependent effects on the levels and activation state of ERK and CREB (Brunzell et al., 2003; Valjent et al., 2004). Acute nicotine administration increases activation of ERK in amygdala and PFC (as measured by levels of phosphorylated ERK (pERK; Valjent et al., 2004). In contrast, chronic nicotine administration increases pERK in the PFC, but decreases both ERK and pERK in the amygdala (Brunzell et al., 2003).

The transcription factor CREB appears to be essential for nicotine-associated cue-dependent learning. Wild-type mice show increased pCREB in VTA in response to acute nicotine exposure, a nicotine conditioned place preference paradigm or exposure to a novel environment that had been paired with nicotine, and knockout mice lacking CREB do not show nicotine conditioned place preference (Walters et al., 2005). The ability of the nicotine-paired chamber to increase phosphorylated or active CREB (pCREB) in the NAc (Walters et al., 2005) suggests that this neuroadaptation could be associated with the ability of nicotine to increase conditioned reinforcement. Chronic nicotine exposure results in upregulation of total CREB levels in the NAc of mice (Brunzell et al., 2003), perhaps further promoting incentive salience of nicotine-associated cues. Post mortem studies on human brain indicate that protein kinase A (PKA) activity is elevated in the NAc and ventral midbrain of smokers (Hope, Nagarkar, Leonard, & Wise, 2007). PKA could promote synaptic plasticity via phosphorylation of CREB leading to CRE-mediated transcription. Reductions in NAc pCREB observed following chronic nicotine in rodents, however, suggest that homeostatic mechanisms occur in the NAc (Brunzell et al., 2003; Pandey et al., 2001).

Both nicotine exposure and withdrawal modulate pCREB levels in the NAc, PFC, VTA, and amygdala (Brunzell et al., 2003; Pandey et al., 2001; Walters et al., 2005). In studies of mice and rats pCREB in the PFC increases with chronic nicotine exposure (Brunzell et al., 2003) and decreases following nicotine withdrawal suggesting that CREB activity may be recruited in the PFC after repeated pairing of nicotine exposure and environmental cues. As indicated above, nicotine-associated cues elicit arc and c-fos immediate early gene activity in the PFC, amygdala, and NAc (Schiltz et al., 2005; Schroeder et al., 2001), suggesting that by virtue of their association with nicotine, cues become capable of altering new gene transcription in areas of the brain that regulate reward.

Conclusions

An incentive motivation theory of nicotine reward can explain why smokers experience intense craving to smoke despite the relatively modest reinforcing value of nicotine (Robinson & Berridge, 1993). Though studies using other psychostimulants provide insights into the mechanisms underlying nicotine-associated effects on incentive motivation, the systems that control incentive motivation for nicotine are less understood. $\beta2^*$nAChRs appear to modulate cue-dependent behavior as well as nicotine-associated enhancement of conditioned reinforcement. nAChRs are expressed in mesolimbic structures that contribute to conditioned reinforcement, but further studies are necessary to identify the specific role that various nAChR subtypes, and their downstream signaling targets, play in incentive sensitization.

Acknowledgments This work was supported by grants DA00436, DA10455, DA14241 and AA15632 from the National Institutes of Health and by NARSAD.

References

Benwell, M. E., & Balfour, D. J. (1992). The effects of acute and repeated nicotine treatment on nucleus accumbens dopamine and locomotor activity. *British Journal of Pharmacology, 105*(4), 849–856.

Bespalov, A. Y., Dravolina, O. A., Sukhanov, I., Zakharova, E., Blokhina, E., Zvartau, et al. (2005). Metabotropic glutamate receptor (mGluR5) antagonist MPEP attenuated cue- and schedule-induced reinstatement of nicotine self-administration behavior in rats. *Neuropharmacology, 49 Suppl*, 167–178.

Bevins, R. A., Besheer, J., & Pickett, K. S. (2001). Nicotine-conditioned locomotor activity in rats: Dopaminergic and GABAergic influences on conditioned expression. *Pharmacology, Biochemistry, and Behavior, 68*(1), 135–145.

Bierut, L. J., Madden, P. A., Breslau, N., Johnson, E. O., Hatsukami, D., Pomerleau, O. F., et al. (2007). Novel genes identified in a high-density genome wide association study for nicotine dependence. *Human Molecular Genetics, 16*(1), 24–35.

Brody, A. L., Mandelkern, M. A., London, E. D., Childress, A. R., Lee, G. S., Bota, R. G., et al. (2002). Brain metabolic changes during cigarette craving. *Archives of General Psychiatry, 59*(12), 1162–1172.

Brody, A. L., Mandelkern, M. A., London, E. D., Olmstead, R. E., Farahi, J., Scheibal, D., et al. (2006). Cigarette smoking saturates brain alpha4 beta2 nicotinic acetylcholine receptors. *Archives General Psychiatry, 63*(8), 907–915.

Brody, A. L., Olmstead, R. E., London, E. D., Farahi, J., Meyer, J. H., Grossman, P., et al. (2004). Smoking-induced ventral striatum dopamine release. *The American Journal of Psychiatry, 161*(7), 1211–1218.

Brunzell, D. H., Chang, J. R., Schneider, B., Olausson, P., Taylor, J. R., & Picciotto, M. R. (2006). Beta2-subunit-containing nicotinic acetylcholine receptors are involved in nicotine-induced increases in conditioned reinforcement but not progressive ratio responding for food in C57BL/6 mice. *Psychopharmacology (Berl), 184*(3–4), 328–338.

Brunzell, D. H., & Picciotto, M. R. (2004). *Non-biased nicotine conditioned place preference requires the beta2-subunit containing nicotinic acetylcholine receptors: Regulation of CREB as a potential mechanism for nicotine reinforcement.* Paper presented at the Society for Neuroscience, 34th Annual Meeting, San Diego, California.

Brunzell, D. H., Russell, D. S., & Picciotto, M. R. (2003). In vivo nicotine treatment regulates mesocorticolimbic CREB and ERK signaling in C57BL/6J mice. *Journal Neurochemistry, 84*(6), 1431–1441.

Cador, M., Taylor, J. R., & Robbins, T. W. (1991). Potentiation of the effects of reward-related stimuli by dopaminergic-dependent mechanisms in the nucleus accumbens. *Psychopharmacology (Berl), 104*(3), 377–385.

Caggiula, A. R., Donny, E. C., Chaudhri, N., Perkins, K. A., Evans-Martin, F. F., & Sved, A. F. (2002a). Importance of nonpharmacological factors in nicotine self-administration. *Physiology & Behavior, 77*(4–5), 683–687.

Caggiula, A. R., Donny, E. C., White, A. R., Chaudhri, N., Booth, S., Gharib, M. A., et al. (2001). Cue dependency of nicotine self-administration and smoking. *Pharmacology, Biochemistry, and Behavior, 70*(4), 515–530.

Caggiula, A. R., Donny, E. C., White, A. R., Chaudhri, N., Booth, S., Gharib, M. A., et al. (2002b). Environmental stimuli promote the acquisition of nicotine self-administration in rats. *Psychopharmacology (Berl), 163*(2), 230–237.

Champtiaux, N., Gotti, C., Cordero-Erausquin, M., David, D. J., Przybylski, C., Lena, C., et al. (2003). Subunit composition of functional nicotinic receptors in dopaminergic neurons investigated with knock-out mice. *The Journal of Neuroscience, 23*(21), 7820–7829.

Chang, K. T., & Berg, D. K. (2001). Voltage-gated channels block nicotinic regulation of CREB phosphorylation and gene expression in neurons. *Neuron, 32*(5), 855–865.

Changeux, J. P., Devillers-Thiery, A., & Chemouilli, P. (1984). Acetylcholine receptor: An allosteric protein. *Science, 225*(4668), 1335–1345.

Cohen, C., Perrault, G., Griebel, G., & Soubrie, P. (2005). Nicotine-associated cues maintain nicotine-seeking behavior in rats several weeks after nicotine withdrawal: Reversal by the cannabinoid (CB1) receptor antagonist, rimonabant (SR141716). *Neuropsychopharmacology, 30*(1), 145–155.

Corrigall, W. A., Coen, K. M., & Adamson, K. L. (1994). Self-administered nicotine activates the mesolimbic dopamine system through the ventral tegmental area. *Brain Research, 653*(1–2), 278–284.

Corrigall, W. A., Franklin, K. B., Coen, K. M., & Clarke, P. B. (1992). The mesolimbic dopaminergic system is implicated in the reinforcing effects of nicotine. *Psychopharmacology (Berl), 107*(2–3), 285–289.

Cui, C., Booker, T. K., Allen, R. S., Grady, S. R., Whiteaker, P., Marks, M. J., et al. (2003). The beta3 nicotinic receptor subunit: A component of alpha-conotoxin MII-binding nicotinic acetylcholine receptors that modulate dopamine release and related behaviors. *The Journal Neuroscience, 23*(35), 11045–11053.

Davis, J. A., & Gould, T. J. (2006). The effects of DhbE and MLA on nicotine-induced enhancement of contextual fear conditioning in C57BL/6 mice. *Psychopharmacology (Berl), 184*, 345–352.

Davis, J. A., & Gould, T. J. (2007). Beta2 subunit-containing nicotinic receptors mediate the enhancing effect of nicotine on trace cued fear conditioning in C57BL/6 mice. *Psychopharmacology (Berl), 190*(3), 343–352.

Di Chiara, G., & Imperato, A. (1988). Drugs abused by humans preferentially increase synaptic dopamine concentrations in the mesolimbic system of freely moving rats. *Proceedings of the National Acadamey of Science of the United States of America, 85*(14), 5274–5278.

Dineley, K. T., Westerman, M., Bui, D., Bell, K., Ashe, K. H., & Sweatt, J. D. (2001). Beta-amyloid activates the mitogen-activated protein kinase cascade via hippocampal alpha7 nicotinic acetylcholine receptors: In vitro and in vivo mechanisms related to alzheimer's disease. *The Journal Neuroscience, 21*(12), 4125–4133.

Due, D. L., Huettel, S. A., Hall, W. G., & Rubin, D. C. (2002). Activation in mesolimbic and visuospatial neural circuits elicited by smoking cues: Evidence from functional magnetic resonance imaging. *American Journal of Psychiatry, 159*(6), 954–960.

Ferrari, R., Le Novere, N., Picciotto, M. R., Changeux, J. P., & Zoli, M. (2002). Acute and long-term changes in the mesolimbic dopamine pathway after systemic or local single nicotine injections. *European Jpurnal of Neuroscience, 15*(11), 1810–1818.

Franklin, T. R., Wang, Z., Wang, J., Sciortino, N., Harper, D., Li, Y., Ehrman, R., et al. (2007). Limbic activation to cigarette smoking cues independent of nicotine withdrawal: A perfusion fMRI study. *Neuropsychopharmacology, 32*(11), 2301–2309.

Gaddnas, H., Pietila, K., & Ahtee, L. (2000). Effects of chronic oral nicotine treatment and its withdrawal on locomotor activity and brain monoamines in mice. *Behavioural Brain Research, 113*(1–2), 65–72.

Gozzi, A., Schwarz, A., Reese, T., Bertani, S., Crestan, V., & Bifone, A. (2005). Region-specific effects of nicotine on brain activity: A pharmacological MRI study in the drug-naive rat. *Neuropsychopharmacology, 31*(8), 1690–1703.

Grady, S., Marks, M. J., Wonnacott, S., & Collins, A. C. (1992). Characterization of nicotinic receptor-mediated [3H]dopamine release from synaptosomes prepared from mouse striatum. *The Journal Neurochemistry, 59*(3), 848–856.

Grady, S. R., Marks, M. J., & Collins, A. C. (1994). Desensitization of nicotine-stimulated [3h]dopamine release from mouse striatal synaptosomes. *The Journal Neurochemistry, 62*(4), 1390–1398.

Grady, S. R., Meinerz, N. M., Cao, J., Reynolds, A. M., Picciotto, M. R., Changeux, J. P., et al. (2001). Nicotinic agonists stimulate acetylcholine release from mouse interpeduncular nucleus: A function mediated by a different nachr than dopamine release from striatum. *The Journal Neurochemistry, 76*(1), 258–268.

Greengard, P. (2001). The neurobiology of slow synaptic transmission. *Science, 294*(5544), 1024–1030.

Grenhoff, J., Aston-Jones, G., & Svensson, T. H. (1986). Nicotinic effects on the firing pattern of midbrain dopamine neurons. *Acta Physiologica Scandinavica, 128*(3), 351–358.

Grottick, A. J., Trube, G., Corrigall, W. A., Huwyler, J., Malherbe, P., Wyler, R., et al. (2000). Evidence that nicotinic alpha7 receptors are not involved in the hyperlocomotor and rewarding effects of nicotine. *The Journal of Pharmacology and Experimental Therapeutics, 294*(3), 1112–1119.

Hope, B. T., Nagarkar, D., Leonard, S., & Wise, R. A. (2007). Long-term upregulation of protein kinase A and adenylate cyclase levels in human smokers. *The Journal of Neuroscience, 27*(8), 1964–1972.

Jentsch, J. D., & Taylor, J. R. (1999). Impulsivity resulting from frontostriatal dysfunction in drug abuse: Implications for the control of behavior by reward-related stimuli. *Psychopharmacology (Berl), 146*(4), 373–390.

Kelley, A. E. (2004). Memory and addiction: Shared neural circuitry and molecular mechanisms. *Neuron, 44*(1), 161–179.

Kelley, A. E. (2006). Worms clear the smoke surrounding nicotine addiction. *Cell, 127*(3), 460–462.

King, S. L., Caldarone, B. J., & Picciotto, M. R. (2004). Beta2-subunit-containing nicotinic acetylcholine receptors are critical for dopamine-dependent locomotor activation following repeated nicotine administration. *Neuropharmacology, 47*(Suppl 1), 132–139.

Klink, R., de Kerchove d'Exaerde, A., Zoli, M., & Changeux, J. P. (2001). Molecular and physiological diversity of nicotinic acetylcholine receptors in the midbrain dopaminergic nuclei. *The Journal of Neuroscience, 21*(5), 1452–1463.

Kulak, J. M., Sum, J., Musachio, J. L., McIntosh, J. M., & Quik, M. (2002). 5-iodo-A-85380 binds to alpha-conotoxin MII-sensitive nicotinic acetylcholine receptors (nAChRs) as well as alpha4beta2* subtypes. *The Journal of Neurochemistry, 81*(2), 403–406.

Lai, A., Parameswaran, N., Khwaja, M., Whiteaker, P., Lindstrom, J. M., Fan, H., et al. (2005). Long-term nicotine treatment decreases striatal alpha6* nicotinic acetylcholine receptor sites and function in mice. *Molecular Pharmacology, 67*(5), 1639–1647.

Laviolette, S. R., & van der Kooy, D. (2003). The motivational valence of nicotine in the rat ventral tegmental area is switched from rewarding to aversive following blockade of the alpha7-subunit-containing nicotinic acetylcholine receptor. *Psychopharmacology (Berl), 166*(3), 306–313.

Le Foll, B., Diaz, J., & Sokoloff, P. (2003). Increased dopamine D3 receptor expression accompanying behavioral sensitization to nicotine in rats. *Synapse, 47*(3), 176–183.

Le Foll, B., Schwartz, J. C., & Sokoloff, P. (2003). Disruption of nicotine conditioning by dopamine D3 receptor ligands. *Molecular Psychiatry, 8*(2), 225–230.

Le Foll, B., Sokoloff, P., Stark, H., & Goldberg, S. R. (2005). Dopamine D3 receptor ligands block nicotine-induced conditioned place preferences through a mechanism that does not involve discriminative-stimulus or antidepressant-like effects. *Neuropsychopharmacology, 30*(4), 720–730.

le Novere, N., Zoli, M., Lena, C., Ferrari, R., Picciotto, M. R., Merlo-Pich, E., et al. (1999). Involvement of alpha6 nicotinic receptor subunit in nicotine-elicited locomotion, demonstrated by in vivo antisense oligonucleotide infusion. *Neuroreport, 10*(12), 2497–2501.

Lesage, M. G., Burroughs, D., Dufek, M., Keyler, D. E., & Pentel, P. R. (2004). Reinstatement of nicotine self-administration in rats by presentation of nicotine-paired stimuli, but not nicotine priming. *Pharmacology, Biochemistry, and Behavior, 79*(3), 507–513.

Liu, X., Koren, A. O., Yee, S. K., Pechnick, R. N., Poland, R. E., & London, E. D. (2003). Self-administration of 5-iodo-A-85380, a beta2-selective nicotinic receptor ligand, by operantly trained rats. *Neuroreport, 14*(11), 1503–1505.

Mansvelder, H. D., Keath, J. R., & McGehee, D. S. (2002). Synaptic mechanisms underlie nicotine-induced excitability of brain reward areas. *Neuron, 33*(6), 905–919.

Markou, A., & Paterson, N. E. (2001). The nicotinic antagonist methyllycaconitine has differential effects on nicotine self-administration and nicotine withdrawal in the rat. *Nicotine & Tobacco Research, 3*(4), 361–373.

Marubio, L. M., Gardier, A. M., Durier, S., David, D., Klink, R., Arroyo-Jimenez, M. M., et al. (2003). Effects of nicotine in the dopaminergic system of mice lacking the alpha4 subunit of neuronal nicotinic acetylcholine receptors. *European Journal of Neuroscience, 17*(7), 1329–1337.

Maskos, U., Molles, B. E., Pons, S., Besson, M., Guiard, B. P., Guilloux, J. P., et al. (2005). Nicotine reinforcement and cognition restored by targeted expression of nicotinic receptors. *Nature, 436*(7047), 103–107.

McCallum, S., Parameswaran, N., Bordia, T., Fan, H., McIntosh, M., & Quik, M. (2006). Differential regulation of mesolimbic alpha3*/alpha6beta2* and alpha4beta2* nAChR sites and function after long-term oral nicotine to monkeys. *The Journal Pharmacology and Experimental Therapeutics, 318*(1), 381–388.

Middleton, L. S., Cass, W. A., & Dwoskin, L. P. (2004). Nicotinic receptor modulation of dopamine transporter function in rat striatum and medial prefrontal cortex. *The Journal Pharmacology and Experimental Therapeutics, 308*(1), 367–377.

Mogg, A. J., Whiteaker, P., McIntosh, J. M., Marks, M., Collins, A. C., & Wonnacott, S. (2002). Methyllycaconitine is a potent antagonist of alpha-conotoxin MII-sensitive presynaptic nicotinic acetylcholine receptors in rat striatum. *The Journal Pharmacology and Experimental Therapeutics, 302*(1), 197–204.

Mugnaini, M., Garzotti, M., Sartori, I., Pilla, M., Repeto, P., Heidbreder, C. A., et al. (2006). Selective down-regulation of [125I]-alpha-conotoxin mii binding in rat mesostriatal dopamine pathway following continuous infusion of nicotine. *Neuroscience, 137*(2), 565–572.

Nakayama, H., Numakawa, T., Ikeuchi, T., & Hatanaka, H. (2001). Nicotine-induced phosphorylation of extracellular signal-regulated protein kinase and CREB in PC12h cells. *The Journal of Neurochemistry, 79*(3), 489–498.

Naqvi, N. H., Rudrauf, D., Damasio, H., & Bechara, A. (2007). Damage to the insula disrupts addiction to cigarette smoking. *Science, 315*(5811), 531–534.

Olausson, P., Jentsch, J. D., & Taylor, J. R. (2003). Repeated nicotine exposure enhances reward-related learning in the rat. *Neuropsychopharmacology, 28*(7), 1264–1271.

Olausson, P., Jentsch, J. D., & Taylor, J. R. (2004a). Nicotine enhances responding with conditioned reinforcement. *Psychopharmacology (Berl), 171*(2), 173–178.

Olausson, P., Jentsch, J. D., & Taylor, J. R. (2004b). Repeated nicotine exposure enhances responding with conditioned reinforcement. *Psychopharmacology (Berl), 173*(1–2), 98–104.

Palmatier, M. I., & Bevins, R. A. (2002). Examination of GABAergic and dopaminergic compounds in the acquisition of nicotine-conditioned hyperactivity in rats. *Neuropsychobiology, 45*(2), 87–94.

Palmatier, M. I., Peterson, J. L., Wilkinson, J. L., & Bevins, R. A. (2004). Nicotine serves as a feature-positive modulator of pavlovian appetitive conditioning in rats. *Behavioural Pharmacology, 15*(3), 183–194.

Pandey, S. C., Roy, A., Xu, T., & Mittal, N. (2001). Effects of protracted nicotine exposure and withdrawal on the expression and phosphorylation of the CREB gene transcription factor in rat brain. *The Journal Neurochemistry, 77*(3), 943–952.

Parker, S. L., Fu, Y., McAllen, K., Luo, J., McIntosh, J. M., Lindstrom, J. M., et al. (2004). Up-regulation of brain nicotinic acetylcholine receptors in the rat during long-term self-administration of nicotine: Disproportionate increase of the alpha6 subunit. *Molecular Pharmacology, 65*(3), 611–622.

Paterson, N. E., & Markou, A. (2005). The metabotropic glutamate receptor 5 antagonist MPEP decreased break points for nicotine, cocaine and food in rats. *Psychopharmacology (Berl), 179*(1), 255–261.

Paterson, N. E., Semenova, S., Gasparini, F., & Markou, A. (2003). The mGlur5 antagonist MPEP decreased nicotine self-administration in rats and mice. *Psychopharmacology (Berl)*, *167*(3), 257–264.

Pauly, J. R., Marks, M. J., Gross, S. D., & Collins, A. C. (1991). An autoradiographic analysis of cholinergic receptors in mouse brain after chronic nicotine treatment. *The Journal Pharmacology and Experimental Therapeutics*, *258*(3), 1127–1136.

Perkins, K. A., Gerlach, D., Vender, J., Grobe, J., Meeker, J., & Hutchison, S. (2001). Sex differences in the subjective and reinforcing effects of visual and olfactory cigarette smoke stimuli. *Nicotine & Tobacco Research*, *3*(2), 141–150.

Picciotto, M. R., Zoli, M., Rimondini, R., Lena, C., Marubio, L. M., Pich, E. M., et al. (1998). Acetylcholine receptors containing the beta2 subunit are involved in the reinforcing properties of nicotine. *Nature*, *391*(6663), 173–177.

Pidoplichko, V. I., DeBiasi, M., Williams, J. T., & Dani, J. A. (1997). Nicotine activates and desensitizes midbrain dopamine neurons. *Nature*, *390*(6658), 401–404.

Pidoplichko, V. I., Noguchi, J., Areola, O. O., Liang, Y., Peterson, J., Zhang, T., et al. (2004). Nicotinic cholinergic synaptic mechanisms in the ventral tegmental area contribute to nicotine addiction. *Learning & Memory*, *11*(1), 60–69.

Rice, M. E., & Cragg, S. J. (2004). Nicotine amplifies reward-related dopamine signals in striatum. *Nature Neuroscience*, *7*(6), 583–584.

Robbins, T. W., & Everitt, B. J. (2002). Limbic-striatal memory systems and drug addiction. *Neurobiology of Learning and Memory*, *78*(3), 625–636.

Robinson, T. E., & Berridge, K. C. (1993). The neural basis of drug craving: An incentive-sensitization theory of addiction. *Brain Research. Brain Research Reviews*, *18*(3), 247–291.

Robinson, T. E., & Berridge, K. C. (2001). Incentive-sensitization and addiction. *Addiction*, *96*(1), 103–114.

Rose, J. E., & Behm, F. M. (2004). Extinguishing the rewarding value of smoke cues: Pharmacological and behavioral treatments. *Nicotine & Tobacco Research*, *6*(3), 523–532.

Rowell, P. P., & Duggan, D. S. (1998). Long-lasting inactivation of nicotinic receptor function in vitro by treatment with high concentrations of nicotine. *Neuropharmacology*, *37*(1), 103–111.

Rowell, P. P., & Hillebrand, J. A. (1994). Characterization of nicotine-induced desensitization of evoked dopamine release from rat striatal synaptosomes. *The Journal Neurochemistry*, *63*(2), 561–569.

Russell, M. A. (1989). Subjective and behavioural effects of nicotine in humans: Some sources of individual variation. *Progress in Brain Research*, *79*, 289–302.

Salminen, O., Murphy, K. L., McIntosh, J. M., Drago, J., Marks, M. J., Collins, A. C., et al. (2004). Subunit composition and pharmacology of two classes of striatal presynaptic nicotinic acetylcholine receptors mediating dopamine release in mice. *Molecular Pharmacology*, *65*(6), 1526–1535.

Salminen, O., Whiteaker, P., Grady, S. R., Collins, A. C., McIntosh, J. M., & Marks, M. J. (2005). The subunit composition and pharmacology of alpha-conotoxin MII-binding nicotinic acetylcholine receptors studied by a novel membrane-binding assay. *Neuropharmacology*, *48*(5), 696–705.

Schiltz, C. A., Kelley, A. E., & Landry, C. F. (2005). Contextual cues associated with nicotine administration increase arc mrna expression in corticolimbic areas of the rat brain. *European Journal of Neuroscience*, *21*(6), 1703–1711.

Schiltz, C. A., Kelley, A. E., & Landry, C. F. (2007). Acute stress and nicotine cues interact to unveil locomotor arousal and activity-dependent gene expression in the prefrontal cortex. *Biological Psychiatry*, *61*(1), 127–135.

Schochet, T. L., Kelley, A. E., & Landry, C. F. (2005). Differential expression of arc mrna and other plasticity-related genes induced by nicotine in adolescent rat forebrain. *Neuroscience*, *135*(1), 285–297.

Schroeder, B. E., Binzak, J. M., & Kelley, A. E. (2001). A common profile of prefrontal cortical activation following exposure to nicotine- or chocolate-associated contextual cues. *Neuroscience*, *105*(3), 535–545.

Schultz, W. (2002). Getting formal with dopamine and reward. *Neuron*, *36*(2), 241–263.

Shiffman, S., Paty, J. A., Gnys, M., Kassel, J. A., & Hickcox, M. (1996). First lapses to smoking: Within-subjects analysis of real-time reports. *Journal of Consulting and Clinical Psychology*, *64*(2), 366–379.

Shoaib, M., Stolerman, I. P., & Kumar, R. C. (1994). Nicotine-induced place preferences following prior nicotine exposure in rats. *Psychopharmacology (Berl)*, *113*(3–4), 445–452.

Silva, A. J., Kogan, J. H., Frankland, P. W., & Kida, S. (1998). CREB and memory. *Annual Review of Neuroscience*, *21*, 127–148.

Sorenson, E. M., Shiroyama, T., & Kitai, S. T. (1998). Postsynaptic nicotinic receptors on dopaminergic neurons in the substantia nigra pars compacta of the rat. *Neuroscience*, *87*(3), 659–673.

Sparks, J. A., & Pauly, J. R. (1999). Effects of continuous oral nicotine administration on brain nicotinic receptors and responsiveness to nicotine in C57BL/6 mice. *Psychopharmacology (Berl)*, *141*(2), 145–153.

Svensson, T. H., Grenhoff, J., & Engberg, G. (1990). Effect of nicotine on dynamic function of brain catecholamine neurons. *Ciba Foundation Symposium*, *152*, 169–180; discussion 180–165.

Sweatt, J. D. (2004). Mitogen-activated protein kinases in synaptic plasticity and memory. *Current Opinion in Neurobiology*, *14*(3), 311–317.

Tapper, A. R., McKinney, S. L., Nashmi, R., Schwarz, J., Deshpande, P., Labarca, C., et al. (2004). Nicotine activation of alpha4* receptors: Sufficient for reward, tolerance, and sensitization. *Science*, *306*(5698), 1029–1032.

Taylor, J. R., & Robbins, T. W. (1984). Enhanced behavioural control by conditioned reinforcers following microinjections of d-amphetamine into the nucleus accumbens. *Psychopharmacology (Berl)*, *84*(3), 405–412.

Taylor, J. R., & Robbins, T. W. (1986). 6-hydroxydopamine lesions of the nucleus accumbens, but not of the caudate nucleus, attenuate enhanced responding with reward-related stimuli produced by intra-accumbens d-amphetamine. *Psychopharmacology (Berl)*, *90*(3), 390–397.

Tiffany, S. T., & Drobes, D. J. (1990). Imagery and smoking urges: The manipulation of affective content. *Addictivity Behaviors*, *15*(6), 531–539.

Valjent, E., Pages, C., Herve, D., Girault, J. A., & Caboche, J. (2004). Addictive and non-addictive drugs induce distinct and specific patterns of erk activation in mouse brain. *European Journal Neuroscience*, *19*(7), 1826–1836.

Walters, C. L., Brown, S., Changeux, J. P., Martin, B., & Damaj, M. I. (2006). The beta2 but not alpha7 subunit of the nicotinic acetylcholine receptor is required for nicotine-conditioned place preference in mice. *Psychopharmacology (Berl)*, *184*(3–4), 339–344.

Walters, C. L., Cleck, J. N., Kuo, Y. C., & Blendy, J. A. (2005). Mu-opioid receptor and CREB activation are required for nicotine reward. *Neuron*, *46*(6), 933–943.

Waters, A. J., Shiffman, S., Bradley, B. P., & Mogg, K. (2003). Attentional shifts to smoking cues in smokers. *Addiction*, *98*(10), 1409–1417.

Wooltorton, J. R., Pidoplichko, V. I., Broide, R. S., & Dani, J. A. (2003). Differential desensitization and distribution of nicotinic acetylcholine receptor subtypes in midbrain dopamine areas. *The Journal Neuroscience*, *23*(8), 3176–3185.

Wu, J., George, A. A., Schroeder, K. M., Xu, L., Marxer-Miller, S., Lucero, L., et al. (2004). Electrophysiological, pharmacological, and molecular evidence for alpha7-nicotinic acetylcholine receptors in rat midbrain dopamine neurons. *The Journal of Pharmacology and Experiemntal Therapeuics*, *311*(1), 80–91.

Zhang, H., & Sulzer, D. (2004). Frequency-dependent modulation of dopamine release by nicotine. *Nature Neuroscience*, *7*(6), 581–582.

Chapter 4
Targeting Reward-Relevant Nicotinic Receptors in the Discovery of Novel Pharmacotherapeutic Agents to Treat Tobacco Dependence

Linda P. Dwoskin, Marharyta Pivavarchyk, B. Matthew Joyce, Nichole M. Neugebauer, Guangrong Zheng, Zhenfa Zhang, Michael T. Bardo, and Peter A. Crooks

Introduction

Tobacco Alkaloids and Tobacco Use

Tobacco dependence is a significant health concern and the most preventable cause of death in the United States. Tobacco (*Nicotiana tabacum*) contains numerous pharmacologically active alkaloids of which nicotine is considered to be the primary alkaloid responsible for tobacco dependence (Balfour, 2002; Pomerleau & Pomerleau, 1992). Studies investigating the effects of minor tobacco alkaloids have demonstrated their pharmacological activity and interaction with nicotinic acetylcholine receptors (nAChRs; Dwoskin et al., 1995; Papke, Dwoskin & Crooks, 2007; Wei et al., 2005). In particular, the minor tobacco alkaloid and nicotine metabolite, nornicotine, likely contributes to tobacco dependence (Crooks & Dwoskin, 1997; Ghosheh, Dwoskin, Li, & Crooks, 1999; Ghosheh, Dwoskin, Miller, & Crooks, 2001) and warrants further investigation.

Nicotinic Receptor-Mediated Dopamine Release in Nicotine Reward

Nicotine acts as an agonist at all known nAChR subtypes. Primarily, nAChRs are located presynaptically, modulating neurotransmitter release (Wonnacott, 1997). Activation of nAChRs on dopamine (DA) terminals in the nucleus accumbens (NAc), medial prefrontal cortex, and striatum evokes the release of DA, which mediates the reward produced by nicotine leading to tobacco dependence (Bonci, Bernardi, Grillner, & Mercuri, 2003; Clarke & Pert, 1985; Corrigall, Franklin, Coen, &

L.P. Dwoskin
Department of Pharmaceutical Sciences, College of Pharmacy, University of Kentucky, Lexington, KY 40536-0082
e-mail: ldwoskin@email.uky.edu

Clarke, 1992; Dani & De Biasi, 2001; Di Chiara, 2000; Koob, 1992; McGehee & Role, 1995; Pidoplichko, DeBiasi, Williams, & Dani, 1997; Pidoplichko et al., 2004; Pontieri, Tanda, Orzi, & Di Chiara, 1996; Spanagel & Weiss, 1999; Stolerman, & Jarvis, 1995; Teng, Crooks, Buxton, & Dwoskin, 1997; Wise, 2000; Wonnacott, 1997; Zhou, Liang, & Dani, 2001; also see Chapter 2, this Volume).

The mesolimbic DA system projects from the ventral tegmental area (VTA) to innervate medium spiny GABAergic neurons in the ventral striatum (Balfour, 2004; Bardo, 1998; Dani, 2003; Dani & Bertrand, 2007; Wonnacott, Sidhpura, & Balfour, 2005). The NAc shell is responsible for the gating of primary appetitive stimuli associated with unconditioned drug reward, including nicotine (Bardo, 1998; Di Chiara et al., 2004; Dani & De Biasi, 2001; Koob, 1999; Wise & Bozarth, 1987). The prefrontal cortex mediates secondary conditioned stimuli, i.e., cues paired with the drug of abuse that produces reward expectancy (Berridge & Robinson, 1998; Brody et al., 2004; Di Chiara et al., 2004; Rose & Behm, 2004; Shima & Tanji, 1998). Integration of this information from the prefrontal cortex occurs in part in the striatum and results in the initiation and execution of movement in reward expectancy and detection of reward (Martin-Soelch et al., 2001).

Sensorimotor and visual cues (e.g., a lit cigarette) act as secondary conditioned stimuli, which leads to an increase in nicotine self-administration in the dependent individual (Niaura et al., 1998; Perkins, Epstein, Grobe, & Fonte, 1994). Comparable findings have been shown in animal models. For example, rats show increased response rates for nicotine self-administration when nicotine is presented in combination with a secondary visual cue, suggesting that nicotine enhances the sensitivity of the neural system to the reward associated with the secondary stimulus (Caggiula et al., 2002; Palmatier et al., 2006; for a detailed discussion of this research see Chapter 6, this Volume). Presentation of the cue may in itself produce some relatively low level of reward which is enhanced with noncontingent exposure to nicotine (Donny et al., 2003). The primary reinforcing effects of nicotine depend on nAChR activity and an expectation of a reinforcing effect, while the reinforcing-enhancement effects of nicotine depend only on the acute action of nicotine at nAChRs (Palmatier, Liu, Caggiula, Donny, & Sved, 2007).

Nicotine interacts with the neural circuitry for mediating the experience of natural rewards, leading to habit formation, compulsive use, and ultimately abuse. Research from animal models employing intravenous (i.v.) nicotine self-administration demonstrates that nicotine lowers the threshold for intracranial self-stimulation, thereby increasing reward sensitivity in the neural circuitry responsible for integrating information on natural, biologically relevant rewards (Kenny & Markou, 2006; Wise, 1996). Neurochemical correlates of the nicotine enhancement of the reinforcing efficacy of both primary and secondary conditioned reward have also been described using fast-scan cyclic voltammetry in rat striatal slices (Rice & Cragg, 2004). Results from these studies show that nicotine enhances DA release during phasic burst firing, but not during tonic neural activity. These findings suggest that nicotine desensitizes nAChRs to suppress DA release during non-reward low firing frequencies and selectively enhances reward-relevant DA release at higher burst-like, tonic firing frequencies. Thus, nicotine is thought to enhance the signal-to-noise when DA neuronal activity switches from tonic to phasic firing, possibly in response to primary rewarding stimuli, as well as to conditioned stimuli associated with reward.

In in vivo microdialysis studies, nicotine has been shown to increase extracellular DA in the NAc, and this nicotine-induced increase in DA release has been associated with reward (Benwell & Balfour, 1992; Di Chiara et al., 2004; Imperato, Mulas, & Di Chiara, 1986; Rahman, Zhang, & Corrigall, 2004). Additionally, 6-hydroxydopamine lesioning of mesolimbic DA neurons, as well as administration of DA receptor antagonists reduce nicotine self-administration, providing support for a primary role for DA in reward produced by nicotine (Corrigall, 1999; Corrigall & Coen, 1989; Corrigall et al., 1992; Di Chiara, 2000; Singer, Wallace, & Hall, 1982). The nicotine-induced increase in extracellular DA in NAc has been shown to be inhibited by systemic or local VTA application of either noncompetitive or competitive nAChR antagonists, e.g., mecamylamine and dihydro-β-erythroidine (DHβE), respectively, demonstrating the involvement of nAChRs in the VTA in mediating the effect of nicotine to increase DA release in NAc (Benwell, Balfour, & Birrell, 1995; Brazell, Mitchell, Joseph, & Gray, 1990; Corrigall, Coen, & Adamson, 1994; Fu, Matta, Gao, & Sharp, 2000; Imperato et al., 1986; Nisell, Nomikos, & Svensson, 1994). Together, these results support a role for nAChR-mediated DA release in the rewarding effects of nicotine.

Nicotinic Receptor Subtypes

Activation of nAChRs modulates presynaptic neurotransmitter release by promoting calcium influx through nAChRs directly, or through subsequent indirect activation of voltage-sensitive calcium channels (Kulak, McIntosh, Yoshikami, & Olivera, 2001; McGehee & Role, 1995; Soliakov & Wonnacott, 1996; Wonnacott, 1997). The existence of 12 genes encoding $\alpha2$-$\alpha10$ and $\beta2$-$\beta4$ subunits leads to enormous complexities in receptor composition, as well as the potential for functional diversity and pharmacological response as a result of the numerous varieties of subunit compositions of nAChRs. nAChRs form pentameric protein structures with a stoichiometry of 2α and 3β (Anand, Conroy, Schoepfer, Whiting & Lindstrom, 1991; Cooper, Couturier & Ballivet, 1991), and these heteromeric nAChRs are the most commonly expressed in the central nervous system (CNS). Of these, $\alpha4\beta2^*$ alone or perhaps in combination with other types of subunits are predominant in the CNS. Note, the asterisk following the subunit designation on nAChRs indicates that the precise composition of subunits is not known for these native receptors.

Immunoprecipitation studies reveal the overlapping CNS distribution of the various types of subunit mRNAs (Deneris, Boulter, Swanson, Patrick, & Heinemann, 1989; Wada, McKinnon, Heinemann, Patrick, & Swanson, 1990; Wada et al., 1989). Individual neurons have been identified that express multiple nAChR subtypes, and combinations of more than two different subunits can form functional nAChRs (Conroy, Vernallis, & Berg, 1992; Forsayeth & Kobrin, 1997; Poth et al., 1997). Studies employing recombinant receptors have shown that when the ratio of subunit pairs is varied, different classes of nAChR subtypes can be formed and their function (e.g., sensitivity to receptor activation) depends on subunit ratio (Lopez-Hernandez et al., 2004; Zwart & Vijverberg, 1998). Exposure to nicotine can also influence nAChR subtype stoichiometry, function, and maturity in recombinant receptor systems (Corringer, Sallette, & Changeux, 2006; Lopez-Hernandez et al., 2004; Nelson, Kuryatov, Choi, Zhou, & Lindstrom, 2003). In addition, individual nigral DA neurons can be categorized based upon the specific subtype compositions expressed (Azam, Winzer-Serhan, Chen, & Leslie, 2002). Thus, the presence of specific subunit mRNAs, the ratio of the expressed subunits and subtypes in individual DA neurons, and the pharmacological history of the organism are all important to neuronal function and may play an important role in the response to nicotine.

nAChR modulation of neurotransmitter release has been reviewed recently (Dani & Bertrand, 2007; Gotti, Zoli, & Clementi, 2006; also see Chapter 2, this Volume). In the striatum and NAc, heteromeric nAChRs containing the $\beta2$ subunit are predominant, and are expressed with either the $\alpha4$ or $\alpha6$ subunit (Jones, Bolam & Wonnacott, 2001; Wonnacott, Kaiser, Mogg, Soliakov, & Jones, 2000; Zoli et al., 2002). Homomeric pentamers comprising $\alpha7*$ nAChRs are the second most abundant nAChRs in the brain (Anand et al., 1991; Flores, Rogers, Pabreza, Wolfe, & Kellar, 1992; Wada et al., 1989). Compared to heteromeric nAChRs, homomeric $\alpha7*$ subtypes are not as sensitive to nicotine. $\alpha7*$ nAChRs are located on glutamatergic presynaptic terminals in the VTA and substantia nigra, and as such may play a role in mediating nicotine-evoked DA release and reward (Mansvelder & McGehee, 2000; Wooltorton, Pidoplichko, Broide & Dani, 2003). Moreover, studies using $\beta2$ knockout mice implicate $\beta2$-containing nAChRs in nicotine-evoked DA release (Grady et al., 2001; Grady et al., 2002; Picciotto et al., 1998; Scholze, Orr-Urtreger, Changeux, McIntosh, & Huck, 2007; Whiteaker et al., 2000; Zhou et al., 2001).

nAChR subtypes including $\alpha4\beta2*$, $\alpha6\beta2*$, and $\alpha4\alpha6\beta2*$ also have been suggested to mediate the dopaminergic response to nicotine (Champtiaux et al., 2003). A comprehensive molecular genetics study in which an individual subunit gene (i.e., $\alpha4$, $\alpha5$, $\alpha7$, $\beta2$, $\beta3$, and $\beta4$) was deleted suggested that at least six different nAChR subtypes mediate nicotine-evoked DA release from mouse striatum, including α-conotoxin-MII (α-CtxMII)-sensitive nAChRs (i.e., $\alpha6\beta2\beta3*$, $\alpha4\alpha6\beta2\beta3*$ and possibly a small amount of $\alpha6\beta2*$ or $\alpha4\alpha6\beta2*$ subtypes) and α-CtxMII-resistant nAChRs (i.e., $\alpha4\beta2*$ and $\alpha4\alpha5\beta2*$ subtypes), whereas deletion of $\beta4$ and $\alpha7$ subunits had no effect (Gotti et al., 2005; Salminen et al., 2004). nAChRs containing $\alpha6$ and $\beta3$ subunits have also been implicated in nicotine-evoked DA release (Cui et al., 2003; Kuryatov, Olale, Cooper, Choi, & Lindstrom, 2000; Le Novere, Zoli, & Changeux, 1996). Importantly, substantia nigra and VTA neurons express high levels of both $\alpha6$ and $\beta3$ mRNA (Charpantier, Barneoud, Moser, Besnard, & Sgard, 1998; Cui et al., 2003; Deneris et al., 1989; Goldner, Dineley, & Patrick, 1997), consistent with the involvement of subtypes containing these subunits in mediating nicotine-evoked DA release. In a recent study, striatal synaptosomes from $\alpha4$ and $\alpha4/\beta3$ knockout mice were used to isolate nAChRs containing the $\alpha6$ subunit and determine their involvement in the effects of nicotine on DA release (Salminen et al., 2007). Results showed an increased EC_{50} value (i.e., the concentration required to produce 50% of the maximal agonist effect) for nicotine to evoke DA release with the deletion of the $\alpha4$ subunit. Furthermore, results from the combined deletion of $\alpha4$ and $\beta3$ subunits showed a 4–7-fold increase in EC_{50} value compared to deletion of only the $\alpha4$ subunit. Taken together with previous reports in the literature, these results support the contention that the $\alpha4\alpha6\beta2\beta3*$ nAChR subtype constitutes about 50% of $\alpha6$-containing nAChRs on DA terminals of wild type mice and is the most sensitive to activation by nicotine, which strongly implicates the $\alpha4\alpha6\beta2\beta3*$ subtype in nicotine-evoked DA release and nicotine reward.

nAChR Antagonists

Ligands that specifically inhibit nAChR subtypes have been investigated for their ability to inhibit nicotine-evoked [^{3}H]DA release from synaptosomes and brain slices. DHβE is an antagonist at $\beta2$-containing nAChR subtypes, whereas methyllycaconitine (MLA) and α-bungarotoxin are relatively selective antagonists for $\alpha7*$ nAChRs (Alkondon, Pereira, Wonnacott, & Albuquerque, 1992; Castro & Albuquerque 1995; Gray, Rajan, Radcliffe, Yakehiro, & Dani, 1996). DHβE has been shown to decrease nicotine self-administration in rats, providing support for the involvement of $\beta2$-containing nAChRs in nicotine reward (Grottick et al., 2000). Peptide neurotoxins isolated from the venom of cone snails have been shown to be selective ligands for a variety of nAChR subtypes (McIntosh, Olivera, & Cruz, 1999; McIntosh, Santos, & Olivera, 1999; Nicke, Wonnacott, & Lewis, 2004). For example, α-conotoxin MII (α-CtxMII) binds $\alpha6$-containing nAChRs with high affinity and binds $\alpha3$-containing nAChRs with lower affinity. It is important to note that $\alpha6$-containing nAChRs comprise 25–30% of the presynaptic nAChRs in rodents, and as much as 70% in non-human primates (Kaiser, Soliakov, Harvey, Luetje, & Wonnacott, 1998; Kulak, Nguyen, Olivera, & McIntosh, 1997; McCallum et al., 2005; Salminen et al., 2004;). α-CtxMII was found to partially inhibit nicotine-evoked DA release from striatal synaptosomes supporting the involvement of at least two different subtypes of nAChRs, at least one of which contains $\alpha6$ and/or $\alpha3$ subunits (Grady, Grun, Marks, & Collins, 1997; Kulak et al.,1997).

Approved Smoking Cessation Pharmacotherapies

Currently, three smoking cessation pharmacotherapies have been approved by the FDA that validate the development of new therapeutic agents that target nAChRs. These are varenicline, marketed as Chantix®; bupropion, marketed as Zyban® and co-indicated as a treatment for depression in addition to smoking cessation; and finally nicotine replacement therapies (NRT), making use of oral and transdermal delivery. The NRT provides nicotine to smokers attempting to quit, with the aim of precluding the need for tobacco consumption. Varenicline has been shown to be a partial agonist at $\alpha4\beta2*$ nAChRs and a full agonist at $\alpha7*$ nAChRs (Coe et al., 2005; Mihalak, Carroll, & Luetje, 2006). In contrast, bupropion inhibits multiple nAChR subtypes, and also inhibits neurotransmitter transporters resulting in accumulation of extracellular DA in the NAc, among other effects (Nomikos, Damsma, Wenkstern, & Fibiger, 1989; Nomikos, Damsma, Wenkstern, & Fibiger, 1992; Rauhut, Neugebauer, Dwoskin, & Bardo, 2003; Slemmer, Martin, & Damaj, 2000; Miller, Sumithran, & Dwoskin, 2002; Vann, Rosecrans, James, Philibin, & Robinson, 2006).

Mecamylamine, a noncompetitive antagonist at nAChRs that lacks subtype selectivity, has been shown to reverse the positive and negative subjective effects resulting from nicotine use in smokers (Lundahl, Henningfield, & Lukas, 2000). The use of mecamylamine in combination with NRTs afforded extended smoking cessation outcomes in comparison with a nicotine patch alone (Rose et al., 1994). However, a major drawback of this therapy is the non-selective nature of mecamylamine, which leads to unwanted peripherally mediated side-effects such as constipation and dry-mouth that contribute to non-compliance and relapse (Rose et al., 1994; Rose, Westman, Behm, Johnson, & Goldberg, 1999). The above smoking cessation strategies have been shown to be limited in efficacy as indicated by high relapse rates. Thus, there remains a need for new pharmacotherapies that target specific nAChR subtypes and that minimize side-effects and relapse (George & O'Malley, 2004; Hurt et al., 2003; Irvin, Hendricks, & Brandon, 2003).

Novel nAChR Antagonists

Studies from our laboratory have focused on the hypothesis that selective antagonists targeting nAChRs that mediate nicotine-evoked DA release will be clinically effective smoking cessation agents, circumventing unwanted side-effects. Because nicotine interacts with all nAChR subtypes, our discovery of subtype-selective nAChR antagonists was initiated using nicotine as the structural scaffold. Simple addition of an N-n-alkyl group converts nicotine from an agonist to an antagonist, and surprisingly, subtype selectivity began to emerge based on the number of methylene groups in the n-alkyl chain (Ayers, Clauset, Schmitt, Dwoskin, & Crooks, 2005; Crooks et al., 2004; Dwoskin et al., 2004; Grinevich et al., 2003; Sumithran et al., 2005; Wilkins, Haubner, Ayers, Crooks, & Dwoskin, 2002; Zheng et al., 2006). In the latter studies, we also investigated structural modifications of the cationic nicotinium head group. The analog with the longest carbon chain, N-n-docecyl-nicotinium iodide (NDDNI, C_{12}), was the most potent ($IC_{50} = 9$ nM) inhibitor of nicotine-evoked [^{3}H]DA overflow, compared with that of DHβE ($IC_{50} = 1.6$ μM). The IC_{50} indicates the analog concentration which decreased nicotine-evoked [^{3}H]DA overflow by 50% of the maximal effect. The results revealed a significant correlation between N-n-alkyl chain length and nicotinium analog-induced inhibition of nicotine-evoked DA release (Wilkins et al., 2002). Unfortunately, with chain lengths of C_9–C_{12}, a loss of selectivity was observed, since these compounds also exhibited significant affinity (Ki = 0.23 – 2.1 μM) for α4β2* nAChRs (Wilkins, Grinevich, Ayers, Crooks, & Dwoskin, 2003). Interestingly, further increases in affinity for the α4β2* nAChR subtype were observed with *N-n*-alkyl chain lengths of C_{13}–C_{20} (unpublished data); however, none of the analogs had high affinity for the α7* subtype (Dwoskin et al., 2004; Crooks et al., 2004; Sumithran et al., 2005; Wilkins et al., 2003; Wilkins, Miller, Ayers, Crooks, & Dwoskin, 2006 and unpublished data). Importantly, these *N-n*-alkylnicotinium analogs exhibited high affinity for the blood–brain barrier choline transporter (Allen, Lockman, Roder, Dwoskin, & Crooks, 2003; Crooks et al., 2004). Subsequent studies with tritiated *N-n*-octylnicotinium iodide (NONI) showed that this *mono*-quaternary ammonium compound was actively transported into the CNS *via* the blood–brain barrier choline transporter. These studies indicate that the above *mono*-quaternary ammonium compounds penetrate the CNS and are considered brain bio available molecules.

Taking into account the classical discovery that the *bis*-tri alkylammonium channel blockers, hexamethonium and decamethonium, exhibited subtype selectivity between ganglionic and muscle type nAChRs, respectively, we adopted a similar approach and generated a sub-library of compounds centered around a *bis*-nicotinium analog structure and incorporating a variety of head groups and diverse linker units which varied in length, unsaturation, and polarity (Ayers et al., 2002; Ayers et al., 2005; Crooks et al., 2004; Dwoskin et al., 2004; Rahman et al., 2007; Zheng et al., 2006; current Chapter). This approach afforded a new lead compound, *N,N'*-dodecyl-1,12-diyl-*bis*-3-picolinium dibromide (bPiDDB), which potently inhibited nicotine-evoked DA release both *in vitro* and *in vivo*, and more-over, decreased nicotine self-administration in rats (Ayers et al., 2002; Ayers et al., 2005; Crooks et al., 2002; Crooks et al., 2004; Dwoskin et al., 2004; Rahman et al., 2007). The latter studies also showed that bPiDDB had no affinity for either the α4β2* or α7* binding sites in rat brain membranes. Utilizing [^{14}C]-bPiDDB, we have also shown that this compound is brain bio available and similar to the *mono*-quaternary ammonium compounds utilizes the blood–brain barrier choline transporter for active transport into the CNS with similar affinity as the natural substrate, choline (Zhang, Lockman, Geldenhuys, Allen, Dwoskin, & Crooks, 2005; Crooks et al., 2004.)

In the evolution of subsequent molecules within this series, we constructed a scaffold incorporating a central phenyl ring from which was appended three identical quaternary ammonium head groups in a 1, 3, 5-orientation, i.e., *tris*-analogs; these head groups were tethered to the phenyl ring *via* linker units to afford *N-N'* inter-atomic distances approximating that in the bPiDDB molecule (Pivavarchyk, Zhang, Crooks & Dwoskin, 2007; Stokes et al., 2007; current Chapter). The linker units were either saturated or contained unsaturation. Further structural elaboration led to the synthesis of the *tetrakis* compounds, in which four quaternary ammonium head groups were similarly arranged around a central phenyl ring in a 1, 2, 4, 5-orientation, incorporating saturated or unsaturated linkers. Each of the above sub-libraries, i.e., *mono*-, *bis*-, *tris*- and *tetrakis*-quaternary ammonium analogs, have provided structure activity (SAR) information of use in developingthe antagonist pharmacophore for nAChRs that mediate nicotine-evoked DA release.

The current chapter illustrates the progressive structural approach and gradual improvement in the hit-rate associated with these novel nAChR antagonists. Using this approach, we have determined the ability of these analogs to alter DA release, and moreover, to inhibit nicotine-evoked DA release from superfused rat striatal slices. Additionally, herein, we report results demonstrating the ability of bPiDDB to decrease nicotine-induced reinstatement of nicotine self-administration in order to assess the effectiveness of this lead compound to inhibit nicotine-seeking behavior in rats.

Methods

Animals

For DA release and behavioral assays, male Sprague-Dawley rats (200 to 225 g) from Harlan Industries (Indianapolis, IN) were used. For blood–brain barrier choline transporter assays, Fischer 344 rats (220–250 g) from Charles River Laboratories (Kingston, NY, USA) were used. Rats had unlimited access to food and water in the home cage, except as noted. Rats were maintained on a 14:10 h light/dark cycle in which the lights came on at 0600 h and went off at 2000 h. All experiments were conducted during the light phase of the cycle. In the behavioral studies, rats were acclimated to the animal colony for at least 5 days and were handled briefly on 3–5 consecutive days prior to the start of the experiment. The Institutional Animal Care and Use Committee of the University of Kentucky approved the conduct of the experiments described herein. The experiments conformed to the guidelines established by the NIH Guide for the Care and Use of Laboratory Animals (1996 Edition).

Synthesis of Analogs

The general strategy for the synthesis of the compounds described involved initial Sonagashira coupling of various halogenated benzenes with 4-pentyn-1-ol. Thus, 1,2-dibromobenzene, 1,3-dibromobenzene or 1,3,5-tribromobenzene was coupled with 4-pentyn-1-ol in the presence of *bis*-(triphenylphosphine)palladium dichloride and cuprous iodide in triethylamine to afford 1,2-benzene-*bis*-1-pentyn-5-ol, 1,3-benzene-*bis*-1-pentyn-5-ol or 1,3,5-benzene-*tris*-1-pentyn-5-ol, respectively. Due to the sluggish reactivity of 1,2,4,5-tetrabromobenzene under Sonagashira coupling conditions, the alternative synthon, 1,2,4,5-tetraiodobenzene, was utilized to afford the desired 1,2,4,5-benzene-*tetrakis*-1-pentyn-5-ol. The pentyn-5-ol side chains of these compounds were then either directly transformed into the corresponding pentynyl bromide derivative or catalytically reduced to the corresponding pentan-1-ol side chains, followed by bromination to afford the corresponding pentanyl bromide derivative. Bromination was achieved in high yield, utilizing a mild bromination procedure employing triphenylphosphine and carbon tetrabromide. Thus, four precursors with pentynyl bromide side chains and four precursors with pentanyl bromide side chains were prepared accordingly. Each of these bromide precursors was reacted with a series of azaheterocycles to yield three sublibraries of *bis-*, *tris-*, or *tetrakis*-quaternary ammonium analogs.

[^{3}H]DA Release Assay

Nicotine-evoked overflow of [^{3}H]DA (28 Ci/mmol, Perkin Elmer, Boston, MA) from striatal slices preloaded with [^{3}H]DA was determined using a previously published method with minor modifications (Grinevich et al., 2003; Sumithran et al., 2005; Wilkins et al., 2002). Briefly, striatal slices were prepared using a McIlwain tissue chopper (Mickle Laboratory Engineering Co Ltd, Surrey, England). Slices were incubated at 34°C in Krebs' buffer containing 118 mM NaCl, 4.7 mM KCl, 1.2 mM MgCl$_2$, 1.0 mM NaH$_2$PO$_4$, 1.3 mM CaCl$_2$, 11.1 mM α-D-glucose, 25 mM NaHCO$_3$, 0.11 mM L-ascorbic acid, and 0.004 mM ethylenediaminetetraacetic acid (EDTA), pH 7.4, saturated with 95%O$_2$/5%CO$_2$ in a metabolic shaker for 30 min. Slices were transferred to fresh buffer, 0.1 μM [^{3}H]DA added and incubation continued for 30 min. Subsequently, slices were rinsed with Krebs' buffer and transferred to superfusion chambers maintained at 34°C (Brandel suprafusion system 2500, Gaithersburg, MD) and were superfused (flow rate = 0.6 ml/min) for 60 min with oxygenated Krebs' buffer containing both nomifensine (10 μM), a DA uptake inhibitor, and pargyline (10 μM), a monoamine oxidase inhibitor. Subsequently, two samples (2.4 ml/sample, sample collection at 4-min intervals) were collected for determination of basal [^{3}H]outflow. Slices were superfused for 36 min in the absence (0 nM; control) or presence of analog (1 nM–10 μM) to determine the effect of the compound alone. Nicotine (10 μM) was added to the buffer, superfusion continued and samples were collected for 36 min to determine the ability of analog to inhibit nicotine-evoked [^{3}H]DA overflow. At the end of the experiment, slices were removed from the chambers and were solubilized with 1 ml TS-2 tissue solubilizer (Research Products International Corp, Prospect, IL). Scintillation cocktail (4 ml) was added to superfusate and solubilized tissue samples. Radioactivity was determined by liquid scintillation spectrometry using a 1600 TR Tri Carb Liquid Scintillation Analyzer (Packard, Downer's Grove, IL). Fractional release was determined by dividing the [^{3}H] in each superfusate sample by the tissue-[^{3}H] at the time of collection and expressed as percent of total tissue tritium. Basal [^{3}H]outflow was defined as the mean of fractional release in the two basal samples collected prior to the introduction of analog in the superfusion buffer. Total [^{3}H]overflow was the sum of fractional release above basal following addition of nicotine to the buffer. A one-way ANOVA with Dunnett's post hoc analysis was used to determine if analog inhibited nicotine-evoked total [^{3}H]DA overflow.

Nicotine-Induced Reinstatement of Nicotine Self-Administration

Experiments were conducted in operant conditioning chambers (ENV-001; Med Associates, St Albans, VT, USA), housed in sound-attenuated outer chambers using a Med Associates Interface model SG-503 with MED-IV software. The end walls of the operant conditioning chamber were aluminum, front and back walls were made of clear Plexiglas and the floor consisted of 18 stainless steel rods (4.8 mm in diameter and placed 1.6 cm apart). Located in the bottom center of one of the end walls was an opening (5 × 4.2 cm) for a recessed food tray, into which a food hopper could dispense sucrose pellets individually. Located on either side of the food tray was a response lever. A 28-V white cue light was located 6 cm above each response lever. An infusion pump (Med-Associates, St. Albans, VT) delivered drug reinforcement *via* a silastic tube attached to a swivel mounted on the outside of the back wall.

For nicotine self-administration, rats were initially given brief lever-press training for food presentations (45 mg Precision Pellets, Bio-Serv, Frenchtown, NJ). Rats were food deprived to 85% of their *ad libitum* weights by restricting their intake of rat chow to 8–10 g per day for 5 days. Rats were then briefly trained to press a lever in a two-lever operant chamber using a fixed ratio 1 (FR 1) schedule, which was increased to a FR 5 across seven sessions (15 min for each session). Rats were given 20 g/day of food following each lever-press training session.

After training for food reinforcement, rats were allowed *ad libitum* access to food in the home cage for 7 days and were then implanted with an indwelling jugular catheter. Rats were anesthetized by injections of ketamine (80 mg/kg, i.p.) and diazepam (5 mg/kg, i.p.) and a silastic catheter was inserted into the jugular vein. The free end of the catheter exited through the skin and was secured to an acrylic head mount attached to the skull. An infusion pump was attached to the head mount *via* silastic tubing that was protected by a metal spring leash during the self-administration sessions. The nicotine self-administration procedure was similar to that described previously (Corrigall & Coen, 1989). Following recovery from catheter surgery (7 days), rats were reintroduced to the operant conditioning chambers for 60-min daily sessions; food restriction was maintained for the duration of the experiment (17–20 g/day, given in the home cage after the session). Responses made on one lever (active) were recorded and were followed by an infusion of nicotine (0.03 mg/kg/infusion, 100 µl delivered over 5.9 sec), whereas responses made on the other lever (inactive) were recorded, but had no scheduled consequence. The unit dose of nicotine (0.03 mg/kg/infusion) was chosen based on previously published work (Corrigall & Coen, 1989). Nicotine was administered i.v. and dose is expressed as the free base weight. This dose produces optimal responding on a FR schedule with limited access. Completion of the FR requirement resulted in simultaneous activation of the infusion pump and cue lights, which signaled a 20-sec time-out period during which responding on either lever had no consequence. The FR 1 schedule was gradually increased across sessions to a terminal FR 5 schedule. Rats were trained on the FR 5 schedule until stable responding was achieved, defined by the following criteria: (1) minimum of 10 infusions per session; (2) less than 20% variability in active lever responding for three consecutive sessions; and (3) minimum of 2:1 (active:inactive) response ratio.

After responding for nicotine stabilized, rats underwent at least 10 extinction sessions during which all cues remained the same and saline was substituted for nicotine. Animals were then assessed for reinstatement following systemic administration of nicotine. Mecamylamine or bPiDDB was administered 5 min prior to nicotine or saline. Animals were placed in the operant chamber 15 min after the nicotine or saline injection in all studies. All reinstatement dose regimens were counterbalanced using a Latin square design. Separate groups of rats were assessed for nicotine-induced reinstatement (0.2 mg/kg), the effects of mecamylamine on nicotine (0.2 mg/kg)-induced reinstatement, and the effects of bPiDDB pretreatment on nicotine (0.2 mg/kg)-induced reinstatement. Data are expressed as the number of lever presses. Separate two-way ANOVAs were used to assess the effect of mecamylamine and bPiDDB on operant responding. For each ANOVA, dose of antagonist was a within-subject factor. Statistical significance was declared at $p < 0.05$.

Results and Discussion

$[^3H]DA$ Release Assay

Our research efforts have focused on identifying analogs which inhibit nicotine-evoked $[^3H]DA$ overflow from superfused rat striatal slices. Of the 283 novel analogs synthesized thus far, 205 analogs have been assayed using a probe concentration of 100 nM to assess inhibition of nicotine-evoked $[^3H]DA$ release. We defined a "hit" as an analog that inhibited nicotine-evoked $[^3H]DA$ release $\geq 40\%$ at a concentration of 100 nM. Of the 205 analogs tested, 67 inhibited nicotine-evoked $[^3H]DA$ release $\geq 40\%$. Thus, 32% of the analogs tested were considered to be "hits." An additional 36 analogs (17% of the total number of analogs assessed) inhibited nicotine-evoked $[^3H]DA$ release between 30–40%, and were considered to be lower priority "hits."

A subset of the above analogs constitutes a new structural motif, in which an additional quaternary ammonium head group is incorporated into the parent *bis*-quaternary ammonium structure, e.g., bPiDDB, to afford a *tris*-quaternary ammonium structure (Fig. 4.1). These *tris*-molecules were constructed using a scaffold incorporating a central phenyl ring from which was appended three identical quaternary ammonium head groups in a 1, 3, 5-orientation, and tethered to the phenyl ring *via* linker units to afford *N-N'* inter-atomic distances approximating that in bPiDDB (Fig. 4.2; Stokes et al., 2007; Pivavarchyk et al., 2007). Also, the linker units were either saturated or unsaturated; the unsaturated linkers incorporating a triple bond conjugated to the central phenyl ring. The rationale was based on the premise that increasing the number of quaternary ammonium head groups from 2 to 3 would result in an increase in the number of ionic interactions with putative negatively charged binding sites on nAChRs mediating nicotine-evoked DA release.

(bPiDDB)   ***bis*-Quaternary Ammonium   *tris*-Quaternary Ammonium Scaffold
                 Scaffold (bPiDDB)

Fig. 4.1 Structure of bPiDDB and the structural scaffolds of *bis*- and *tris*-quaternary ammonium analogs

GZ 551B and GZ 558C contain nicotinium head groups, whereas other analogs contain the 3-picolinium (GZ 555A and GZ 550A) moiety present in the lead candidate compound, bPiDDB, as well as related isomeric picolinium (GZ 554A, GZ 555B, GZ 554B, GZ 555C), and lutidinium (GZ553A, GZ 553B, GZ 557A, GZ 557B) moieties. More bulky quaternary ammonium head groups also were introduced, such as 3-n-butylpyridinium (GZ 558B and GZ 551A), isoquinolinium (GZ 552B and GZ 556B), quinolinium (GZ 552A and GZ 556A), and phenylpyridinium groupings (GZ 550B and GZ 558A). The availability of both the saturated and unsaturated linker units in these *tris*-quaternary ammonium compounds provides information on the importance of conformational flexibility and the extent of the area of coplanarity in the center of the molecule with respect to the ability of these compounds to interact with critical nAChR binding sites to inhibit nicotine-evoked DA release.

Figure 4.3 shows the *tris*-analog-induced inhibition of [^{3}H]DA release evoked by 10 μM nicotine. Each of the 20 *tris*-analogs evaluated was assessed at 100 nM. *tris*-Analogs afforded decreases in nicotine-evoked [^{3}H]DA release in the range of 24–70% of control (control represents the effect of nicotine in the absence of analog); however, six of these analogs, including two quinolinium analogs (GZ 552A and GZ 556A), a 3-phenylpyridinium analog (GZ 558A), a nicotinium analog (GZ 558C), and two isomeric lutidinium analogs (GZ 557A and GZ 553B), did not inhibit nicotine-evoked [^{3}H]DA release. Nine analogs were identified as hits ($\geq$30% inhibition). One commonality in the chemical structure of several of the hits (i.e., GZ 550A, GZ 554A, GZ 554B, GZ 555A, and GZ 555C) is the presence of a 2-, 3- or 4-picolinium head group, with a saturated or unsaturated linker. In terms of SAR,

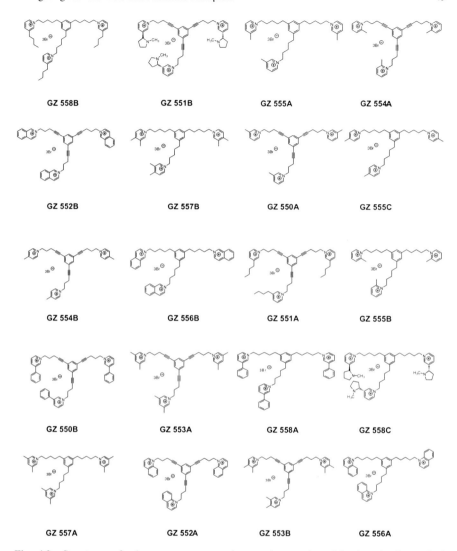

Fig. 4.2 Structures of *tris*-quaternary ammonium analogs evaluated in the nicotine-evoked dopamine release assay

the position of the methyl group in these picolinium analogs did not appear to be critical. However, the 2-picolinium derivative with a saturated linker produced 25% inhibition and was not considered a hit. Generally, inclusion of a second methyl group into the pyridinium ring to afford a lutidinium analog appears to significantly reduce activity. The other four hits had more diversity in head group structure, in that they had either a nicotinium (GZ 551B), a 3,4-lutidinium (GZ 557B), an isoquinolinium (GZ 552B) or a 3-*n*-butylpyridinium head group (GZ 558B). Of note, the *tris*-analogs containing quinolinium head groups (GZ 552A and GZ 556A),

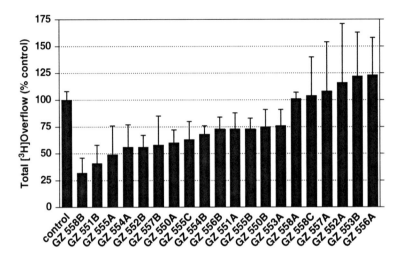

Fig. 4.3 The inhibitory activity of *tris*-quaternary ammonium analogs in the nicotine (10 μM)-evoked dopamine release assay. Compounds were evaluated at a probe concentration of 100 nM in triplicate, and results are expressed as percentage inhibition compared to control (absence of drug)

incorporating either unsaturated or saturated linker units, respectively, produced no inhibition of nicotine-evoked [³H]DA release. Generally, the *tris*-picolinium analogs were pharmacologically active and the structural relationship to bPiDDB is apparent.

The most potent analog, GZ 558B, which contained a *tris*-3-*n*-butylpyridinium head group, exhibited 70% inhibition of nicotine-evoked DA release and incorporated a saturated linker connecting the head groups to the 1, 3, and 5 positions of the central phenyl ring. However, if this linker was changed to an unsaturated triple bond containing linker (i.e., GZ 551A), which increases the area of planarity of the central core moiety of the molecule, then inhibition was reduced to 25%. This indicates the importance of conformational flexibility in the linker unit. Surprisingly, the opposite was observed with the unsaturated isoquinolinium analog (GZ 552B), which exhibited about 48% inhibition of nicotine-evoked DA release and contained the more rigid triple bond linker units. When the triple bonds were reduced to give the saturated isoquinolinium analog (GZ 556B), inhibition was reduced to 26%. Similarly, the more rigid nicotinium analog (GZ 551B) was one of the most potent compounds in the series producing 60% inhibition; however, when the triple bonds were reduced to afford the more flexible nicotinium analog (GZ 558C), all inhibitory activity was lost, indicating the important role of linker geometry in combination with the nature of the head group in these molecules. In summary, *tris*-analogs with 3-alkylpyridinium head groups containing saturated linkers exhibit robust inhibitory activity, whereas *tris*-analogs with quinolinium and nicotinium head groups containing saturated linkers exhibit poor inhibitory activity.

To further investigate the effect of increasing the number of quaternary ammonium head groups in the molecule, a series of novel *tetrakis* quaternary ammonium

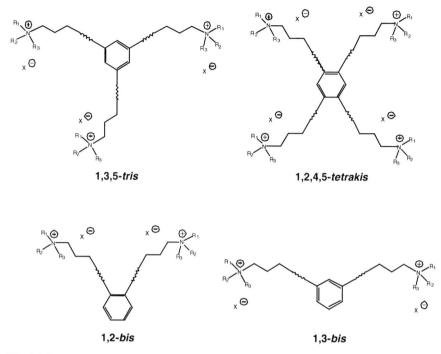

Fig. 4.4 Comparative structural scaffolds of *tris-*, *tetrakis-*, 1,2-*bis-*, and 1,3-*bis*-quaternary ammonium analogs

analogs was synthesized incorporating quaternary ammonium head groups at the 1, 2, 4, and 5 positions around the central phenyl ring (Fig. 4.4). The *tetrakis*-analogs were pursued in order to increase the number of interactions with anionic binding sites on nAChRs mediating nicotine-evoked DA release. The same approach that was used in the *tris*-analog series was followed, and new quaternary ammonium head groups were incorporated into the molecules (Fig. 4.5). These *tetrakis*-analogs were evaluated at 100 nM for inhibition of nicotine-evoked DA release. The effect of increasing the head groups from three to four resulted in a slightly greater number of hits, i.e., a 50% hit rate, compared to the *tris* series (Fig. 4.6). Three of the most potent inhibitors contained fully saturated linker units and incorporated similar head groups to the active *tris* compounds, i.e., isoquinolinium (ZZ 208G), 4-picolinium (ZZ 208B) and 3,5-lutidinium (ZZ 208D). Additional saturated analogs with new head groups included a 1-([3-hydroxy]propyl)pyridinium analog (ZZ 208F), and a 3-benzylpyridinium analog (ZZ 208H). Other active saturated analogs contained nicotinium (ZZ 208E) and 3,4-lutidinium (ZZ 208C) head groups. Several unsaturated analogs were also active, including the 1-([3-hydroxy]propyl)pyridinium analog (ZZ 204 J), the 3-phenylpyridinium analog (ZZ 204G), and the isoquinolinium analog (ZZ 204H). All of the above active saturated linker analogs lost their inhibitory activity on incorporation of a triple bond into the linker units. ZZ 204A,

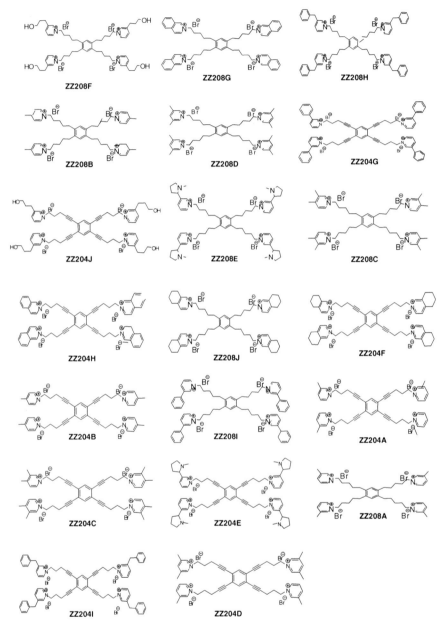

Fig. 4.5 Structures of *tetrakis*-quaternary ammonium analogs evaluated in the nicotine-evoked dopamine release assay

the *tetrakis* analog of GZ 550A (the most potent *tris* analog), exhibited only 16% inhibition at 100 nM. However, it must be emphasized that the *tetrakis* series does not contain within their structure the 1, 3, 5 phenyl substitution pattern of the *tris* scaffold (Fig. 4.4). Thus, the spatial arrangement of the linkers around the central

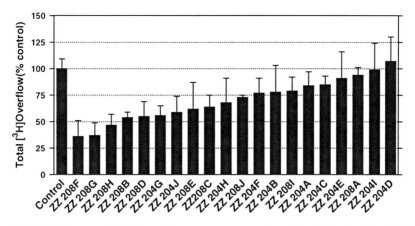

Fig. 4.6 The inhibitory activity of *tetrakis*-quaternary ammonium analogs in the nicotine (10 μM)-evoked dopamine release assay. Compounds were evaluated at a probe concentration of 100 nM in triplicate, and results are expressed as percentage inhibition compared to control (absence of drug)

phenyl ring may also be important in determining activity. Nevertheless, it is clear that in the *tetrakis* series, the more potent compounds have more flexible linkers. Considering the higher number of "hits" in this series, it will be important to perform full concentration response analyses to fully elucidate the SAR in this promising sub-library of compounds.

We have also evaluated 1,3-*bis*-analogs that are fragments of both the *tris* and *tetrakis* analogs to determine if the number of head groups and/or the spatial location of the head groups around the phenyl ring are important structural factors (Fig. 4.4). In the 1,3-*bis* series (Fig. 4.7), only four compounds exhibited inhibition greater than 30% at 100 nM (Fig. 4.8). This demonstrates a significant reduction in the number of active compounds (lower "hit" rate) when the third quaternary ammonium head group was removed from the 5-position on the phenyl ring in the *tris*-series, or when the third and fourth quaternary ammonium head groups were removed from the 2,4-position on the phenyl ring in the *tetrakis* series (Fig. 4.4). Again, this structural change dramatically decreases the hit rate compared to that observed in the *tetrakis* series. In the 1,3-*bis* series, three of the most active analogs had a picolinium or lutidinium head group and saturated linker units (i.e., GZ 577A, GZ 577B, and GZ578B, Figs. 4.7 and 4.8). Of note, GZ 577A is a close structure analog of the lead *bis*-compound, bPiDDB.

bis-Fragments of the *tetrakis* analogs containing head groups at the 1 and 2 positions around the central phenyl ring were also evaluated (Fig. 4.4). Generally, the same approach was used in the 1,2-*bis* analogs series as in the 1,3-*bis* analog series, and new quaternary ammonium head groups were also employed (Fig. 4.9). Similarly, the hit rate was also significantly reduced in this series compared to the *tetrakis* series (Fig. 4.10). In the 1,2-*bis* series of compounds, the most active analogs were those containing isoquinolinium (GZ 585B), 3,5-lutidinium (GZ 584A), 3-picolinium (GZ 508A) and pyridinium (GZ 586C) head groups. Of note,

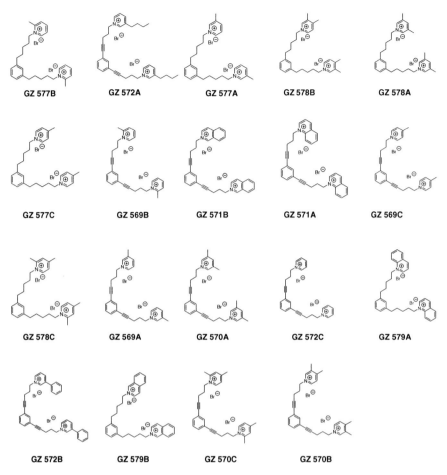

Fig. 4.7 Structures of the 1,3-*bis*-quaternary ammonium analogs [*bis*-1,3-(*n*-pentyl-4-ammonium) benzene and *bis*-1,3-(*n*-pent-1-ynyl-4-ammonium) benzene analogs] evaluated in the nicotine-evoked dopamine release assay

the two most active compounds, GZ 585B and GZ 584A, contained head groups attached to saturated linkers, where the third most active compound, GZ 580A, contained a 3-picolinum head group and an unsaturated linker.

Thus, through an iterative process of structural modification and the use of a rapid through put assay, we have identified a subset of quaternary ammonium molecules which affords a substantially improved hit rate for inhibition of nicotine-evoked DA release. This evolution has clearly indicated that as one progresses from the simple *bis*-quaternary ammonium compounds, such as bPiDDB, to the more complex *tris*- and *tetrakis*-sub-libraries of analogs, one obtains a more diverse selection of lead candidate molecules. A limitation of these SAR investigations is that thus far, only a single concentration of each candidate compound has been investigated, and a clear picture of the structure–activity relationships will only be evident once the full

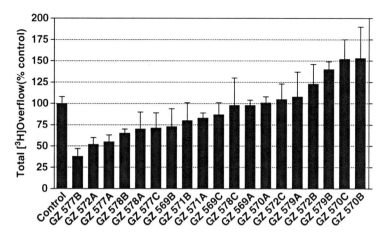

Fig. 4.8 The inhibitory activity of the 1,3-*bis*-quaternary ammonium analogs [*bis*-1,3-(*n*-pentyl-4-ammonium) benzene and *bis*-1,3-(*n*-pent-1-ynyl-4-ammonium) benzene analogs] in the nicotine (10 μM)-evoked dopamine release assay. Compounds were evaluated at a probe concentration of 100 nM in triplicate, and results are expressed as percentage inhibition compared to control (absence of drug)

concentration response and IC_{50} values are generated. Nevertheless, the neurochemical data generated thus far suggests that both the number of quaternary ammonium head groups in the molecule and the spatial location of these head groups are critical, when there is a central planar phenyl core in the molecule. For example, with respect to the importance of spatial location, in the 1,3-*bis* series, the 2- and 3-picolinium analogs with saturated linkers were highly potent inhibitors of nicotine-evoked DA release (Fig. 4.7), whereas the corresponding analogs in the 1,2-*bis* series were inactive (Fig. 4.9). Obtaining IC_{50} values within these series of compounds, and further elucidating the mechanism of inhibition will determine the importance of number and type of quaternary ammonium head groups, conformational requirements for the linker units, and the spatial arrangement of the quaternary ammonium moieties around the central phenyl core. These data can be utilized to optimize potency and subtype selectivity of the interaction of these novel nAChR antagonists with nAChRs mediating nicotine-evoked DA release.

Nicotine-Induced Reinstatement of Nicotine Self-Administration

The current study establishes a rodent model of reinstatement in order to assess the potential of novel nicotinic receptor antagonists to attenuate relapse. Two groups of rats were used to assess the ability of a well characterized classical nAChR antagonist (mecamylamine) and our lead compound (bPiDDB) to attenuate nicotine-induced reinstatement of extinguished nicotine self-administration (i.e., nicotine-seeking behavior). Mecamylamine (3 mg/kg) pretreatment significantly attenuated nicotine (0.2 mg/kg)-seeking behavior, while having no effect when

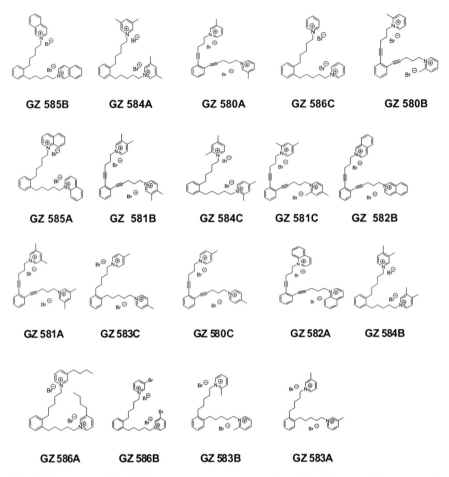

GZ 585B   GZ 584A   GZ 580A   GZ 586C   GZ 580B

GZ 585A   GZ 581B   GZ 584C   GZ 581C   GZ 582B

GZ 581A   GZ 583C   GZ 580C   GZ 582A   GZ 584B

GZ 586A   GZ 586B   GZ 583B   GZ 583A

Fig. 4.9 Structures of the 1,2-*bis*-quaternary ammonium analogs [*bis*-1,2-(*n*-pentyl-4-ammonium) benzene and *bis*-1,2-(*n*-pent-1-ynyl-4-ammonium) benzene analogs] evaluated in the nicotine-evoked dopamine release assay

administered alone (Fig. 4.11). A time-course analysis of nicotine-induced reinstatement revealed that the reinstatement was more pronounced during the latter portion of the session, and that this effect was attenuated by mecamylamine (Fig. 4.12). Nicotine (0.2 mg/kg) administration significantly increased responding at 30, 45, and 60 min time points compared to responding observed following administration of saline. Mecamylamine (3 mg/kg) pretreatment reduced responding at 15 min compared to saline–saline and saline–nicotine (0.2 mg/kg) groups, as well as significantly attenuating the nicotine-induced increase in responding at 30 and 60 min. Similar to the results observed following mecamylamine administration, pretreatment with bPiDDB significantly attenuated nicotine (0.2 mg/kg)-induced drug seeking across the 60-min session at both doses tested (1 and 3 mg/kg;

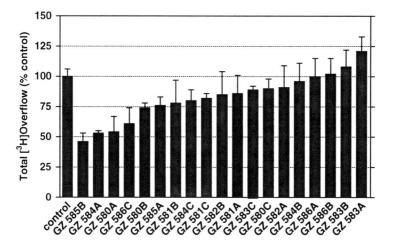

Fig. 4.10 The inhibitory activity of the 1,2-*bis*-quaternary ammonium analogs [*bis*-1,2-(*n*-pentyl-4-ammonium) benzene and *bis*-1,2-(*n*-pent-1-ynyl-4-ammonium) benzene analogs] in the nicotine (10 μM)-evoked dopamine release assay. Compounds were evaluated at a probe concentration of 100 nM in triplicate, and results are expressed as percentage inhibition compared to control (absence of drug)

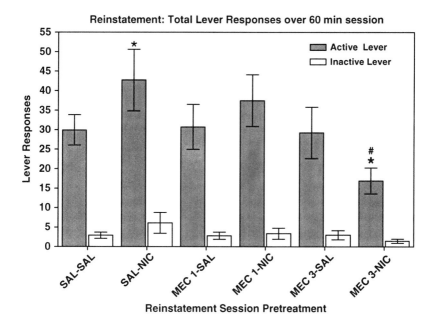

Fig. 4.11 Mean (±SEM) number of responses on the active and inactive levers for each of six treatment conditions. SAL=saline; NIC=nicotine, 0.2 mg/kg; MEC 1= mecamylamine, 1 mg/kg; and MEC 3= mecamylamine, 3 mg/kg. * indicates significant difference from SAL–SAL active lever (p<0.05). # indicates significant difference from SAL–NIC active lever (p<0.05)

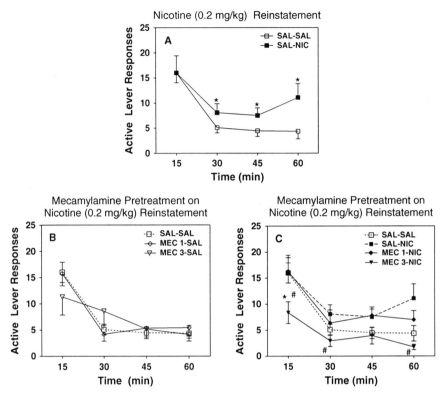

Fig. 4.12 Mean (±SEM) number of responses on the active lever for each treatment condition across 15-min time intervals within the session. **Panel A**: effect of nicotine (0.2 mg/kg) alone; **Panel B**: mecamylamine (1 or 3 mg/kg) pretreatment alone; and **Panel C**: effect of nicotine (0.2 mg/kg) in the presence and absence of mecamylamine (1 or 3 mg/kg). SAL=saline; NIC=nicotine, 0.2 mg/kg; MEC 1= mecamylamine, 1 mg/kg; and MEC 3= mecamylamine, 3 mg/kg. *indicates significant difference from SAL–SAL active lever (p<0.05). # indicates significant difference from SAL–NIC active lever (p<0.05)

Fig. 4.13). A time-course analysis also revealed that bPiDDB (1 and 3 mg/kg) pretreatment significantly decreased the number of active lever responses during the first 15 min of the reinstatement session compared to saline–saline and saline–nicotine (0.2 mg/kg) groups (Fig. 4.14). Interestingly, these doses of bPiDDB have been shown previously to decrease nicotine self-administration acutely (Neugebauer, Zhang, Crooks, Dwoskin, & Bardo, 2006). In addition, these results showing an attenuation of nicotine-induced reinstatement of nicotine seeking by both mecamylamine and bPiDDB extend previous work showing that mecamylamine attenuates cue-induced reinstatement (Liu et al., 2007). Taken together, the effectiveness of bPiDDB in decreasing both nicotine self-administration (Neugebauer et al., 2006) and nicotine-stimulated reinstatement (current study) suggest that nicotinic receptor antagonists may be a useful tobacco dependence pharmacotherapy to reduce relapse.

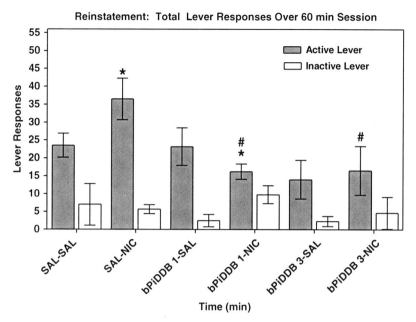

Fig. 4.13 Mean (±SEM) number of responses on the active and inactive levers for each of six treatment conditions. SAL=saline; NIC=nicotine, 0.2 mg/kg; bPiDDB 1 indicates 1 mg/kg; and bPiDDB 3 indicates 3 mg/kg. *indicates significant difference from SAL–SAL active lever ($p < 0.05$). # indicates significant difference from SAL–NIC active lever ($p < 0.05$)

The current approach in identifying nAChR antagonists that may have benefit in treating tobacco dependence employed the nicotine-evoked striatal DA release assay to assess analogs for their ability to inhibit the effect of nicotine. However, a relatively large literature minimizes the role of the presynaptic nAChRs located in the dopaminergic terminal regions as mediating nicotine-evoked DA release, and rather implicates nAChRs in the dopaminergic cell body regions as being critically involved. Our own findings, in part, support this contention. Similar to mecamylamine, bPiDDB (1 or 3 mg/kg) produced a dose-dependent blockade of the nicotine-induced increase in extracellular NAc DA (Rahman et al., 2007). The anatomical localization of the critical bPiDDB-sensitive nAChRs involved in regulating nicotine-evoked DA release in NAc was assessed using reverse dialysis (Rahman, Zhang, Papke, Crooks, Dwoskin & Bardo, 2008). The increase in extracellular DA in NAc following systemic nicotine (0.4 mg/kg, sc) was blocked completely by bPiDDB (1 µM) infused directly into the VTA, but not by bPiDDB infused into the NAc, suggesting that *in vivo* the nAChRs critical for mediating nicotine-stimulated DA release are located in the VTA.

Nicotine activates and rapidly desensitizes nAChRs on DA neurons in the VTA, and these nAChRs predominantly are high affinity α4β2* nAChRs (Mansvelder & McGehee, 2002; Picciotto et al., 1998; Pidoplichko et al., 1997; Tapper et al., 2004). Also, VTA DA neurons are activated indirectly through nicotine stimulation of α7*

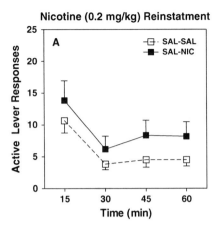

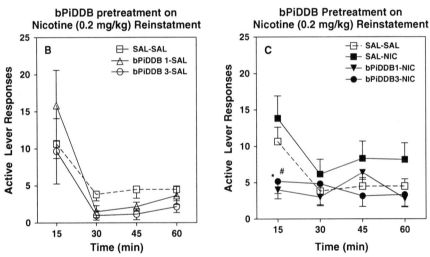

Fig. 4.14 Mean (±SEM) number of responses on the active lever for each treatment condition across 15-min time intervals within the session. **Panel A**: effect of nicotine (0.2 mg/kg) alone; **Panel B**: bPiDDB (1 or 3 mg/kg) pretreatment alone; and **Panel C**: effect of nicotine (0.2 mg/kg) in the presence and absence of bPiDDB (1 or 3 mg/kg). SAL=saline; NIC=nicotine, 0.2 mg/kg; bPiDDB 1 indicates 1 mg/kg; and bPiDDB 3 indicates 3 mg/kg.*indicates significant difference from SAL–SAL active lever (p<0.05). # indicates significant difference from SAL–NIC active lever (p<0.05)

nAChRs located on glutamatergic presynaptic terminals leading to glutamate release and subsequent excitation of VTA DA neurons (Dani & Harris, 2005; Mansvelder & McGehee, 2000; Wooltorton et al., 2003). These $\alpha7^*$ nAChRs have a lower affinity for nicotine and are not desensitized at nicotine concentrations experienced by tobacco smokers, which leads to long-term potentiation and prolonged excitation of the VTA DA neurons (Dani & Bertrand, 2007). Electrophysiological results demonstrate that nicotine enhances excitation of the DA neurons by interacting with α7* nAChRs on excitatory glutamatergic neurons that are not readily desensitized; nicotine also activates, but more importantly, desensitizes α4β2* nAChRs located on GABAergic terminals, which impinge on the DA neurons, leading to disinhibition of the DA neurons (Bonci et al., 2003; Dani, Ji, & Zhou, 2001; Klink, de Kerchove d'Exaerde, Zoli, & Changeux, 2001; McGehee, Heath, Gelber, Devay, & Role, 1995; Mansvelder, Keath, & McGehee, 2002; Mansvelder & McGehee, 2000; Mansvelder & McGehee, 2002).

While some data support the importance of α7* nAChRs on glutamatergic presynaptic terminals in mediating nicotine effects on DA release, other studies suggest that the role of α7* nAChRs is of lesser importance. Specifically, administration of α7* nAChR agonists (AR-R 17779 and DMAC) to non-tolerant and nicotine-sensitized rats failed to increase locomotion, in contrast with the hyperactivity observed following nicotine or an α4β2*-selective agonist (SIB 1765F). These results suggest that α7* nAChRs do not play a role in nicotine-induced hyperlocomotion (Grottick et al., 2000). Furthermore, the latter study showed that MLA did not decrease nicotine self-administration, in contrast to the effects of DHβE, which decreased nicotine self-administration, again suggesting that α7* nAChRs do not play a role in nicotine reward (also see Markou & Paterson, 2001). Another study reported that β2 subunit deletion or DHβE administration to wild type mice blocked nicotine conditioned place preference (CPP), whereas α7 subunit deletion or MLA administration to wild type mice did not alter nicotine CPP (Walters, Brown, Changeux, Martin, & Damaj, 2006). In a very recent microdialysis study, DHβE was shown to decrease nicotine-induced DA release when co-administered locally in the NAc in freely moving rats, implicating a role for presynaptic nAChRs in the DA terminal region (Quarta et al., 2007). In the latter study, the DA receptor agonist, quinpirole, blocked the nicotine-induced increase in DA release in NAc and interestingly, D2 receptors were shown to co-immunoprecipitate with β2 nAChR subunits from rat striatum, suggesting the close association of the D2 receptor with β2-containing nAChRs in striatum. Although the majority of studies implicates nAChRs in the dopaminergic cell body regions as regulating nicotine-evoked DA release in the terminal regions, the latter *in vivo* study provides support for nAChRs in the terminal regions as playing a role in nicotine-stimulated DA release, and further, supports the use of nAChRs in DA terminal regions as valid targets in the discovery of therapeutic candidates for the treatment of tobacco dependence. In summary, the effectiveness of the nAChR antagonist bPiDDB to decrease both nicotine self-administration (Neugebauer et al., 2006) and nicotine-stimulated reinstatement (current study) in rats provides *in vivo* preclinical evidence that bPiDDB and the subsequent generations of structurally related analogs such as those described in this Chapter will provide novel, clinically effective treatments for nicotine dependence.

Acknowledgments This work was supported by a National Cooperative Drug Discovery Group research grant NIH U19 DA017548.

References

Alkondon, M., Pereira, E. F., Wonnacott, S., & Albuquerque, E. X. (1992). Blockade of nicotinic currents in hippocampal neurons defines methyllycaconitine as a potent and specific receptor antagonist. *Molecular Pharmacology, 41*(4), 802–808.

Allen, D. D., Lockman, P. R., Roder, K. E., Dwoskin, L. P., & Crooks, P. A. (2003). Active transport of high affinity choline and nicotine analogs into the central nervous system by the blood brain barrier choline transporter. *Journal of Pharmacology and Experimental Therapeutics, 304*, 1268–1274.

Anand, R., Conroy, W. G., Schoepfer, R., Whiting, P., & Lindstrom, J. (1991). Neuronal nicotinic acetylcholine receptors expressed in *Xenopus* oocytes have a pentameric quaternary structure. *Journal of Biological Chemistry, 266*(17), 11192–11198.

Ayers, J. T., Clauset, A., Schmitt, J. D., Dwoskin, L. P., & Crooks, P. A. (2005). Molecular modeling of *mono-* and *bis*-quaternary ammonium salts as ligands at the alpha4beta2 nicotinic acetylcholine receptor subtype using nonlinear techniques. *The AAPS Journal, 7*(3), E678–E685.

Ayers, J. T., Dwoskin, L. P., Deaciuc, A. G., Grinevich, V. P., Zhu, J., & Crooks, P. A. (2002). *Bis*-Azaaromatic quaternary ammonium analogues: ligands for alpha4beta2* and alpha 7* subtypes of neuronal nicotinic receptors. *Bioorganic & Medicinal Chemistry Letters, 12*(21), 2067–3071.

Azam, L., Winzer-Serhan, U. H., Chen, Y., & Leslie, F. M. (2002). Expression of neuronal nicotinic acetylcholine receptor subunit mRNAs within midbrain dopamine neurons. *Journal of Comparative Neurology, 444*(3), 260–274.

Balfour, D. J. (2002). The neurobiology of tobacco dependence: a commentary. *Respiration, 69*, 7–11.

Balfour, D. J. (2004). The neurobiology of tobacco dependence: a preclinical perspective on the role of the dopamine projections to the nucleus accumbens. *Nicotine & Tobacco Research, 6*(6), 899–912.

Bardo, M. T. (1998). Neuropharmacological mechanisms of drug reward: beyond dopamine in the nucleus accumbens. *Critical Reviews in Neurobiology, 12*(1–2), 37–67.

Benwell, M. E., & Balfour, D. J. (1992). The effects of acute and repeated nicotine treatment on nucleus accumbens dopamine and locomotor activity. *British Journal of Pharmacology, 105*(4), 849–456.

Benwell, M. E., Balfour, D. J., & Birrell, C. E. (1995). Desensitization of the nicotine-induced mesolimbic dopamine responses during constant infusion with nicotine. *British Journal of Pharmacology, 114*(2), 454–460.

Berridge, K. C., & Robinson, T. E. (1998). What is the role of dopamine in reward: hedonic impact, reward learning, or incentive salience? *Brain Research Brain Research Reviews, 28*, 309–369.

Bonci, A., Bernardi, G., Grillner, P., & Mercuri, N. B. (2003). The dopamine-containing neuron: maestro or simple musician in the orchestra of addiction? *Trends in Pharmacological Sciences, 24*(4), 172–177.

Brazell, M. P., Mitchell, S. N., Joseph, M. H., & Gray, J. A. (1990). Acute administration of nicotine increases the in vivo extracellular levels of dopamine, 3,4-dihydroxyphenylacetic acid and ascorbic acid preferentially in the nucleus accumbens of the rat: comparison with caudate-putamen. *Neuropharmacology, 29*(12), 1177–1185.

Brody, A. L., Mandelkern, M. A., Lee, G., Smith, E., Sadeghi, M., Saxena, S., et al. (2004). Attenuation of cue-induced cigarette craving and anterior cingulate cortex activation in bupropion-treated smokers: a preliminary study. *Psychiatry Research, 130*(3), 269–281.

Caggiula, A. R., Donny, E. C., White, A. R., Chaudhri, N., Booth, S., Gharib, M. A., et al. (2002). Environmental stimuli promote the acquisition of nicotine self-administration in rats. *Psychopharmacology, 163*: 230–237.

Castro, N. G., & Albuquerque, E. X. (1995). alpha-Bungarotoxin-sensitive hippocampal nicotinic receptor channel has a high calcium permeability. *Biophysical Journal, 68*(2), 516–524.

Champtiaux, N., Gotti, C., Cordero-Erausquin, M., David, D. J., Przybylski, C., Lena, C., et al., (2003). Subunit composition of functional nicotinic receptors in dopaminergic neurons investigated with knock-out mice. *The Journal of Neuroscience, 23*(21), 7820–7829.

Charpantier, E., Barneoud, P., Moser, P., Besnard, F., & Sgard, F. (1998). Nicotinic acetylcholine subunit mRNA expression in dopaminergic neurons of the rat substantia nigra and ventral tegmental area. *Neuroreport, 9*(13), 3097–3101.

Clarke, P. B., & Pert, A. (1985). Autoradiographic evidence for nicotine receptors on nigrostriatal and mesolimbic dopaminergic neurons. *Brain Research, 348*(2), 355–358.

Coe, J. W., Brooks, P. R., Vetelino, M. G., Wirtz, M. C., Arnold, E. P., Huang, J., et al. (2005). Varenicline: an alpha4beta2 nicotinic receptor partial agonist for smoking cessation. *Journal of Medicinal Chemistry, 48*(10), 3474–3477.

Conroy, W. G., Vernallis, A. B., & Berg, D. K. (1992). The alpha 5 gene product assembles with multiple acetylcholine receptor subunits to form distinctive receptor subtypes in brain. *Neuron, 9*(4), 670–691.

Cooper, E., Couturier, S., & Ballivet, M. (1991). Pentameric structure and subunit stoichiometry of a neuronal acetylcholine receptor. *Nature, 350*(6315), 235–238.

Corrigall, W. A. (1999). Nicotine self-administration in animals as a dependence model. *Nicotine & Tobacco Research, 1*(1), 11–20.

Corrigall, W. A., & Coen, K. M. (1989). Nicotine maintains robust self-administration in rats on a limited-access schedule. *Psychopharmacology (Berl), 99*(4), 473–478.

Corrigall, W. A., Coen, K. M., & Adamson, K. L. (1994). Self-administered nicotine activates the mesolimbic dopamine system through the ventral tegmental area. *Brain Research, 653*(1–2), 278–284.

Corrigall, W. A., Franklin, K. B., Coen, K. M., & Clarke, P. B. (1992). The mesolimbic dopaminergic system is implicated in the reinforcing effects of nicotine. *Psychopharmacology (Berl),107*(2–3), 285–289.

Corringer, P. J., Sallette, J., & Changeux, J. P. (2006). Nicotine enhances intracellular nicotinic receptor maturation: a novel mechanism of neural plasticity? *Journal of Physiology, Paris, 99*(2–3), 162–171.

Crooks P. A., & Dwoskin L. P. (1997). Contribution of CNS nicotine metabolites to the neuropharmacological effects of nicotine and tobacco smoking. *Biochemical Pharmacology, 54*, 743–753.

Crooks, P. A., Ayers, J. T., Haubner, A. J., Grinevich, V. P., Sumithran, S. P., Deaciuc, A. G., et al. (2002) The *bis*-picolinium salt, bPiDDB, is a potent and selective antagonist at nicotinic acetylcholine receptors mediating nicotine-evoked dopamine release in rat striatum. *Drug and Alcohol Dependence, 64*, 38.

Crooks, P. A., Ayers, J. T., Xu, R., Sumithran, S. P., Grinevich, V. P., Wilkins, L. H., Deaciuc, A. G., Allen, D. D., & Dwoskin, L. P. (2004). Development of subtype-selective ligands as antagonists at nicotinic receptors mediating nicotine-evoked dopamine release. *Bioorganic & Medicinal Chemistry Letters, 14*(8), 1869–1874.

Cui, C., Booker, T. K., Allen, R. S., Grady, S. R., Whiteaker, P., Marks, M. J., et al. (2003). The β3 nicotinic receptor subunit: A component of α-conotoxin MII-binding nicotinic acetylcholine receptors that modulate dopamine release and related behaviors. *Journal of Neuroscience, 23*, 11045–11053.

Dani, J. A. (2003). Roles of dopamine signaling in nicotine addiction. *Molecular Psychiatry, 8*(3), 255–256.

Dani, J. A., & Bertrand, D. (2007). Nicotinic acetylcholine receptors and nicotinic cholinergic mechanisms of the central nervous system. *Annual Review of Pharmacology and Toxicology, 47*, 699–729.

Dani, J. A., & De Biasi, M. (2001). Cellular mechanisms of nicotine addiction. *Pharmacology, Biochemistry and Behavior, 70*(4), 439–446.

Dani, J. A., & Harris, R. A. (2005). Nicotine addiction and comorbidity with alcohol abuse and mental illness. *Nature Neuroscience, 8*(11), 1465–1470.

Dani, J. A., Ji, D., & Zhou, F. M. (2001). Synaptic plasticity and nicotine addiction. *Neuron, 31*(3), 349–352.

Deneris, E. S., Boulter, J., Swanson, L. W., Patrick, J., & Heinemann, S. (1989). Beta 3: a new member of nicotinic acetylcholine receptor gene family is expressed in the brain. *Journal of Biological Chemistry, 264*(11), 6268–6272.

Di Chiara, G. (2000). Role of dopamine in the behavioural actions of nicotine related to addiction. *European Journal of Pharmacology, 393*, 295–314.

Di Chiara, G., Bassareo, V., Fenu, S., De Luca, M. A., Spina, L., Cadoni, C., Acquas, E., Carboni, E., Valentini, V., & Lecca, D. (2004). Dopamine and drug addiction: the nucleus accumbens shell connection. *Neuropharmacology, 47*, 227–241.

Dwoskin, L. P., Sumithran, S. P., Zhu, J., Deaciuc, A. G., Ayers, J. T., & Crooks, P. A. (2004). Subtype-selective nicotinic receptor antagonists: potential as tobacco use cessation agents. *Bioorganic & Medicinal Chemistry Letters, 14*, 1863–1867.

Dwoskin, L. P., Teng, L. H., Buxton, S. T., Ravard, A., Deo, N., & Crooks, P. A. (1995). Minor alkaloids of tobacco release [³H]dopamine release from superfused rat striatal slices. *European. Journal of. Pharmacology, 276*,195–199.

Donny, E. C., Chaudhri, N., Caggiula, A. R., Evans-Martin, F. F., Booth, S., Gharib, M. A., et al. (2003). Operant responding for a visual reinforcer in rats in enhanced by noncontingent nicotine: implications for nicotine self-administration and reinforcement. *Psychopharmacology (Berl), 169*(1), 68–76.

Flores, C. M., Rogers, S. W., Pabreza, L. A., Wolfe, B. B., & Kellar, K. J. (1992). A subtype of nicotinic cholinergic receptor in rat brain is composed of alpha 4 and beta 2 subunits and is up-regulated by chronic nicotine treatment. *Molecular Pharmacology, 41*(1), 31–37.

Forsayeth, J. R., & Kobrin, E. (1997). Formation of oligomers containing the beta 3 and beta 4 subunits of the rat nicotinic receptor. *Journal of Neuroscience, 17*(5), 1531–1538.

Fu, Y., Matta, S. G., Gao, W., & Sharp, B. M. (2000). Local alpha-bungarotoxin-sensitive nicotinic receptors in the nucleus accumbens modulate nicotine-stimulated dopamine secretion in vivo. *Neuroscience, 101*(2), 369–375.

Ghosheh, O., Dwoskin, L. P., Li, W. K., & Crooks, P. A. (1999). Residence time and half-lives of nicotine metabolites in rat brain after acute peripheral administration of [2'-¹⁴C]nicotine. *Drug Metabolism and Disposition, 27*, 1448–1455.

Ghosheh O. A., Dwoskin L. P., Miller D. K. and Crooks P. A. (2001). Accumulation of nicotine and its metabolites in rat brain after intermittent or continuous peripheral administration of [2'-¹⁴C]-nicotine. *Drug Metabolism and Disposition, 29*, 645–651.

George, T. P., & O'Malley, S. S. (2004). Current pharmacological treatments for nicotine dependence. *Trends in Pharmacological Sciences, 25*(1), 42–48.

Goldner, F. M., Dineley, K. T., & Patrick, J. W. (1997). Immunohistochemical localization of the nicotinic acetylcholine receptor subunit alpha 6 to dopaminergic neurons in the substantia nigra and ventral tegmental area. *Neuroreport, 8*(12), 2739–2742.

Gotti, C., Moretti, M., Clementi, F., Riganti, F., McIntosh, J. M., Collins, A. C., et al. (2005). Expression of nigrostriatal α6-containing nicotinic acetylcholine receptors is selectively reduced, but not eliminated, by β3 subunit gene deletion. *Molecular Pharmacology, 67*, 2007–2015.

Gotti, C., Zoli, M., & Clementi, F. (2006). Brain nicotinic acetylcholine receptors: native subtypes and their relevance. *Trends in Pharmacological Sciences, 27*(9), 482–491.

Grady, S. R., Grun, E. U., Marks, M. J., & Collins, A. C. (1997). Pharmacological comparisons of transient and persistent [³H]dopamine release from mouse striatal synaptosomes and response to chronic L-nicotine treatment. *The Journal of Pharmacology and Experimental Therapeutics, 282*, 32–43.

Grady, S. R., Meinerz, N. M., Cao, J., Reynolds, A. M., Picciotto, M. R., Changeux, J-P., et al. (2001). Nicotinic agonists stimulate acetylcholine release from mouse interpeduncular nucleus: a function mediated by a different nAChR than dopamine release from striatum. *Journal of Neurochemistry, 76*, 258–226.

Grady, S. R., Murphy, K. L., Cao, J., Marks, M. J., McIntosh, J. M., & Collins, A. C. (2002). Characterization of nicotinic agonist-induced [(3)H]dopamine release from synaptosomes prepared from four mouse brain regions. *Journal of Pharmacology and Experimental Therapeutics*, *301*(2), 651–660.

Gray, R., Rajan, A. S., Radcliffe, K. A., Yakehiro, M., & Dani, J. A. (1996). Hippocampal synaptic transmission enhanced by low concentrations of nicotine. *Nature*, *383*(6602), 713–716.

Grinevich, V. P., Crooks, P. A., Sumithran, S. P., Haubner, A. J., Ayers, J. T., & Dwoskin, L. P. (2003). N-*n*-Alkylpyridinium analogs, a novel class of nicotinic receptor antagonists: selective inhibition of nicotine-evoked [3H]dopamine overflow from superfused rat striatal slices. *The Journal of Pharmacology and Experimental Therapeutics*, *306*(3), 1011–1020.

Grottick, A. J., Trube, G., Corrigall, W. A., Huwyler, J., Malherbe, P., Wyler, R., et al. (2000). Evidence that nicotinic alpha(7) receptors are not involved in the hyperlocomotor and rewarding effects of nicotine. *The Journal of Pharmacology and Experimental Therapeutics*, *294*(3), 1112–1119.

Hurt, R. D., Krook, J. E., Croghan, I. T., Loprinzi, C. L., Sloan, J. A., Novotny, P. J., et al. (2003). Nicotine patch therapy based on smoking rat followed by bupropion for prevention of relapse to smoking. *Journal of Clinical Oncology*, *21*(5), 914–920.

Imperato, A., Mulas, A., & Dichiara, G. (1986). Nicotine preferentially stimulates dopamine release in the limbic system of freely moving rats. *European Journal of Pharmacology*, *132* (2–3), 337–338.

Irvin, J. E., Hendricks, P. S., & Brandon, T. H. (2003). The increasing recalcitrance of smokers in clinical trials II: Pharmacotherapy trials. *Nicotine & Tobacco Research*, *5*(1), 27–35.

Jones, I. W., Bolam, J. P., & Wonnacott, S. (2001). Presynaptic localization of the nicotinic acetylcholine receptor beta 2 subunit immunoreactivity in rat nigrostriatal dopaminergic neurons. *The Journal of Comparative Neurology*, *439*(2), 235–247.

Kaiser, S. A., Soliakov, L., Harvey, S. C., Luetje, C. W., & Wonnacott, S. (1998). Differential inhibition by α-conotoxin-MII of the nicotinic stimulation of [^{3}H]dopamine release from rat striatal synaptosomes and slices. *Journal of Neurochemistry*, *70*, 1069–1076.

Kenny, P. J., & Markou, A. (2006). Nicotine self-administration acutely activates brain reward systems and induces a long-lasting increase in reward sensitivity. *Neuropsychopharmacology*, *31*, 1203–1211.

Klink, R., de Kerchove d'Exaerde, A., Zoli, M., & Changeux, J. P. (2001). Molecular and physiological diversity of nicotinic acetylcholine receptors in the midbrain dopaminergic nuclei. *Journal of Neuroscience*, *21*(5), 1452–1463.

Koob, G. F. (1992). Neural mechanisms of drug reinforcement. *Annals of New York Academy of Sciences*, *654*, 171–191.

Koob, G. F. (1999). The role of the striatopallidal and extended amygdala systems in drug addiction. *Annals of New York Academy of Sciences*, *877*, 445–46.

Kulak, J. M., McIntosh, J. M., Yoshikami, D., & Olivera, B. M. (2001). Nicotine-evoked transmitter release from synaptosomes: functional association of specific presynaptic acetylcholine receptors and voltage-gated calcium channels. *Journal of Neurochemistry*, *77*, 1581–1589.

Kulak, J. M., Nguyen, T. A., Olivera, B. M., & McIntosh, J. M. (1997). Alpha-conotoxin MII blocks nicotine-stimulated dopamine release in rat striatal synaptosomes. *Journal of Neuroscience*, *17*(14), 5263–5270.

Kuryatov, A., Olale, F., Cooper, J., Choi, C., & Lindstrom, J. (2000). Human alpha6 AChR subtypes: subunit composition, assembly and pharmacological responses. *Neuropharmacology*, *38*(13), 2570–2590.

Le Novere, N., Zoli, M., & Changeux, J. P. (1996). Neuronal nicotinic receptor alpha 6 subunit mRNA is selectively concentrated in catecholaminergic nuclei of the rat brain. *European Journal of Neuroscience*, *8*(11), 2428–2439.

Liu, X., Caggiula, A. R., Yee, S. K., Nobuta, H., Sved, A. F., Pechnick, R. N., et al. (2007). Mecamylamine attenuates cue-induced reinstatement of nicotine-seeking behavior in rats. *Neuropsychopharmacology*, *32*(3), 710–718.

Lopez-Hernandez, G. Y., Sanchez-Padilla, J., Ortiz-Acevedo, A., Lizardi-Ortiz, J., Salas-Vincenty, J., Rojas, L. V., et al. (2004). Nicotine-induced up-regulation and desensitization of alpha4beta2 neuronal nicotinic receptors depend on subunit ratio. *Journal of Biological Chemistry, 279*(36), 38007–38015.

Lundahl, L. H., Henningfield, J. E., & Lukas, S. E. (2000). Mecamylamine blockade of both positive and negative effects of IV nicotine in human volunteers. *Pharmacology, Biochemistry, and Behavior, 66*(3), 637–643.

Mansvelder, H. D., Keath, J. R., & McGehee, D. S. (2002). Synaptic mechanisms underlie nicotine-induced excitability of brain reward areas. *Neuron, 33*(6), 905–919.

Mansvelder, H. D., & McGehee, D. S. (2000). Long-term potentiation of excitatory inputs to brain reward areas by nicotine. *Neuron, 27*(2), 349–357.

Mansvelder, H. D., & McGehee, D. S. (2002). Cellular and synaptic mechanisms of nicotine addiction. *Journal of Neurobiology, 53*(4), 606–617.

Markou, A., & Paterson, N. E. (2001). The nicotinic antagonist methyllycaconitine has differential effects on nicotine self-administration and nicotine withdrawal in the rat. *Nicotine and Tobacco Research, 3*(4), 361–373.

Martin-Soelch, C., Leenders, K. L., Chevalley, A. F., Missimer, J., Kunig, G., Magyar, S., et al. (2001). Reward mechanisms in the brain and their role in dependence: Evidence from neurophysiological and neuroimaging studies. *Brain Research Review, 26*(2–3), 139–149.

McCallum, S. E., Parameswaran, N., Bordia, T., McIntosh, J. M., Grady, S. R., & Quik, M. (2005). Decrease in alpha3*/alpha6* nicotinic receptors but not nicotine-evoked dopamine release in monkey brain after nigrostriatal damage. *Molecular Pharmacology, 68*(3), 737–746.

McGehee, D. S., Heath, M. J., Gelber, S., Devay, P., & Role, L. W. (1995). Nicotine enhancement of fast excitatory synaptic transmission in CNS by presynaptic receptors. *Science, 269*(5231), 1681–1682.

McGehee, D. S., & Role, L. W. (1995). Physiological diversity of nicotinic acetylcholine receptors expressed by vertebrate neurons. *Annual Review of Physiology, 57*, 521–546.

McIntosh, J. M., Olivera, B. M., & Cruz, L. J. (1999). *Conus* peptides as probes for ion channels. *Methods in Enzymology, 294*, 605–624.

McIntosh, J. M., Santos, A. D., & Olivera, B. M. (1999). *Conus* peptides targeted to specific nicotinic acetylcholine receptor subtypes. *Annual Review of Biochemistry, 68*, 59–88.

Mihalak, K. B., Carroll, F. I., & Luetje, C. W. (2006). Varenicline is a partial agonist at alpha4beta2 and a full agonist at alpha7 neuronal nicotinic receptors. *Molecular Pharmacology, 70*(3), 801–805.

Miller, D. K., Sumithran, S. P., & Dwoskin, L. P. (2002). Bupropion inhibits nicotine-evoked [^{3}H]overflow from rat striatal slices preloaded with [^{3}H]dopamine and from rat hippocampal slices preloaded with [^{3}H]norepinephrine. *The Journal of Pharmacology and Experimental Therapeutics, 203*(3), 1113–1122.

Nelson, M. E., Kuryatov, A., Choi, C. H., Zhou, Y., & Lindstrom, J. (2003). Alternate stoichiometries of alpha4beta2 nicotinic acetylcholine receptors. *Molecular Pharmacology, 63*(2), 332–341.

Neugebauer, N. M., Zhang, Z., Crooks, P. A., Dwoskin, L. P., & Bardo, M. T. (2006). Effect of a novel nicotinic receptor antagonist, *N,N*'dodecane-1,12-diyl-*bis*-3-picolinium dibromide, on nicotine self-administration and hyperactivity in rats. *Psychopharmacology (Berl), 184*(3–4), 426–434.

Niaura, R., Shadel, W. G., Abrams, D. B., Monti, P. M., Rohsenow, D. J., & Sirota, A. (1998). Individual differences in cue reactivity among smokers trying to quit: effects of gender and cue type. *Addictive Behaviors, 23*(2), 209–224.

Nicke, A., Wonnacott, S., & Lewis, R. J. (2004). Alpha-conotoxins as tools for the elucidation of structure and function of neuronal nicotinic acetylcholine receptor subtypes. *European Journal of Biochemistry, 271*(12), 2305–2319.

Nisell, M., Nomikos, G. G., & Svensson, T. H. (1994). Systemic nicotine-induced dopamine release in the rat nucleus accumbens is regulated by nicotinic receptors in the ventral tegmental area. *Synapse, 16*(1), 36–44.

Nomikos ,G. G., Damsma, G., Wenkstern, D., & Fibiger, H. C. (1989). Acute effects of bupropion on extracellular dopamine concentrations in rat striatum and nucleus accumbens studied by in vivo microdialysis. *Neuropsychopharmacology, 2*(4), 273–279.

Nomikos, G. G., Damsma, G., Wenkstern, D., & Fibiger, H. C. (1992). Effects of chronic bupropion on interstitial concentrations of dopamine in rat nucleus accumbens and striatum. *Neuropsychopharmacology, 7*(1), 7–14.

Palmatier, M. I., Evans-Martin, F. F., Hoffman, A., Caggiula, A. R., Chaudhri, N., Donny, E. C., et al., (2006). Dissociating the primary reinforcing and reinforcement-enhancing effects of nicotine using a rat self-administration paradigm with concurrently available drug and environmental reinforcers. *Psychopharmacology, 184*, 391–400.

Palmatier, M. I., Liu, X., Caggiula, A. R., Donny, E. C., & Sved, A. F. (2007). The role of nicotinic acetylcholine receptors in the primary reinforcing and reinforcement-enhancing effects of nicotine. *Neuropsychopharmacology, 32*, 1098–1108.

Papke, R. L., Dwoskin, L. P., & Crooks, P. A. (2007). The pharmacological fingerprint of nAChRs subtypes utilizing nicotine and nornicotine: relevance to nicotine dependence and drug discovery. *Journal of Neurochemistry, 101*(1), 160–167.

Perkins, K. A., Epstein, L. H., Grobe, J., & Fonte, C. (1994). Tobacco abstinence, smoking cues, and the reinforcing value of smoking. *Pharmacology, Biochemistry, and Behavior, 47*(1), 107–112.

Picciotto, M. R., Zoli, M., Rimondini, R., Lena, C., Marubio, L. M., Pich, E. M., et al. (1998). Acetylcholine receptors containing the beta2 subunit are involved in the reinforcing properties of nicotine. *Nature, 391*(6663), 173–177.

Pidoplichko, V. I., DeBiasi, M., Williams, J. T., & Dani, J. A. (1997). Nicotine activates and desensitizes midbrain dopamine neurons. *Nature, 390*(6658), 401–404.

Pidoplichko, V. I., Noguchi, J., Areola, O. O., Liang, Y., Peterson, J., Zhang, T., et al. (2004). Nicotinic cholinergic synaptic mechanisms in the ventral tegmental area contribute to nicotine addiction. *Learning and Memory, 11*(1), 60–69.

Pivavarchyk, M., Zhang, Z., Crooks, P. A., & Dwoskin, L. P. (2007). Tetrakis quaternary ammonium salts: novel nicotinic receptor antagonists which inhibit nicotine-evoked [^{3}H]dopamine overflow from superfused rat striatal slices. *Society for Neuroscience Abstract, 37*, 78.12.

Pomerleau, C. S., & Pomerleau, O. F. (1992). Euphoriant effects of nicotine in smokers. *Pychopharmacology (Berl), 108*, 460–465.

Pontieri, F. E., Tanda, G., Orzi, F., & Di Chiara, G. (1996). Effects of nicotine on the nucleus accumbens and similarity to those of addictive drugs. *Nature, 382*(6588), 255–257.

Poth, K., Nutter, T. J., Cuevas, J., Parker, M. J., Adams, D. J., & Luetje, C. W. (1997). Heterogeneity of nicotinic receptor class and subunit mRNA expression among individual parasympathetic neurons from rat intracardiac ganglia. *Journal of Neuroscience, 17*(2), 586–596.

Quarta, D., Ciruela, F., Patkar, K., Borycz, J., Solinas, M., Lluis, C., et al. (2007). Heteromeric nicotinic acetylcholine-dopamine autoreceptor complexes modulate striatal dopamine release. *Neuropsychopharmacology, 32*(1), 35–42.

Rahman, S., Neugebauer, N. M., Zhang, Z., Crooks, P. A., Dwoskin, L. P., & Bardo, M. T. (2007). The effects of a novel nicotinic receptor antagonist *N,N*'-dodecane-1,12-diyl-*bis*-3-picolinium dibromide (bPiDDB) on acute repeated nicotine-induced increases in extracellular dopamine in rat nucleus accumbens. *Neuropharmacology, 52*(3), 755–763.

Rahman, S., Zhang, J., & Corrigall, W. A. (2004). Effects of nicotine preexposure on sulpiride-induced dopamine release in the nucleus accumbens. *European Journal of Pharmacology, 494*(1), 31–34.

Rahman, S., Zhang, Z., Papke, R. L., Crooks, P. A., Dwoskin, L. P., & Bardo, M. T. (2008). Region-specific effects of *N,N*'dodecane-1,12-diyl-*bis*-3-picolinium dibromide (bPiDDB) on nicotine-induced increase in extracellular dopamine *in vivo*. *British Journal of Pharmacology, 153*, 792–804.

Rauhut, A. S., Neugebauer, N., Dwoskin, L. P., & Bardo, M. T. (2003). Effect of bupropion on nicotine self-administration in rats. *Psychopharmacology (Berl), 169*, 1–9.

Rice, M. E., & Cragg, S. J. (2004). Nicotine amplifies reward-related dopamine signals in striatum. *Nature Neuroscience, 7*(6), 583–584.

Rose, J. E., & Behm, F. M. (2004). Extinguishing the rewarding value of smoke cues: pharmacological and behavioral treatments. *Nicotine & Tobacco Research, 6*(3), 523–532.

Rose, J. E., Behm, F. M., Westman, E. C., Levin, E. D., Stein, R. M., & Ripka, G. V. (1994). Mecamylamine combined with nicotine skin patch facilitates smoking cessation beyond nicotine patch treatment alone. *Clinical Pharmacology and Therapeutics, 56*(1), 86–99.

Rose, J. E., Westman, E. C., Behm, F. M., Johnson, M. P., & Goldberg, J. S. (1999). Blockade of smoking satisfaction using the peripheral nicotinic antagonist trimethaphan. *Pharmacology, Biochemistry, and Behavior, 62*(1), 165–172.

Salminen, O., Drapeau, J. A., McIntosh, J. M., Collins, A. C., Marks, M. J., & Grady, S. R. (2007). Pharmacology of α-conotoxin MII-sensitive subtypes of nicotinic acetylcholine receptors isolated by breeding of null mutant mice. *Molecular Pharmacology, 71*, 1563–1571.

Salminen, O., Murphy, K. L., McIntosh, J. M., Drago, J., Marks, M. J., Collins, A. C., et al. (2004). Subunit composition and pharmacology of two classes of striatal presynaptic nicotinic acetylcholine receptors mediating dopamine release in mice. *Molecular Pharmacology, 65*, 1526–1535.

Scholze, P., Orr-Urtreger, A., Changeux, J. P., McIntosh, J. M., & Huck, S. (2007). Catecholamine outflow from mouse and rat brain slice preparations evoked by nicotinic acetylcholine receptor activation and electrical field stimulation. *British Journal of Pharmacology, 151*(3), 414–422.

Shima, K., & Tanji, J. (1998). Role for cingulated motor area cells in voluntary movement selection based on reward. *Science, 282*, 1335–1338.

Singer, G., Wallace, M., & Hall, R. (1982). Effects of dopaminergic nucleus accumbens lesions on the acquisition of schedule induced self injection of nicotine in the rat. *Pharmacology, Biochemistry, and Behavior, 17*(3), 579–581.

Slemmer, J. E., Martin, B. R., & Damaj, M. I. (2000). Bupropion is a nicotinic antagonist. *The Journal of Pharmacology and Experimental Therapeutics, 295*(1), 321–327.

Soliakov, L., & Wonnacott, S. (1996). Voltage-sensitive Ca^{2+} channels involved in nicotinic receptor-mediated [^{3}H]dopamine release from rat striatal synaptosomes. *Journal of Neurochemistry, 67*, 163–170.

Spanagel, R., & Weiss, F. (1999). The dopamine hypothesis of reward: past and current status. *Trends in Neuroscience, 22*(11), 521–527.

Stokes, C., Dwoskin, L. P., Crooks, P. A., Jacobs, L. B., McIntosh, J. M., & Papke, R. L. (2007). The identification of selective competitive and noncompetitive nAChR antagonists using alpha6 nicotinic acetylcholine receptor chimeras. *Society for Neuroscience Abstract, 37*, 574.4.

Stolerman, I. P., & Jarvis, M. J. (1995). The scientific case that nicotine is addictive. *Psychopharmacology, 117*(1), 2–10.

Sumithran, S. P., Crooks, P. A., Xu, R., Zhu, J., Deaciuc, A. G., Wilkins, L. H., et al. (2005). Introduction of unsaturation into the *N-n*-alkyl chain of the nicotinic receptor antagonists, NONI and NDNI: effect on affinity and selectivity. *American Association of Pharmaceutical Scientists Journal, 7*(1), E201–217.

Tapper, A. R., McKinney, S. L., Nashmi, R., Schwarz, J., Deshpande, P., Labarca, C., et al. (2004). Nicotine activation of alpha4* receptors: sufficient for reward, tolerance, and sensitization. *Science, 306*(5698), 983–985.

Teng, L., Crooks, P. A., Buxton, S. T., & Dwoskin, L. P. (1997). Nicotinic-receptor mediation of S(-)nornicotine-evoked [^{3}H]overflow from rat striatal slices preloaded with [^{3}H]dopamine: differential inhibition of synaptosomal and vesicular [^{3}H]dopamine uptake. *The Journal of Pharmacology and Experimental Therapeutics, 280*(3), 1432–1444.

Vann, R. E., Rosecrans, J. A., James, J. R., Philibin, S. D., & Robinson, S. E. (2006). Neurochemical and behavioral effects of bupropion and mecamylamine in the presence of nicotine. *Brain Research, 1117*, 18–24.

Wada, E., McKinnon, D., Heinemann, S., Patrick, J., & Swanson, L. W. (1990). The distribution of mRNA encoded by a new member of the neuronal nicotinic acetylcholine receptor family (alpha 5) in the rat central nervous system. *Brain Research, 526*(1), 45–53.

Wada, E., Wada, K., Boulter, J., Deneris, E., Heinemann, S., Patrick, J., et al. (1989). Distribution of alpha 2, alpha 3, alpha 4, and beta 2 neuronal nicotinic receptor subunit mRNAs in the central nervous system: a hybridization histochemical study in the rat. *The Journal Comparative Neurology, 284*(2), 314–335.

Walters, C. L., Brown, S., Changeux, J. P., Martin, B., & Damaj, M. I. (2006). The beta2 but not alpha7 subunit of the nicotinic acetylcholine receptor is required for nicotine-conditioned place preference in mice. *Psychopharmacology, 184*(3–4), 339–344.

Wei, X., Sumithran, S. P., Deaciuc, A. G., Burton, H. R., Bush, L. P., Dwoskin, L. P., et al. (2005). Identification and synthesis of novel alkaloids from the root system of *Nicotiana tabacum*: Affinity for neuronal nicotinic acetylcholine receptors. *Life Sciences, 78*, 495–505.

Whiteaker, P., Marks, M. J., Grady, S. R., Lu, Y., Picciotto, M. R., Changeux, J. P., et al. (2000). Pharmacological and null mutation approaches reveal nicotinic receptor diversity. *European Journal of Pharmacology, 393*(1–3), 123–135.

Wilkins, L. H., JR., Grinevich, V. P., Ayers, J. T., Crooks, P. A., & Dwoskin, L. P. (2003). N-*n*-Alkylnicotinium analogs, a novel class of nicotinic receptor antagonists: interaction with α4β2* and α7* neuronal nicotinic receptors. *The Journal of Pharmacology and Experimental Therapeutics, 304*(1), 400–410.

Wilkins, L. H., Haubner, A., Ayers, J. T., Crooks, P. A., & Dwoskin, L. P. (2002). N-*n*-Alkylnicotinium analogs, a novel class of nicotinic receptor antagonist: inhibition of S(-)-nicotine-evoked [^{3}H]dopamine overflow from superfused rat striatal slices. *The Journal of Pharmacology and Experimental Therapeutics, 301*(3), 1088–1096.

Wilkins, L. H., Miller, D. K., Ayers, J. T., Crooks, P. A., & Dwoskin, L. P. (2006). N-*n*-Alkylnicotinium analogs, a novel class of antagonists at alpha 4 beta 2* nicotinic receptors: inhibition of S(-)-nicotine-evoked ^{86}Rb$^+$ efflux from rat thalamic synaptosomes. *American Association of Pharmaceutical Scientists Journal, 7*(4), E922–930.

Wise, R. A. (1996). Neurobiology of addiction. *Current Opinion in Neurobiology, 6*(2), 243–251.

Wise, R. A. (2000). Addiction becomes a brain disease. *Neuron, 26*, 27–33.

Wise, R. A., & Bozarth, M. A. (1987). A psychomotor stimulant theory of addiction. *Psychological Review, 94*(4), 469–492.

Wonnacott, S. (1997). Presynaptic nicotinic Ach receptors. *Trends in Neuroscience, 20*(2), 92–98.

Wonnacott, S., Kaiser, S., Mogg, A., Soliakov, L., & Jones, I. W. (2000). Presynaptic nicotinic receptors modulating dopamine release in the rat striatum. *European Journal of Pharmacology, 393*(1–3), 51–58.

Wonnacott, S., Sidhpura, N., & Balfour, D. J. (2005). Nicotine: from molecular mechanisms to behaviour. *Current Opinion in Pharmacology, 5*(1), 53–59.

Wooltorton, J. R.A., Pidoplichko, V. I., Broide, R. S., & Dani, J. A. (2003). Differential desensitization and distribution of nicotinic acetylcholine receptor subtypes in midbrain dopamine areas. *Journal of Neuroscience, 23*(8), 3176–3185.

Zheng, F., Bayram, E., Sumithran, S. P., Ayers, J. T., Zhan, C. G., Schmitt, J. D., et al. (2006). QSAR modeling of *mono-* and *bis*-quaternary ammonium salts that act as antagonists at neuronal nicotinic acetylcholine receptors mediating dopamine release. *Bioorganic & Medicinal Chemistry, 14*(9), 3017–3037.

Zhang, Z., Lockman, P. R., Geldenhuys, W. J., Allen, D. D., Dwoskin, L. P., & Crooks, P. A. (2005). Synthesis of *bis*-pyridinium analogs and structurally related cyclophanes with high affinity for the blood brain barrier choline transporter. *American Association Pharmaceutical Scientists, PharmSci (Supplement), 7*(S2), Abstract W4079.

Zhou, F. M., Liang, Y., & Dani, J. A. (2001). Endogenous nicotinic cholinergic activity regulates dopamine release in the striatum. *Nature Neuroscience, 4*(12), 1224–1229.

Zoli, M., Moretti, M., Zanardi, A., McIntosh, J. M., Clementi, F., & Gotti, C. (2002). Identification of the nicotinic receptor subtypes expressed on dopaminergic terminals in the rat striatum. *Journal of Neuroscience, 22*(20), 8785–8789.

Zwart, R., & Vijverberg, H. P. (1998). Four pharmacologically distinct subtypes of alpha4beta2 nicotinic acetylcholine receptor expressed in *Xenopus laevis* oocytes. *Molecular Pharmacology, 54*(6), 1124–1131.

Chapter 5
Multiple Motivational Forces Contribute to Nicotine Dependence

Athina Markou and Neil E. Paterson

Introduction

Approximately 40% of current smokers attempt to quit each year (Centers for Disease Control and Prevention, 2005), but only 10–15% succeed (Fiore, Smith, Jorenby, & Baker, 1994), with relapse to smoking often occurring during the first few days or weeks of abstinence (al'Absi, Hatsukami, Davis, & Wittmers, 2004; Piasecki, Jorenby, Smith, Fiore, & Baker, 2003). The low success rate of quit attempts suggests that there are powerful motivational forces that maintain the tobacco smoking habit. One of the main psychoactive ingredients in tobacco smoke that is responsible for its highly addictive properties is nicotine (Bardo, Green, Crooks, & Dwoskin, 1999; Crooks & Dwoskin, 1997; Dwoskin, Teng, Buxton, & Crooks, 1999; Stolerman & Jarvis, 1995). Thus, much psychological and neurobiological research is focused on understanding the factors that contribute to nicotine dependence in order to shed light onto the factors that underlie addiction to tobacco smoking.

In this chapter, we review evidence primarily from rat studies demonstrating that there are several primary and conditioned motivational forces that contribute to the maintenance of nicotine dependence, and consequently to the tobacco smoking habit. First, there are the primary rewarding effects of nicotine that have incentive-motivational value. However, these alone cannot explain the persistence of nicotine self-administration behavior in humans and experimental animals. Second, it has been hypothesized that the reward-enhancing effects of nicotine (i.e., nicotine-induced enhancement of the reward value of other primary and conditioned stimuli; see below and Caggiula, Donny, Palmatier, Liu, Chaudhri and Sved, this volume; Balfour, Wright, Benwell, & Birrell, 2000; Di Chiara, 2002; Rose, 2006) provides an additional motivational force leading to nicotine consumption. Third, the aversive affective and somatic signs of nicotine withdrawal provide the substrate for negative reinforcement to occur through nicotine administration. Finally, an additional

A. Markou
Department of Psychiatry, M/C 0603, School of Medicine, University of California, San Diego, 9500 Gilman Drive, La Jolla, San Diego, CA 92093-0603, USA
e-mail: amarkou@ucsd.edu

R.A. Bevins, A.R. Caggiula (eds.), *The Motivational Impact of Nicotine and its Role in Tobacco Use*, DOI: 10.1007/978-0-387-78748-0_5, © Springer Science+Business Media, LLC 2009

source of motivation underlying nicotine dependence may be the cognitive-enhancing effects of nicotine. These cognitive-enhancing effects of nicotine may constitute positive reinforcement (i.e., cognitive enhancement in healthy individuals), or negative reinforcement (i.e., alleviation of cognitive impairment in those suffering from mental illness, and also in nicotine-dependent individuals experiencing nicotine withdrawal). Importantly, all of these primary motivational forces can bestow conditioned motivational properties to previously neutral environmental stimuli (either discrete cues or contextual stimuli) through predictive temporal associations. Accordingly, environmental stimuli may acquire conditioned rewarding and reward-enhancing properties may lead to conditioned nicotine withdrawal and may induce conditioned cognitive enhancement. Preclinical experimental evidence demonstrating these motivational forces and how these forces play a crucial role in maintaining compulsive nicotine use are reviewed below.

Rewarding Effects of Nicotine

Primary Rewarding Effects of Nicotine

Despite early difficulties in establishing nicotine self-administration in experimental animals (for reviews, see Corrigall, 1999; Stolerman & Jarvis, 1995), it has now been shown repeatedly that nicotine is self-administered intravenously by non-human primates (e.g., Goldberg, Spealman, & Goldberg, 1981), dogs (e.g., Risner & Goldberg, 1983), rats (e.g., Corrigall & Coen, 1989; DeNoble & Mele, 2006; Donny, Caggiula, Knopf, & Brown, 1995; Watkins, Epping-Jordan, Koob, & Markou, 1999) and mice (e.g., Picciotto et al., 1998). Furthermore, rats will self-administer nicotine under a broad range of access conditions (Corrigall & Coen, 1989; DeNoble & Mele, 2006; Kenny & Markou, 2006; LeSage et al., 2002; Paterson & Markou, 2004; Valentine, Hokanson, Matta, & Sharp, 1997) and reinforcement schedules (e.g., Donny et al., 1999; Markou & Paterson, 2001; Paterson, Froestl, & Markou, 2004). Across species, intravenous self-administration of nicotine under fixed-ratio schedules of reinforcement (where a nicotine infusion is delivered after emission of a fixed number of instrumental responses) occurs with a relatively flattened inverted U-shaped dose-response function (e.g., Risner & Goldberg, 1983; Sannerud, Prada, Goldberg, & Goldberg, 1994; Watkins et al., 1999; Panel A in Fig. 5.1) compared to self-administration of other psychostimulant substances, such as cocaine (e.g., Pickens & Thompson, 1968; Caine & Koob, 1995). Under progressive-ratio schedules of reinforcement, where a nicotine infusion is delivered after emission of an increasing number of instrumental responses until the response requirements for the subsequent infusion become so high that the subject ceases to respond, the nicotine dose-response function is linear for the range of doses that are reliably self-administered (Donny et al., 1999; Paterson et al., 2004; Panel B in Fig. 5.1), similar to the function obtained with cocaine (Depoortere, Li, Lane, & Emmett-Oglesby, 1993; Paterson & Markou, 2003). Fixed- and progressive-ratio schedules,

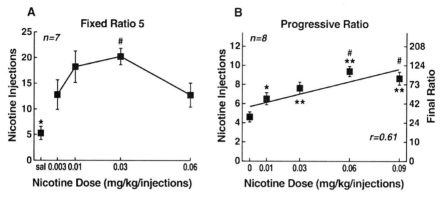

Fig. 5.1 Nicotine self-administration dose-response curves. Panel A: Nicotine self-administration dose-response curve under a fixed-ratio 5 schedule of reinforcement in Wistar rats. The number of infusions earned when the various nicotine doses (base) were available is shown as mean ± SEM. Asterisk (*p<0.05) indicates significantly lower responding compared to all nicotine doses; pound sign (#p<0.05) indicates significantly higher responding compared to 0.003 and 0.06 mg/kg/injection nicotine. Adapted with permission from Watkins, Epping-Jordan, Koob & Markou 1999. **Panel B**: Nicotine self-administration dose-response curve under a progressive-ratio schedule of reinforcement in Wistar rats. The number of infusions earned (mean ± SEM) is shown on the left y-axis, and the final ratio completed (i.e., breaking point, mean ± SEM) is shown on the right y-axis. Asterisks (*p<0.05, **p<0.01) and pound signs (#p<0.05) indicate significant differences compared to saline or 0.01 mg/kg/injection nicotine, respectively. Adapted with permission from Paterson, Froestl & Markou, 2004

while not the only schedules of reinforcement utilized in self-administration studies, have been used most commonly. It has been suggested that progressive-ratio schedules of reinforcement provide a more direct measure of the motivation to obtain a drug compared to fixed-ratio schedules that provide a direct measure of drug intake (Arnold & Roberts, 1997; Markou et al., 1993; McGregor & Roberts, 1995; Rowlett, 2000).

Patterns of responding for nicotine infusions in rats under fixed-ratio schedules of reinforcement are broadly similar to responding for intravenous nicotine in humans, as indicated in Fig. 5.2. It should be noted that the tightly regulated and precisely timed patterns of intravenous self-administration of cocaine seen during 1–3 hours long self-administration sessions in rats (Markou, unpublished observations) are not seen in rats and humans that self-administer nicotine intravenously. Intravenous self-administration of nicotine has a flatter dose-response function (Watkins et al., 1999; Panel A in Fig. 5.1) and more irregular patterns of intake (Fig. 5.2) than self-administration of cocaine. Cocaine has a shorter half-life than nicotine that, together with other poorly understood factors, leads to a more distinctly inverted U-shaped dose-response function than nicotine. Taken together, the nicotine self-administration data suggest that the primary rewarding properties of nicotine lead to the initiation and maintenance of nicotine self-administration, and are one of the motivational factors contributing to nicotine dependence.

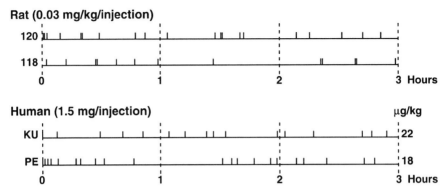

Fig. 5.2 Individual nicotine self-administration records in Wistar rats and humans during 3 hour sessions. Each upwards tick represents delivery of a nicotine infusion. Rat data adapted from Watkins et al., 1999, and human data adapted from Henningfield, Miyasato & Jasinski, 1983

Conditioned Rewarding Effects of Stimuli Associated with Nicotine Administration

Neutral environmental stimuli that are associated in a predictive manner with the primary rewarding effects of nicotine acquire conditioned rewarding properties that also have motivational significance and are likely to contribute to the maintenance of nicotine dependence. The motivational significance of such conditioned stimuli to maintain nicotine-seeking behaviors has been demonstrated in experimental animals. When rats trained to self-administer a drug, such as nicotine, are given access to saline rather than the drug (i.e., extinction conditions), response rates dramatically decrease (Chiamulera, Borgo, Falchetto, Valerio, & Tessari, 1996; See, Grimm, Kruzich, & Rustay, 1999; Shaham, Adamson, Grocki, & Corrigall, 1997; Watkins et al., 1999). If specific environmental stimuli are presented with each drug infusion (e.g., brief illumination of a light above the active lever whose depression leads to the drug infusion) and continue to be presented during the extinction phase contingent upon the performance of the operant response, levels of responding take significantly longer to decline under extinction conditions for the drug, than if these conditioned environmental stimuli are removed during the extinction phase (Fig. 5.3). Resistance to extinction is one of the classic measures of the motivational impact of environmental stimuli. Thus, the resistance to extinction exhibited when environmental stimuli previously paired with nicotine self-administration continue to be presented is consistent with the notion that these stimuli have acquired conditioned motivational properties that maintain the drug-seeking behavior.

The acquired motivational properties of such nicotine-associated cues are also demonstrated by the fact that contingent presentation of such conditioned stimuli elicits reinstatement of previously extinguished nicotine-seeking behavior, even when nicotine continues not to be available (Caggiula et al., 2002; LeSage, Burroughs, Dufek, Keyler, & Pentel, 2004; Liu et al., 2006; Paterson, Froestl, &

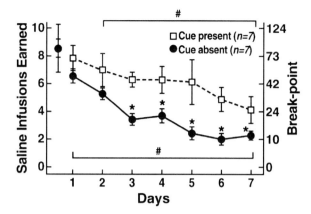

Fig. 5.3 Presentation of conditioned stimuli associated with nicotine administration retards extinction of nicotine-seeking behavior under a progressive-ratio schedule of reinforcement. Data are expressed as mean ± SEM. The left axis shows the number of saline infusions (i.e., extinction conditions) earned, and the right axis shows the corresponding final ratio completed (i.e., break-points). Asterisks (*p<0.05) indicate significantly lower responding in the group that was not presented with the stimulus previously associated with nicotine administration (i.e., cue-absent group) compared to responding in the group that was presented with the nicotine-associated cue upon completion of a required ratio (i.e., cue-present group). Pound sign (#p<0.05) indicates significantly lower responding compared to pre-extinction baseline levels of responding within groups (Paterson & Markou, previously unpublished observations)

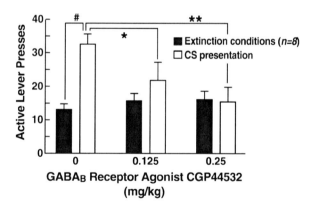

Fig. 5.4 Presentation of conditioned stimuli previously associated with nicotine adminis-tration induces reinstatement of nicotine-seeking behavior. Data are presented as number of lever presses (mean ± SEM). *Black* and *white* bars represent responding under cue-absent (i.e., extinction conditions) and cue-present (i.e., CS presentation upon completion of a fixed-ratio 5) conditions, respectively. Pound sign (#p<0.05) indicates significant differences between the test day (CS presentation) compared to the preceding 3-day baseline (i.e., baseline under extinction conditions), and thus demonstrates that the contingent presentation of stimuli previously asso-ciated with nicotine administration reinstates nicotine-seeking behavior in Wistar rats. Asterisks (*p<0.05, **p<0.01) indicate significant differences from saline pretreatment, and indicate that administration of the GABA$_B$ receptor agonist CGP44532 reversed cue-induced reinstatement of nicotine-seeking. Adapted with permission from Paterson, Froestl & Markou, 2005

Markou, 2005; Fig. 5.4), similar to that seen after presentation of stimuli associated with other drugs of abuse (for review, see Shaham, Shalev, Lu, De Wit, & Stewart, 2003).

Reward-Enhancing Effects of Nicotine

Primary Reward-Enhancing Effects of Nicotine

A property of psychomotor stimulant drugs that may also contribute to drug dependence is the reward-enhancing effect of these drugs. That is, nicotine and other psychomotor stimulant drugs enhance the reward value of other primary and conditioned rewarding stimuli (e.g., Taylor & Robbins, 1984). Brief electrical stimulation of numerous subcortical brain sites, and in particular sites along the medial forebrain bundle, is extremely rewarding for animals (Olds & Milner, 1954). Using a variety of procedures, one may derive quantitative measures of brain reward function by assessing the current-intensity or frequency thresholds for the stimulation that will support responding (Markou & Koob, 1992). Administration of almost all drugs of abuse (for review, see Markou & Kenny 2002), including nicotine, lowers the reward threshold value thereby providing a quantitative measure of the reward-enhancing effects of nicotine (Harrison, Gasparini, & Markou, 2002; Fig. 5.5).

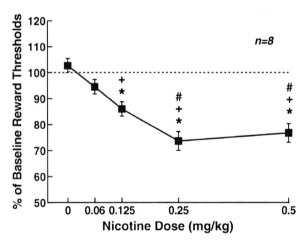

Fig. 5.5 Acute experimenter-administered nicotine enhances brain reward function as reflected in a dose-dependent lowering of intracranial self-stimulation (ICSS) reward thresholds. Reward threshold data (mean ± SEM) are expressed as a percent of the previous baseline day's threshold (drug-free). Asterisks ($*p < 0.05$) denote statistically significant differences from thresholds after saline treatment. Crosses ($+p < 0.05$) denote statistically significant differences from thresholds after administration of 0.06 mg/kg nicotine base. Pound signs ($\#p < 0.05$) denote statistically significant differences from thresholds after administration of 0.125 mg/kg nicotine base. Adapted with permission from Harrison, Gasparini & Markou, 2002

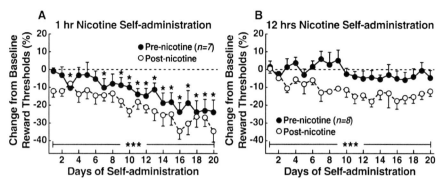

Fig. 5.6 Self-administered nicotine enhances brain reward function as reflected in lowering of intracranial self-stimulation (ICSS) reward thresholds. Data (mean ± SEM) are expressed as percent change from baseline reward thresholds. Wistar rats were allowed to self-administer nicotine for 1 hour (**Panel A**) or 12 hours (**Panel B**) daily, and their reward thresholds were assessed 1 hour before (pre-nicotine) and 15 min (post-nicotine) after the daily nicotine self-administration session. Asterisks indicate significantly lower pre-nicotine thresholds compared with baseline thresholds (i.e., thresholds assessed before the initiation of nicotine self-administration, *p<0.05), and main effects of nicotine on reward thresholds in a two-way repeated measures ANOVA (***p<0.001). Adapted with permission from Kenny & Markou, 2006

Recently, the reward-enhancing effects of experimenter-administered nicotine have been extended to self-administered nicotine (Kenny & Markou, 2006; Paterson, Balfour & Markou 2007). Nicotine, self-administered intravenously for either 1, 6, or 12 hours daily, reliably and consistently lowered brain reward thresholds compared to thresholds measured immediately before self-administration (Fig. 5.6). Another demonstration of the reward-enhancing effects of experimenter- or self-administered nicotine is the increased responding for a primary reinforcing compound visual stimulus in rats when nicotine is administered (see Caggiula, Donny, Palmatier, Liu, Chaudhri and Sved, this volume;Caggiula et al., 2002; Chaudhri et al., 2006). These reward-enhancing properties of nicotine are likely to provide an additional motivational factor that drives continued use of nicotine, and thus maintain nicotine dependence, as people may seek the reward-enhancing effects of nicotine.

Conditioned Reward-Enhancing Effects of Psychomotor Stimulants

In addition to the primary reward-enhancing effects of acute nicotine, it is likely that stimuli paired with nicotine administration also acquire reward-enhancing properties. Although the conditioned reward-enhancing effects of nicotine have just begun to be explored in experimental studies (see below), we hypothesize that there are such conditioned rewarding effects based on similar effects observed for cocaine-associated stimuli and the demonstrated ability of nicotine withdrawal-associated conditioned stimuli to inhibit brain reward function (see below under Nicotine

Withdrawal). A study with cocaine as the psychomotor stimulant drug has demonstrated how stimuli predictably paired with the reward-enhancing effects of cocaine gradually acquire reward-enhancing properties and lead to conditioned reward enhancement. Brain reward thresholds were assessed in two consecutive 30 min sessions in rats. Immediately after the first session and 10 min before the second session rats were injected with cocaine for 20 consecutive days. Although pre-injection thresholds remained stable, post-cocaine thresholds were lowered compared to both pre-injection and baseline thresholds, reflecting the cocaine-induced enhancement of brain reward function (Kenny, Koob, & Markou, 2003). After completion of the cocaine administration phase, saline injections administered at the same time and under the same conditions as cocaine were administered during the preceding days, significantly lowered brain reward thresholds for 3 consecutive days, while pre-injection thresholds remained unchanged as during the cocaine treatment phase (Fig. 5.7). These results demonstrate that neutral discrete

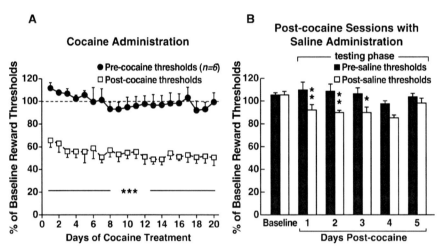

Fig. 5.7 Conditioned enhancement of brain reward function. Data (mean ± SEM) are expressed as percent of baseline reward thresholds defined as the mean value for each subject obtained over the last five intracranial self-stimulation (ICSS) sessions prior to the initiation of the cocaine administration phase of the experiment. Wistar rats were tested in two consecutive daily sessions in the ICSS procedure (i.e., pre-cocaine and post-cocaine sessions). **Panel A**: For 20 consecutive days, rats were experimentally administered intraperitoneally 10 mg/kg cocaine salt immediately after the first ICSS session and 10 min before the second ICSS session. Asterisks (***p<0.001) indicate a main effect of cocaine in the ANOVA reflecting the fact that cocaine administration led to lower reward thresholds in the second daily session compared to the daily pre-cocaine session. **Panel B**: After the termination of the 20-day cocaine administration procedure, rats continued to be tested twice daily in the ICSS procedure for 5 consecutive days and a saline, instead of cocaine, injection was administered to the subjects between sessions. Asterisks (*p<0.05, **p<0.01, ***p<0.001) indicate significantly lower thresholds after saline administration (post-saline session) compared to thresholds before the saline administration (pre-saline session). This effect demonstrates that both the daily injection and the second daily ICSS session that were previously associated with cocaine-induced enhancement of brain reward function, induced conditioned reward enhancement even after the discontinuation of the daily cocaine injections. Adapted with permission from Kenny, Koob & Markou, 2003

and contextual environmental stimuli, such as the injection procedure and the second daily assessment of brain reward thresholds, when paired with the reward-enhancing properties of psychomotor stimulant drugs, acquire conditioned reward-enhancing properties. These conditioned reward-enhancing properties may be an additional motivational factor that leads to the approach of these conditioned stimuli. Because these conditioned stimuli are often predictably and temporally associated with the availability of the primary drug reward, the motivation to approach such conditioned stimuli is likely to lead to drug consumption. Indeed, recent experimental data have demonstrated that nicotine enhances the motivational effects of conditioned stimuli that earned their conditioned reinforcing properties by temporal associations with the primary reinforcer nicotine (see Caggiula, Donny, Palmatier, Liu, Chaudhri and Sved, this volume). Such effects provide the basis for a feed-forward loop whereby previously neutral stimuli acquire conditioned rewarding properties by temporal association with nicotine administration and subsequent nicotine administration amplifies those conditioned reinforcing effects.

Nicotine Withdrawal

Decreased Brain Reward Function during Nicotine Withdrawal

Cessation of chronic nicotine exposure in both humans and experimental animals leads to a constellation of unpleasant signs termed the nicotine withdrawal syndrome. The negative aspects of nicotine withdrawal constitute another important motivational factor that contributes to nicotine dependence by providing the substrate for negative reinforcement processes to occur. That is, alleviation of the aversive aspects of nicotine withdrawal by further nicotine administration provides negative reinforcement. In both humans and rodents, nicotine withdrawal is characterized by somatic and affective components. These affective and somatic components of nicotine withdrawal have been observed in both rats (e.g., Malin et al., 1992; Epping-Jordan, Watkins, Koob & Markou, 1998; Irvine, Cheeta, & File, 2001) and humans (e.g., al'Absi et al., 2004; Glassman et al., 1990; Hughes & Hatsukami, 1986; Parrott, 1993; West, Jarvis, Russell, Carruthers, & Feyerabend, 1984). The affective component of the nicotine withdrawal syndrome in humans comprises anhedonia (i.e., diminished interest or pleasure in normally rewarding stimuli), dysphoria and anxiety (American Psychiatric Association 1994).

The nicotine withdrawal syndrome is characterized by both behavioral and neurochemical changes that have been extensively characterized (e.g., Carboni, Bortone, Giua & Di Chiara, 2000; Hildebrand, Nomikos, Hertel, Schilstrom & Svensson, 1998; Paterson et al., 2007; Smolka, Budde, Karow & Schmidt, 2004) As described above and shown in Figs. 5.5 and 5.6 (Harrison, Liem & Markou, 2001; Kenny & Markou, 2006), acute nicotine administration lowers brain reward thresholds reflecting an enhancement of brain reward function, while nicotine withdrawal is associated with elevations in brain reward thresholds reflecting diminished interest in the rewarding electrical stimuli (i.e., anhedonia; e.g., Epping-Jordan,

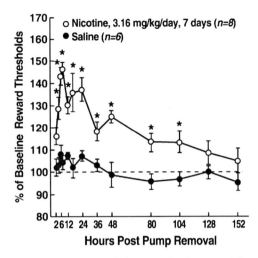

Fig. 5.8 Spontaneous nicotine withdrawal decreases brain reward function as reflected in elevations in ICSS reward thresholds. Wistar rats were treated with nicotine (3.16 mg/kg/day, base) or saline via subcutaneous osmotic minipumps for 7 days. Upon removal of the minipumps, previously nicotine-treated rats exhibited significant elevations in intracranial self-stimulation (ICSS) reward thresholds, reflecting an anhedonic state, while thresholds of saline-treated control rats were stable. Asterisks (*$p < 0.05$) indicate statistically significant differences between nicotine- and saline-treated groups after minipump removal. Data (mean ± SEM) are expressed as a percentage of baseline thresholds prior to the implantation of the minipumps. Adapted with permission from Epping-Jordan, Watkins, Koob & Markou 1998

Watkins, Koob & Markou, 1998; Fig. 5.8). The elevations of brain reward thresholds associated with the cessation of nicotine administration (i.e., nicotine withdrawal) are an operational measure of the symptom of anhedonia (Geyer & Markou, 1995; Kenny & Markou, 2001; Markou, Kosten, & Koob, 1998) seen in nicotine withdrawal and in major depression in humans (American Psychiatric Association 1994). Removal of osmotic minipumps that delivered 3.16 mg/kg/day nicotine base over 7 days resulted in the appearance of elevations in brain reward thresholds within 4 hours of pump removal that persisted until 104 hours post-pump in this study. Thresholds of saline-treated control rats remained stable. This phenomenon of elevations in brain reward thresholds during nicotine withdrawal has been replicated multiple times and extended to additional times of exposure and nicotine doses by several investigators in our laboratory (e.g., Cryan, Bruijnzeel, Skjei, & Markou, 2003; Harrison et al., 2001; Kenny, Gasparini & Markou, 2003; Lindblom et al., 2005; Paterson et al., 2007; Paterson et al., 2005; Semenova & Markou, 2003; Skjei & Markou, 2003). Furthermore, similar brain reward threshold elevations were seen after cessation of repeated non-contingent administration of subcutaneous nicotine injections (Bozarth, Pudiak, & KuoLee, 1998). The dose of nicotine administered by minipump produces venous plasma nicotine levels of approximately 40 ng/ml in rats (Murrin, Ferrer, Zeng, & Haley, 1987) equal to the upper limit of the range of nicotine levels in human smokers (Benowitz & Jacob,

1984), and lower than the peak plasma nicotine levels (65–75 ng/ml) observed in rats allowed to self-administer nicotine for 1 or 2 hours daily (Shoaib & Stolerman, 1999). Administration of both the broad spectrum nicotinic acetylcholine receptor antagonist mecamylamine (Watkins, Stinus, Koob & Markou 2000) or the nicotinic acetylcholine receptor antagonist dihydro-β-erythroidine that has some selectivity for α4β2 nicotinic receptors (Epping-Jordan, Watkins, Koob & Markou 1998) dose-dependently elevated brain reward thresholds in nicotine- but not saline- treated rats. Administration of nicotine via minipumps at a dose sufficient to induce the anhe-donic component of withdrawal upon cessation of the infusion also results in the emergence of the somatic component of nicotine withdrawal (see below). Similar reward threshold elevations are also seen during withdrawal from all major drugs of abuse, such as cocaine (Markou & Koob, 1991), morphine (Schulteis, Markou, Gold, Stinus & Koob, 1994), amphetamine (Paterson, Myers & Markou, 2000), ethanol (Schulteis, Markou, Cole & Koob, 1995) and phencyclidine (Spielewoy & Markou, 2003).

The Somatic Aspects of Nicotine Withdrawal

Increased number of somatic signs was one of the first preclinical measures of nicotine withdrawal in rodents. Malin and coworkers recognized a nicotine with-drawal syndrome in rats that emerged after the cessation of continuous nicotine administration and comprised a constellation of somatic signs (e.g., gasps, writhes, teeth-chattering, ptosis) that are a subset of, and milder in intensity than, some of the somatic signs of opiate withdrawal (Malin et al., 1994; Malin et al., 1992). Nicotine administration attenuates somatic signs of nicotine withdrawal (Malin et al., 1996), while administration of the non-selective nicotinic acetylcholine receptor antagonist mecamylamine (Hildebrand, Nomikos, Bondjers, Nisell, & Svensson, 1997; Malin et al., 1994; Watkins et al., 2000) reliably precipitates the somatic components of nicotine withdrawal in nicotine-treated rats (Fig. 5.9).

Motivational Significance of Anhedonic Versus Somatic Components of Drug Withdrawal

When chlorisondamine, a nicotinic acetylcholine receptor antagonist that does not readily cross the blood–brain barrier, was administered directly into the brain, (Gosling & Lu, 1969), it precipitated somatic signs of nicotine withdrawal and brain reward threshold elevations in nicotine-treated rats (Malin et al., 1997; Watkins et al., 2000). Systemic chlorisondamine administration, at doses that do not cross the blood–brain barrier, only precipitated the somatic signs of nicotine withdrawal and not the threshold elevations (Watkins et al., 2000). Similarly, systemic admin-istration of hexamethonium, a nicotinic acetylcholine receptor antagonist that also does not cross the blood–brain barrier readily in mice, induced increased somatic signs of withdrawal in mice chronically treated with nicotine (Damaj, Kao, &

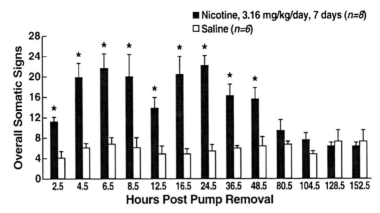

Fig. 5.9 Spontaneous nicotine withdrawal increases somatic signs of withdrawal. Wistar rats were treated with nicotine (3.16 mg/kg/day, base) or saline via subcutaneous osmotic minipumps for 7 days. Upon removal of the minipumps, previously nicotine-treated rats exhibited significant increases in somatic signs of withdrawal while the number of somatic signs observed in saline-treated rats remained low and stable. Data (mean ± SEM) are expressed as overall number of somatic signs of withdrawal observed. Asterisks (*$p < 0.05$) indicate statistically significant differences between nicotine- and saline-treated groups at each time-point after minipump removal. Adapted with permission from Epping-Jordan et al., 1998

Martin, 2003). In addition, Hildebrand and coworkers (Hildebrand et al., 1997) reversed mecamylamine-precipitated somatic signs of withdrawal by administering the peripherally active nicotinic acetylcholine receptor agonist tetramethylammonium (Engberg & Hajos, 1994). Overall the vast majority of available evidence suggests that the somatic signs of nicotine withdrawal are primarily peripherally mediated, while the withdrawal-associated anhedonia is centrally mediated. Nevertheless, both aspects of nicotine withdrawal are likely to be significant motivational factors that contribute to continued nicotine use to alleviate either or both of these affective aspects of withdrawal. It is also highly likely that all other affective aspects of nicotine withdrawal, such as anxiety, are centrally mediated. Recent evidence indicates that an antagonist at corticotropin-releasing factor receptors prevented the threshold elevations associated with precipitated withdrawal, but did not reverse the threshold elevations associated with spontaneous nicotine withdrawal in rats (Bruijnzeel, Zislis, Wilson, & Gold, 2007). This pattern of results suggests that anxiety aspects of nicotine withdrawal may contribute to the initiation of the anhedonic component of nicotine withdrawal.

These findings in nicotine withdrawal, coupled with data from cocaine and heroin self-administration studies (see below), led these authors to hypothesize that the affective aspects of nicotine withdrawal may constitute a more important motivational factor in drug dependence than the somatic aspects of drug withdrawal (Koob & Le Moal, 2005; Markou et al., 1998). Specifically, escalation of cocaine intake in rats allowed extended access to cocaine self-administration was associated with a progressive decrement of brain reward function prior to daily self-administration

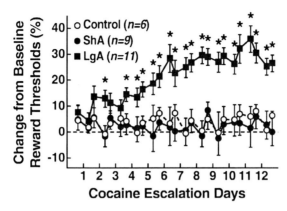

Fig. 5.10 Escalation of cocaine intake in self-administering rats is associated with progressive impairment of brain reward function. Rats with access to saline (control) for 1 hour (short access rats; ShA) or 6 hours (long-access rats; LgA) were tested daily 1 hour before their daily cocaine self-administration session in the intracranial self-stimulation (ICSS) procedure. As cocaine intake gradually escalated in the LgA rats (self-administration data not shown here), there was an accompanying elevation in brain reward thresholds reflecting the development of an anhedonic state. Indeed, the threshold elevations preceded by a few days the escalation in cocaine intake, suggesting that this anhedonic state may have motivational properties that drive increased drug consumption. Asterisks (*p<0.05) indicate elevated brain reward thresholds of LgA rats compared to thresholds of control and ShA rats. Adapted with permission from Ahmed, Kenny, Koob & Markou 2002

sessions (Ahmed, Kenny, Koob, & Markou, 2002; Fig. 5.10). These data suggest that the increased intake of cocaine may be motivated by decreased brain reward function as the rat attempts to return brain reward function towards pre-drug baseline levels by self-administering increasing amounts of cocaine.

Conditioned Nicotine Withdrawal

It has been shown that presentation of a compound visual and auditory cue previously paired with nicotinic receptor antagonist-precipitated nicotine withdrawal led to significant elevations in brain reward thresholds, reflecting conditioned withdrawal, in nicotine-treated rats (Kenny & Markou 2005; Fig. 5.11). The same cues had no effect on brain reward thresholds in rats exposed to the cues and also subjected to nicotine withdrawal in an unpaired fashion (i.e., un-paired rats), or in nicotine-naïve rats.

Another measure of conditioned nicotine withdrawal is the avoidance of an environment that was previously associated with nicotine withdrawal; this measure is termed conditioned place aversion. An aversive state is necessary to induce a conditioned place aversion response, and therefore the expression of a conditioned place aversion indicates both the prior induction of a primary aversive state and the acquired aversive properties of an environment previously paired with that aversive state. Such a state can be induced by repeated administration of a nicotinic

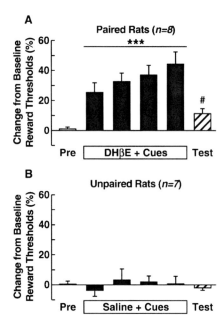

Fig. 5.11 Conditioned nicotine withdrawal impairs brain reward function. Data (mean ± SEM) are expressed as percent change from baseline intracranial self-stimulation (ICSS) reward thresholds. Rats made dependent on nicotine via chronic exposure to nicotine-containing subcutaneous osmotic minipumps were treated with the nicotinic acetylcholine receptor antagonist dihydro-β-erythroidine (DHβE) and simultaneously presented with a visual cue (**Panel A**; Paired Rats) or were treated with saline and presented with the same cue (**Panel B**; Unpaired Rats) for 4 consecutive days. The unpaired rats were treated with DHβE in their home cage so that they had the same DHβE-precipitated withdrawal experiences as the paired rats. Additional control groups were also included in this study whose data are not shown here. 'Pre' indicates the preconditioning day and 'Test' indicates the test day when all rats were presented with the cues and injected with saline. Asterisks (***p<0.001) indicate a main effect of DHβE + Cues on reward thresholds as revealed by an ANOVA. Pound sign (#p<0.05) indicates elevated reward thresholds on the test day compared with the preconditioning day (paired *t* test). Adapted with permission from Kenny & Markou, 2005

acetylcholine receptor antagonist in rats chronically treated with nicotine (Suzuki, Ise, Tsuda, Maeda & Misawa, 1996; Watkins et al., 2000; Fig. 5.12). Conditioned place aversion responses have only been demonstrated in response to antagonist-precipitated withdrawal, due to: (a) the impracticality of surgically removing and re-implanting osmotic minipumps to repeatedly induce and resolve spontaneous nicotine withdrawal in rats; and (b) precise temporal pairing of the aversive subjective state with the discrete environment in order for the association to be formed.

Theses findings with conditioned nicotine withdrawal extend previous findings showing that presentation of discrete environmental stimuli paired with antagonist-precipitated opiate withdrawal in humans, non-human primates, or rats precipitated somatic or behavioral manifestations of opiate withdrawal (Baldwin & Koob, 1993; Goldberg & Schuster, 1967; O'Brien, Testa, O'Brien, Brady, & Wells, 1977).

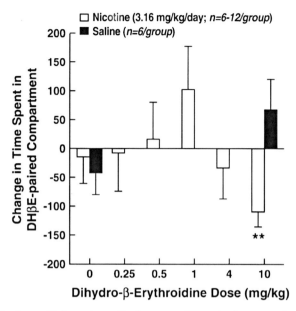

Fig. 5.12 Nicotine withdrawal results in a conditioned place aversion. Nicotine- or saline-treated rats were injected with the nicotinic acetylcholine receptor antagonist dihydro-β-erythroidine (DHβE) and confined in one compartment of a three-compartment place preference/aversion apparatus. On alternate days, rats were injected with saline and confined in a different compartment of the apparatus. On the test day (day 10 of nicotine/saline exposure), rats were allowed to freely explore the three-compartment apparatus, and the difference in time (mean±SEM) spent in the DHβE-paired compartment before conditioning versus after conditioning was recorded. Asterisks (**p< 0.01) indicate a statistically significant decrease in the time spent in the DHβE-paired compartment before conditioning compared with the time spent after conditioning. This result indicates that nicotine withdrawal is associated with a negative state that can be associated with the context in which this state was experienced. Accordingly, exposure to the context previously associated with the negative state of nicotine withdrawal leads to conditioned nicotine withdrawal. Adapted with permission from Watkins et al., 2000

Thus, presentation of environmental stimuli that are repeatedly paired with nicotine withdrawal can induce a conditioned negative affective state (i.e., conditioned nicotine withdrawal seen as either conditioned threshold elevations or conditioned place aversion), and thus provide a source of motivation to resume nicotine use. Indeed, in the case of opiate withdrawal, it has been shown that conditioned withdrawal leads to increased heroin intake, reflecting the motivational value of conditioned withdrawal and its potentially critical role in drug addiction. Pairing of a compound stimulus with naloxone-precipitated opiate withdrawal in rats resulted in impaired brain reward function (Kenny, Chen, Kitamura, Markou & Koob, 2006). Most interestingly, after repeated pairing of the compound stimulus with administration of the opiate receptor antagonist naloxone in heroin-dependent rats allowed to self-administer heroin for 23 hours per day, presentation of the compound stimulus alone increased responding for heroin, indicating the motivational significance of the conditioned withdrawal state (Kenny et al., 2006; Fig. 5.13). Presentation of

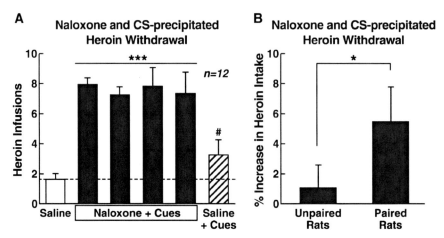

Fig. 5.13 Conditioned heroin withdrawal increases heroin intake in self-administering rats. Rats trained to self-administer heroin increased the number of heroin infusions (mean ± SEM) earned when administered the opiate receptor antagonist naloxone and exposed to discrete cues (CS). **Panel A**: After four pairings of naloxone administration with the cues, presentation of the cues alone led to a conditioned increase in heroin intake presumably due to the induction of conditioned opiate withdrawal that could be alleviated by increased heroin intake. These data clearly demonstrate that conditioned withdrawal has motivational significance that leads to increased drug intake. Asterisks (***p<0.001) indicate a significant main effect of naloxone+cues on heroin intake compared to heroin intake after administration of saline. Pound sign (#p<0.05) indicates significantly increased heroin intake after saline+cues compared with intake after saline administration. **Panel B**: Asterisk (*p<0.05) indicates significant increase in heroin intake on the test day (saline+cues presentation) in rats that previously experienced naloxone administration paired with the cues and allowed to increase their intake (paired rats whose data are also shown in Panel A), and rats that had equal exposure to naloxone and cues but these two stimuli were unpaired (unpaired rats). Adapted with permission from Kenny, Chen, Kitamura, Markou & Koob 2006

the same compound stimulus had no effect in heroin-dependent rats that had not experienced the pairing of the compound stimulus with administration of the opiate antagonist naloxone. Thus, these data indicate that environmental stimuli previously paired with a withdrawal state can increase drug intake when subsequently presented to dependent individuals, presumably by inducing a conditioned opiate withdrawal state.

Considered in the context of the elevations in brain reward thresholds seen in rats that gradually escalate their cocaine intake (Ahmed et al., 2002; Fig. 5.10) and the conditioned elevations in brain reward thresholds in nicotine-dependent rats presented with stimuli previously associated with precipitated nicotine withdrawal (Kenny & Markou 2005; Fig. 5.11), it seems likely that impaired brain reward function motivates increased drug self-administration. It is worth noting that in the heroin study (Kenny et al. 2006), the rats received only naloxone when heroin was available and these rats became gradually dependent on heroin due to extended access to heroin self-administration. These two features of the procedure allowed the subjects to learn that increased heroin intake counteracted the effects of unconditioned and conditioned withdrawal, consistent with findings by Everitt and colleagues (Hellemans, Dickinson & Everitt, 2006; Hutcheson, Everitt, Robbins & Dickinson, 2001) who used non-contingent heroin to induce dependence. In the first of these studies, it was shown that prior experience with heroin-taking during withdrawal was required for increased heroin-seeking behavior when dependent rats subsequently experienced withdrawal (Hutcheson et al., 2001). Similarly, prior experience of heroin-taking in the presence of a withdrawal-paired conditioned stimulus was required to observe increased heroin-seeking behavior during subsequent conditioned stimulus exposure (Hellemans, Dickinson & Everitt 2006). In both studies, animals with no prior experience of the withdrawal-alleviating effects of heroin exhibited suppression, rather than enhancement, of heroin-seeking during subsequent withdrawal states. The data obtained from the heroin studies (Hellemans et al., 2006; Hutcheson et al., 2001; Kenny et al., 2006) likely explain the lack of increased nicotine self-administration during nicotine withdrawal after chronic non-contingent nicotine exposure (Paterson & Markou, 2004) in rats that had no prior experience of withdrawal alleviation by increased nicotine intake. Future work should examine whether experience with nicotine self-administration during the withdrawal state may lead to increased nicotine intake during spontaneous or precipitated or conditioned nicotine withdrawal.

Recently, we reported that prolonged abstinence from extended nicotine self-administration access was associated with lowered brain reward thresholds, reflecting an enhancement of brain reward function (Kenny & Markou, 2006; Fig. 5.14). This finding was unexpected considering the presence of the somatic signs of nicotine withdrawal in rats that allowed extended access to nicotine self-administration (Paterson & Markou, 2004; Paterson et al., 2007). Thus, these data provide further evidence that the somatic and anhedonic components of nicotine withdrawal are dissociable and mediated by different substrates, as previously suggested by the studies that used different nicotinic acetylcholine receptor antagonists to precipitate the various aspects of nicotine withdrawal (Epping-Jordan, Watkins, Koob & Markou 1998; Watkins et al., 2000). Most importantly, the data shown in Fig. 5.14 and reported in Kenny & Markou, 2006 demonstrate enhanced, rather than decreased, brain reward function after cessation of daily intravenous nicotine self-administration in rats. This effect may be attributable to the stable low levels of nicotine self-administration observed (0.38–1.36 mg/kg/day base), which result in lower nicotine intake per day than that delivered passively via subcutaneous osmotic minipumps (>3.16 mg/kg/day base) that resulted in decreased brain reward function upon cessation of administration of these higher nicotine doses (e.g., Epping-Jordan et al., 1998; Skjei & Markou, 2003). Thus, low daily nicotine intake may lead to long-term enhancement of brain reward function, similar to that seen after acute nicotine administration (e.g., Harrison et al., 2002; Fig. 5.5; Kenny and Markou, 2006); this effect appears to be long-lasting (up to 36 days of testing) and outlasts the acute effects of nicotine. By contrast, cessation of daily administration of higher nicotine doses (>3.16 mg/kg/day base) results in deficits in brain reward function. Ongoing studies are exploring factors such as daily nicotine dose, length of exposure, type of exposure (intermittent versus continuous infusion)

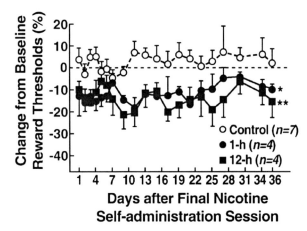

Fig. 5.14 Abstinence from low dose nicotine self-administration results in enhanced brain reward function. Rats were allowed to self-administer nicotine (0.03 mg/kg/injection base) during 1-hour or 12-hour daily sessions. Control rats were prepared with intravenous catheters and food-trained but were not exposed to the self-administration apparatus. Termination of nicotine self-administration resulted in lowering of brain reward thresholds compared to pre-nicotine thresholds and thresholds of control rats. Intracranial self-stimulation (ICSS) reward threshold data (mean ± SEM) are expressed as percent change from baseline reward thresholds (defined as the mean value for each subject obtained during the last five ICSS sessions prior to the initiation of the self-administration phase of the experiment). Asterisks (*$p<0.05$, **$p<0.01$) indicate significantly lowered ICSS thresholds compared with control rats over the entire testing period of 36 days with tests of simple main effects. Thus, the increased sensitivity in brain reward systems seen after cessation of self-administration of a relatively low nicotine dose appears to be long-lasting. This effect has been replicated and presented twice by Kenny & Markou (2006), and also by a second experimenter (Paterson & Markou, unpublished observations). Adapted with permission from Kenny & Markou 2006

and route of administration (intravenous versus subcutaneous) that may determine whether enhancement of brain reward function or deficits in brain reward function would be observed after cessation of nicotine administration. Such studies may provide critical information about the conditions that lead to nicotine dependence, as well as the nature of the long-lasting effects of nicotine that may be associated with the development and maintenance of dependence, and potentially relapse states.

Cognitive-Enhancing Effects of Nicotine

The cognitive-enhancing effects of nicotine (Jones, Sahakian, Levy, Warburton, & Gray, 1992; Levin et al., 1998) or the decline in cognitive function experienced during nicotine withdrawal (Snyder & Henningfield, 1989) are likely to provide additional sources of motivation to consume nicotine. For example, it has been demonstrated in rats using procedures that assess attentional performance, such as the 5-choice serial reaction time task (Grottick & Higgins, 2000; Mirza & Stolerman, 1998), and procedures that assess working memory (Levin & Simon,

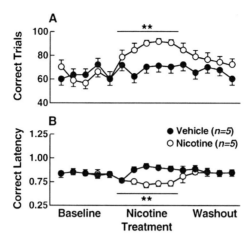

Fig. 5.15 Nicotine enhances attentional performance and speed of responding in the 5-choice serial reaction time task. Data points reflect the mean ± SEM number of trials in which the rats emitted a correct response (**Panel A**) and mean ± SEM latency to emit a correct response (**Panel B**) over consecutive treatment (nicotine or saline) days. Asterisks (**p<0.01) indicate a significant main effect of nicotine treatment compared to performance in saline-treated rats. Adapted with permission from Grottick & Higgins 2000

1998) that nicotine enhances cognitive performance. Figure 5.15 shows the cognitive-enhancing effects of nicotine in the 5-choice serial reaction time task in rats, where chronic nicotine increased both the correct number of responses and the latency to respond correctly (Grottick & Higgins, 2000). Such cognitive-enhancing effects of nicotine may be considered to be positive reinforcing effects in healthy individuals.

Conversely, cognitive function declines during nicotine withdrawal in human smokers (Snyder & Henningfield, 1989) and rodents (Semenova, Stolerman, & Markou, 2007; Shoaib & Bizarro, 2005). Nicotine use restored cognitive function back to normal (Snyder and Henningfield 1989) in these abstinent smokers. Therefore, the normalizing effect of nicotine in this context acts as negative reinforcement by alleviating the negative consequences of nicotine withdrawal. Nicotine may also improve impaired cognitive function in individuals suffering from diseases such as schizophrenia (Sacco et al., 2005) or Alzheimer's disease (Jones et al., 1992; Levin & Rezvani, 2002). Interestingly, the data in Fig. 5.15 showing enhancement of attentional function after nicotine administration in rats were obtained from a set of rats that were selected for poor performance of the task from a larger pool of subjects (Grottick & Higgins, 2000). Thus, these data may represent nicotine-induced normalization of impaired cognitive function.

Conclusions

This chapter reviewed experimental evidence primarily from rat studies demonstrating that there are multiple primary motivational forces that are likely to contribute to both the initiation and maintenance of nicotine dependence.

Furthermore, experimental evidence was presented showing that these primary motivational forces can be associated with discrete or contextual environmental stimuli that, through these predictive associations, acquire conditioned motivational properties. In the naturalistic environment of humans, contact with such conditioned stimuli is frequent and can greatly contribute, together with the primary unconditional forces, to the maintenance of the harmful tobacco habit.

Acknowledgments AM was supported by Research Grant 15RT-0022 from the Tobacco-Related Disease Research Program of the State of California, and NIH grants U01 MH69062, R01 DA11946 and R01 DA023209. NEP was supported by postdoctoral fellowship 14FT-0056 from the Tobacco-Related Disease Research Program of the State of California and the Peter F. McManus Charitable Trust. The authors would like to thank Mr. Michael Arends for editorial assistance, and Ms. Janet Hightower for graphics. Finally, the authors would like to thank Drs. John Cryan, Adrie Bruijnzeel, Mark Epping-Jordan, Amanda Harrison, Paul Kenny, Svetlana Semenova, Cecile Spielewoy, Serge Ahmed and Shelly Watkins for their great experimental and intellectual contribution to this research program.

References

Ahmed, S. H., Kenny, P. J., Koob, G. F., & Markou, A. (2002). Neurobiological evidence for hedonic allostasis associated with escalating cocaine use. *Nature Neuroscience, 5*(7), 625–626.

al'Absi, M., Hatsukami, D., Davis, G. L., & Wittmers, L. E. (2004). Prospective examination of effects of smoking abstinence on cortisol and withdrawal symptoms as predictors of early smoking relapse. *Drug and Alcohol Dependence, 73*(3), 267–278.

American Psychiatric Association. (1994). *Diagnostic and Statistical Manual of Mental Disorders* (4th ed.). Washington, DC: American Psychiatric Press.

Arnold, J. M., & Roberts, D. C. S. (1997). A critique of fixed and progressive ratio schedules used to examine the neural substrates of drug reinforcement. *Pharmacology Biochemistry and Behavior, 57*(3), 441–447.

Baldwin, H. A., & Koob, G. F. (1993). Rapid induction of conditioned opiate withdrawal in the rat. *Neuropsychopharmacology, 8*(1), 15–21.

Balfour, D. J., Wright, A. E., Benwell, M. E., & Birrell, C. E. (2000). The putative role of extrasynaptic mesolimbic dopamine in the neurobiology of nicotine dependence. *Behavioural Brain Research, 113*(1–2), 73–83.

Bardo, M. T., Green, T. A., Crooks, P. A., & Dwoskin, L. P. (1999). Nornicotine is self-administered intravenously by rats. *Psychopharmacology (Berl), 146*(3), 290–296.

Benowitz, N. L., & Jacob, P., 3rd. (1984). Daily intake of nicotine during cigarette smoking. *Clinical Pharmacology and Therapeutics, 35*(4), 499–504.

Bozarth, M. A., Pudiak, C. M., & KuoLee, R. (1998). Effect of chronic nicotine on brain stimulation reward. II. An escalating dose regimen. *Behavioural Brain Research, 96*(1–2), 189–194.

Bruijnzeel, A. W., Zislis, G., Wilson, C., & Gold, M. S. (2007). Antagonism of CRF receptors prevents the deficit in brain reward function associated with precipitated nicotine withdrawal in rats. *Neuropsychopharmacology, 32*(4), 955–963.

Caggiula, A. R., Donny, E. C., White, A. R., Chaudhri, N., Booth, S., Gharib, M. A., et al. (2002). Environmental stimuli promote the acquisition of nicotine self-administration in rats. *Psychopharmacology (Berl), 163*(2), 230–237.

Caine, S. B., & Koob, G. F. (1995). Pretreatment with the dopamine agonist 7-OH-DPAT shifts the cocaine self-administration dose-effect function to the left under different schedules in the rat. *Behavioural Pharmacology, 6*(4), 333–347.

Carboni, E., Bortone, L., Giua, C., & Di Chiara, G. (2000). Dissociation of physical abstinence signs from changes in extracellular dopamine in the nucleus accumbens and in the prefrontal cortex of nicotine dependent rats. *Drug and Alcohol Dependence, 58*(1–2), 93–102.

Centers for Disease Control and Prevention (2005). Cigarette smoking among adults–United States, 2004. *Morbidity and Mortality Weekly Report, 54*(44), 1121–1124.

Chaudhri, N., Caggiula, A. R., Donny, E. C., Palmatier, M. I., Liu, X., & Sved, A. F. (2006). Complex interactions between nicotine and nonpharmacological stimuli reveal multiple roles for nicotine in reinforcement. *Psychopharmacology (Berl), 184*(3–4), 353–366.

Chiamulera, C., Borgo, C., Falchetto, S., Valerio, E., & Tessari, M. (1996). Nicotine reinstatement of nicotine self-administration after long-term extinction. *Psychopharmacology (Berl), 127*(2), 102–107.

Corrigall, W. A. (1999). Nicotine self-administration in animals as a dependence model. *Nicotine and Tobacco Research, 1*(1), 11–20.

Corrigall, W. A., & Coen, K. M. (1989). Nicotine maintains robust self-administration in rats on a limited-access schedule. *Psychopharmacology (Berl), 99*(4), 473–478.

Crooks, P. A., & Dwoskin, L. P. (1997). Contribution of CNS nicotine metabolites to the neuropharmacological effects of nicotine and tobacco smoking. *Biochemical Pharmacology, 54*(7), 743–753.

Cryan, J. F., Bruijnzeel, A. W., Skjei, K. L., & Markou, A. (2003). Bupropion enhances brain reward function and reverses the affective and somatic aspects of nicotine withdrawal in the rat. *Psychopharmacology (Berl), 168*(3), 347–358.

Damaj, M. I., Kao, W., & Martin, B. R. (2003). Characterization of spontaneous and precipitated nicotine withdrawal in the mouse. *Journal of Pharmacology and Experimental Therapeutics, 307*(2), 526–534.

DeNoble, V. J., & Mele, P. C. (2006). Intravenous nicotine self-administration in rats: Effects of mecamylamine, hexamethonium and naloxone. *Psychopharmacology (Berl), 184*(3–4), 266–272.

Depoortere, R. Y., Li, D. H., Lane, J. D., & Emmett-Oglesby, M. W. (1993). Parameters of self-administration of cocaine in rats under a progressive-ratio schedule. *Pharmacology Biochemistry and Behavior, 45*(3), 539–548.

Di Chiara, G. (2002). Nucleus accumbens shell and core dopamine: Differential role in behavior and addiction. *Behavioural Brain Research, 137*(1–2), 75–114.

Donny, E. C., Caggiula, A. R., Knopf, S., & Brown, C. (1995). Nicotine self-administration in rats. *Psychopharmacology (Berl), 122*(4), 390–394.

Donny, E. C., Caggiula, A. R., Mielke, M. M., Booth, S., Gharib, M. A., Hoffman, A., et al. (1999). Nicotine self-administration in rats on a progressive ratio schedule of reinforcement. *Psychopharmacology (Berl), 147*(2), 135–142.

Dwoskin, L. P., Teng, L., Buxton, S. T., & Crooks, P. A. (1999). (*S*)-(-)-Cotinine, the major brain metabolite of nicotine, stimulates nicotinic receptors to evoke [^{3}H]dopamine release from rat striatal slices in a calcium-dependent manner. *Journal of Pharmacology and Experimental Therapeutics, 288*(3), 905–911.

Engberg, G., & Hajos, M. (1994). Nicotine-induced activation of locus coeruleus neurons: an analysis of peripheral versus central induction. *Naunyn Schmiedeberg's Archives of Pharmacology, 349*(5), 443–446.

Epping-Jordan, M. P., Watkins, S. S., Koob, G. F., & Markou, A. (1998). Dramatic decreases in brain reward function during nicotine withdrawal. *Nature, 393*(6680), 76–79.

Fiore, M. C., Smith, S. S., Jorenby, D. E., & Baker, T. B. (1994). The effectiveness of the nicotine patch for smoking cessation. A meta-analysis. *Journal of the American Medical Association, 271*(24), 1940–1947.

Geyer, M. A., & Markou, A. (1995). Animal models of psychiatric disorders. *In: Psychopharmacology: The Fourth Generation of Progress.*: Raven Press New York, NY. pp 787–798.

Glassman, A. H., Helzer, J. E., Covey, L. S., Cottler, L. B., Stetner, F., Tipp, J. E., et al. (1990). Smoking, smoking cessation, and major depression. *Journal of the American Medical Association, 264*(12), 1546–1549.

Goldberg, S. R., & Schuster, C. R. (1967). Conditioned suppression by a stimulus associated with nalorphine in morphine-dependent monkeys. *Journal of the Experimental Analysis of Behavior, 10*(3), 235–242.

Goldberg, S. R., Spealman, R. D., & Goldberg, D. M. (1981). Persistent behavior at high rates maintained by intravenous self-administration of nicotine. *Science, 214*(4520), 573–575.

Gosling, J. A., & Lu, T. C. (1969). Uptake and distribution of some quaternary ammonium compounds in the central nervous system of the rat. *Journal of Pharmacology and Experimental Therapeutics, 167*(1), 56–62.

Grottick, A. J., & Higgins, G. A. (2000). Effect of subtype selective nicotinic compounds on attention as assessed by the five-choice serial reaction time task. *Behavioural Brain Research, 117*(1–2), 197–208.

Harrison, A. A., Gasparini, F., & Markou, A. (2002). Nicotine potentiation of brain stimulation reward reversed by DHβE and SCH 23390, but not by eticlopride, LY 314582 or MPEP in rats. *Psychopharmacology (Berl), 160*(1), 56–66.

Harrison, A. A., Liem, Y. T., & Markou, A. (2001). Fluoxetine combined with a serotonin-1A receptor antagonist reversed reward deficits observed during nicotine and amphetamine withdrawal in rats. *Neuropsychopharmacology, 25*(1), 55–71.

Hellemans, K. G., Dickinson, A., & Everitt, B. J. (2006). Motivational control of heroin seeking by conditioned stimuli associated with withdrawal and heroin taking by rats. *Behavioral Neuroscience, 120*(1), 103–114.

Hildebrand, B. E., Nomikos, G. G., Bondjers, C., Nisell, M., & Svensson, T. H. (1997). Behavioral manifestations of the nicotine abstinence syndrome in the rat: Peripheral versus central mechanisms. *Psychopharmacology (Berl), 129*(4), 348–356.

Hildebrand, B. E., Nomikos, G. G., Hertel, P., Schilstrom, B., & Svensson, T. H. (1998). Reduced dopamine output in the nucleus accumbens but not in the medial prefrontal cortex in rats displaying a mecamylamine-precipitated nicotine withdrawal syndrome. *Brain Research, 779*(1–2), 214–225.

Hughes, J. R., & Hatsukami, D. (1986). Signs and symptoms of tobacco withdrawal. *Archives of General Psychiatry, 43*(3), 289–294.

Hutcheson, D. M., Everitt, B. J., Robbins, T. W., & Dickinson, A. (2001). The role of withdrawal in heroin addiction: enhances reward or promotes avoidance? *Nature Neuroscience, 4*(9), 943–947.

Irvine, E. E., Cheeta, S., & File, S. E. (2001). Tolerance to nicotine's effects in the elevated plus-maze and increased anxiety during withdrawal. *Pharmacology Biochemistry and Behavior, 68*(2), 319–325.

Jones, G. M., Sahakian, B. J., Levy, R., Warburton, D. M., & Gray, J. A. (1992). Effects of acute subcutaneous nicotine on attention, information processing and short-term memory in Alzheimer's disease. *Psychopharmacology (Berl), 108*(4), 485–494.

Kenny, P. J., Chen, S. A., Kitamura, O., Markou, A., & Koob, G. F. (2006). Conditioned withdrawal drives heroin consumption and decreases reward sensitivity. *Journal of Neuroscience, 26*(22), 5894–5900.

Kenny, P. J., Gasparini, F., & Markou, A. (2003). Group II metabotropic and α-amino-3-hydroxy-5-methyl-4-isoxazole propionate (AMPA)/kainate glutamate receptors regulate the deficit in brain reward function associated with nicotine withdrawal in rats. *Journal of Pharmacology and Experimental Therapeutics, 306*(3), 1068–1076.

Kenny, P. J., Koob, G. F., & Markou, A. (2003). Conditioned facilitation of brain reward function after repeated cocaine administration. *Behavioral Neuroscience, 117*(5), 1103–1107.

Kenny, P. J., & Markou, A. (2001). Neurobiology of the nicotine withdrawal syndrome. *Pharmacology Biochemistry and Behavior, 70*(4), 531–549.

Kenny, P. J., & Markou, A. (2005). Conditioned nicotine withdrawal profoundly decreases the activity of brain reward systems. *Journal of Neuroscience, 25*(26), 6208–6212.

Kenny, P. J., & Markou, A. (2006). Nicotine self-administration acutely activates brain reward systems and induces a long-lasting increase in reward sensitivity. *Neuropsychopharmacology, 31*(6), 1203–1211.

Koob, G. F., & Le Moal, M. (2005). *Neurobiology of Addiction.* London: Academic Press.

LeSage, M. G., Burroughs, D., Dufek, M., Keyler, D. E., & Pentel, P. R. (2004). Reinstatement of nicotine self-administration in rats by presentation of nicotine-paired stimuli, but not nicotine priming. *Pharmacology Biochemistry and Behavior, 79*(3), 507–513.

LeSage, M. G., Keyler, D. E., Shoeman, D., Raphael, D., Collins, G., & Pentel, P. R. (2002). Continuous nicotine infusion reduces nicotine self-administration in rats with 23-h/day access to nicotine. *Pharmacology Biochemistry and Behavior, 72*(1–2), 279–289.

Levin, E. D., Conners, C. K., Silva, D., Hinton, S. C., Meck, W. H., March, J., et al. (1998). Transdermal nicotine effects on attention. *Psychopharmacology (Berl), 140*(2), 135–141.

Levin, E. D., & Rezvani, A. H. (2002). Nicotinic treatment for cognitive dysfunction. *Current Drug Targets. CNS and Neurological Disorders, 1*(4), 423–431.

Levin, E. D., & Simon, B. B. (1998). Nicotinic acetylcholine involvement in cognitive function in animals. *Psychopharmacology (Berl), 138*(3–4), 217–230.

Lindblom, N., de Villiers, S. H., Semenova, S., Kalayanov, G., Gordon, S., Schilstrom, B., et al. (2005). Active immunisation against nicotine blocks the reward facilitating effects of nicotine and partially prevents nicotine withdrawal in the rat as measured by dopamine output in the nucleus accumbens, brain reward thresholds and somatic signs. *Naunyn-Schmiedeberg's Archives of Pharmacology, 372*(3), 182–194.

Liu, X., Caggiula, A. R., Yee, S. K., Nobuta, H., Poland, R. E., & Pechnick, R. N. (2006). Reinstatement of nicotine-seeking behavior by drug-associated stimuli after extinction in rats. *Psychopharmacology (Berl), 184*(3–4), 417–425.

Malin, D. H., Lake, J. R., Carter, V. A., Cunningham, J. S., Hebert, K. M., Conrad, D. L., et al. (1994). The nicotinic antagonist mecamylamine precipitates nicotine abstinence syndrome in the rat. *Psychopharmacology (Berl), 115*(1–2), 180–184.

Malin, D. H., Lake, J. R., Newlin-Maultsby, P., Roberts, L. K., Lanier, J. G., Carter, V. A., et al. (1992). Rodent model of nicotine abstinence syndrome. *Pharmacology Biochemistry and Behavior, 43*(3), 779–784.

Malin, D. H., Lake, J. R., Payne, M. C., Short, P. E., Carter, V. A., Cunningham, J. S., et al. (1996). Nicotine alleviation of nicotine abstinence syndrome is naloxone-reversible. *Pharmacology Biochemistry and Behavior, 53*(1), 81–85.

Malin, D. H., Lake, J. R., Schopen, C. K., Kirk, J. W., Sailer, E. E., Lawless, B. A., et al. (1997). Nicotine abstinence syndrome precipitated by central but not peripheral hexamethonium. *Pharmacology Biochemistry and Behavior, 58*(3), 695–699.

Markou, A., & Kenny, P. J. (2002). Neuroadaptations to chronic exposure to drugs of abuse: relevance to depressive symptomatology seen across psychiatric diagnostic categories. *Neurotoxicology Research, 4*(4), 297–313.

Markou, A., & Koob, G. F. (1991). Postcocaine anhedonia: An animal model of cocaine withdrawal. *Neuropsychopharmacology, 4*(1), 17–26.

Markou, A., & Koob, G. F. (1992). Construct validity of a self-stimulation threshold paradigm: effects of reward and performance manipulations. *Physiology and Behavior, 51*(1), 111–119.

Markou, A., Kosten, T. R., & Koob, G. F. (1998). Neurobiological similarities in depression and drug dependence: a self-medication hypothesis. *Neuropsychopharmacology, 18*(3), 135–174.

Markou, A., & Paterson, N. E. (2001). The nicotinic antagonist methyllycaconitine has differential effects on nicotine self-administration and nicotine withdrawal in the rat. *Nicotine and Tobacco Research, 3*(4), 361–373.

Markou, A., Weiss, F., Gold, L. H., Caine, S. B., Schulteis, G., & Koob, G. F. (1993). Animal models of drug craving. *Psychopharmacology (Berl), 112*(2–3), 163–182.

McGregor, A., & Roberts, D. C. S. (1995). Effect of medial prefrontal cortex injections of SCH 23390 on intravenous cocaine self-administration under both a fixed and progressive ratio schedule of reinforcement. *Behavioural Brain Research, 67*(1), 75–80.

Mirza, N. R., & Stolerman, I. P. (1998). Nicotine enhances sustained attention in the rat under specific task conditions. *Psychopharmacology (Berl), 138*(3–4), 266–274.

Murrin, L. C., Ferrer, J. R., Zeng, W. Y., & Haley, N. J. (1987). Nicotine administration to rats: Methodological considerations. *Life Sciences, 40*(17), 1699–1708.

O'Brien, C. P., Testa, T., O'Brien, T. J., Brady, J. P., & Wells, B. (1977). Conditioned narcotic withdrawal in humans. *Science, 195*(4282), 1000–1002.

Olds, J., & Milner, P. (1954). Positive reinforcement produced by electrical stimulation of septal area and other regions of rat brain. *Journal of Comparative and Physiological Psychology, 47*(6), 419–427.

Parrott, A. C. (1993). Cigarette smoking: effects upon self-rated stress and arousal over the day. *Addictive Behaviors, 18*(4), 389–395.

Paterson, N. E., Balfour, D. J., & Markou, A. (2007). Chronic bupropion attenuated the anhedonic component of nicotine withdrawal in rats via inhibition of dopamine reuptake in the nucleus accumbens shell. *European Journal of Neuroscience, 25*(10), 3099–3108.

Paterson, N. E., Bruijnzeel, A. W., Kenny, P. J., Wright, C. D., Froestl, W., & Markou, A. (2005). Prolonged nicotine exposure does not alter GABA$_B$ receptor-mediated regulation of brain reward function. *Neuropharmacology, 49*(7), 953–962.

Paterson, N. E., Froestl, W., & Markou, A. (2004). The GABA$_B$ receptor agonists baclofen and CGP44532 decreased nicotine self-administration in the rat. *Psychopharmacology (Berl), 172*(2), 179–186.

Paterson, N. E., Froestl, W., & Markou, A. (2005). Repeated administration of the GABA$_B$ receptor agonist CGP44532 decreased nicotine self-administration, and acute administration decreased cue-induced reinstatement of nicotine-seeking in rats. *Neuropsychopharmacology, 30*(1), 119–128.

Paterson, N. E., & Markou, A. (2003). Increased motivation for self-administered cocaine after escalated cocaine intake. *Neuroreport, 14*(17), 2229–2232.

Paterson, N. E., & Markou, A. (2004). Prolonged nicotine dependence associated with extended access to nicotine self-administration in rats. *Psychopharmacology (Berl), 173*(1–2), 64–72.

Paterson, N. E., Myers, C., & Markou, A. (2000). Effects of repeated withdrawal from continuous amphetamine administration on brain reward function in rats. *Psychopharmacology (Berl), 152*(4), 440–446.

Piasecki, T. M., Jorenby, D. E., Smith, S. S., Fiore, M. C., & Baker, T. B. (2003). Smoking withdrawal dynamics: II. Improved tests of withdrawal-relapse relations. *Journal of Abnormal Psychology, 112*(1), 14–27.

Picciotto, M. R., Zoli, M., Rimondini, R., Lena, C., Marubio, L. M., Pich, E. M., et al. (1998). Acetylcholine receptors containing the β_2 subunit are involved in the reinforcing properties of nicotine. *Nature, 391*(6663), 173–177.

Pickens, R., & Thompson, T. (1968). Cocaine-reinforced behavior in rats: Effects of reinforcement magnitude and fixed-ratio size. *Journal of Pharmacology and Experimental Therapeutics, 161*(1), 122–129.

Risner, M. E., & Goldberg, S. R. (1983). A comparison of nicotine and cocaine self-administration in the dog: fixed-ratio and progressive-ratio schedules of intravenous drug infusion. *Journal of Pharmacology and Experimental Therapeutics, 224*(2), 319–326.

Rose, J. E. (2006). Nicotine and nonnicotine factors in cigarette addiction. *Psychopharmacology (Berl), 184*(3–4), 274–285.

Rowlett, J. K. (2000). A labor-supply analysis of cocaine self-administration under progressive-ratio schedules: antecedents, methodologies, and perspectives. *Psychopharmacology (Berl), 153*(1), 1–16.

Sacco, K. A., Termine, A., Seyal, A., Dudas, M. M., Vessicchio, J. C., Krishnan-Sarin, S., et al. (2005). Effects of cigarette smoking on spatial working memory and attentional deficits in schizophrenia: involvement of nicotinic receptor mechanisms. *Archives of General Psychiatry, 62*(6), 649–659.

Sannerud, C. A., Prada, J., Goldberg, D. M., & Goldberg, S. R. (1994). The effects of sertraline on nicotine self-administration and food-maintained responding in squirrel monkeys. *European Journal of Pharmacology, 271*(2–3), 461–469.

Schulteis, G., Markou, A., Cole, M., & Koob, G. F. (1995). Decreased brain reward produced by ethanol withdrawal. *Proceedings of the National Academy of Sciences of the United States of America, 92*(13), 5880–5884.

Schulteis, G., Markou, A., Gold, L. H., Stinus, L., & Koob, G. F. (1994). Relative sensitivity to naloxone of multiple indices of opiate withdrawal: A quantitative dose-response analysis. *Journal of Pharmacology and Experimental Therapeutics, 271*(3), 1391–1398.

See, R. E., Grimm, J. W., Kruzich, P. J., & Rustay, N. (1999). The importance of a compound stimulus in conditioned drug-seeking behavior following one week of extinction from self-administered cocaine in rats. *Drug and Alcohol Dependence, 57*(1), 41–49.

Semenova, S., & Markou, A. (2003). Clozapine treatment attenuated somatic and affective signs of nicotine and amphetamine withdrawal in subsets of rats exhibiting hyposensitivity to the initial effects of clozapine. *Biological Psychiatry, 54*(11), 1249–1264.

Semenova, S., Stolerman, I. P., & Markou, A. (2007). Chronic nicotine administration improves attention while nicotine withdrawal induces performance deficits in the 5-choice serial reaction time task in rats. *Pharmacology Biochemistry and Behavior, 87*(3), 360–368.

Shaham, Y., Adamson, L. K., Grocki, S., & Corrigall, W. A. (1997). Reinstatement and spontaneous recovery of nicotine seeking in rats. *Psychopharmacology (Berl), 130*(4), 396–403.

Shaham, Y., Shalev, U., Lu, L., De Wit, H., & Stewart, J. (2003). The reinstatement model of drug relapse: History, methodology and major findings. *Psychopharmacology (Berl), 168*(1–2), 3–20.

Shoaib, M., & Bizarro, L. (2005). Deficits in a sustained attention task following nicotine withdrawal in rats. *Psychopharmacology (Berl), 178*(2–3), 211–222.

Shoaib, M., & Stolerman, I. P. (1999). Plasma nicotine and cotinine levels following intravenous nicotine self-administration in rats. *Psychopharmacology (Berl), 143*(3), 318–321.

Skjei, K. L., & Markou, A. (2003). Effects of repeated withdrawal episodes, nicotine dose, and duration of nicotine exposure on the severity and duration of nicotine withdrawal in rats. *Psychopharmacology (Berl), 168*(3), 280–292.

Smolka, M. N., Budde, H., Karow, A. C., & Schmidt, L. G. (2004). Neuroendocrinological and neuropsychological correlates of dopaminergic function in nicotine dependence. *Psychopharmacology (Berl), 175*(3), 374–381.

Snyder, F. R., & Henningfield, J. E. (1989). Effects of nicotine administration following 12 h of tobacco deprivation: assessment on computerized performance tasks. *Psychopharmacology (Berl), 97*(1), 17–22.

Spielewoy, C., & Markou, A. (2003). Withdrawal from chronic phencyclidine treatment induces long-lasting depression in brain reward function. *Neuropsychopharmacology, 28*(6), 1106–1116.

Stolerman, I. P., & Jarvis, M. J. (1995). The scientific case that nicotine is addictive. *Psychopharmacology (Berl), 117*(1), 2–10; discussion 14–20.

Suzuki, T., Ise, Y., Tsuda, M., Maeda, J., & Misawa, M. (1996). Mecamylamine-precipitated nicotine-withdrawal aversion in rats. *European Journal of Pharmacology, 314*(3), 281–284.

Taylor, J. R., & Robbins, T. W. (1984). Enhanced behavioural control by conditioned reinforcers following microinjections of d-amphetamine into the nucleus accumbens. *Psychopharmacology (Berl), 84*(3), 405–412.

Valentine, J. D., Hokanson, J. S., Matta, S. G., & Sharp, B. M. (1997). Self-administration in rats allowed unlimited access to nicotine. *Psychopharmacology (Berl), 133*(3), 300–304.

Watkins, S. S., Epping-Jordan, M. P., Koob, G. F., & Markou, A. (1999). Blockade of nicotine self-administration with nicotinic antagonists in rats. *Pharmacology Biochemistry and Behavior, 62*(4), 743–751.

Watkins, S. S., Stinus, L., Koob, G. F., & Markou, A. (2000). Reward and somatic changes during precipitated nicotine withdrawal in rats: Centrally and peripherally mediated effects. *Journal of Pharmacology and Experimental Therapeutics, 292*(3), 1053–1064.

West, R. J., Jarvis, M. J., Russell, M. A., Carruthers, M. E., & Feyerabend, C. (1984). Effect of nicotine replacement on the cigarette withdrawal syndrome. *British Journal of Addiction, 79*(2), 215–219.

Chapter 6
The Role of Nicotine in Smoking: A Dual-Reinforcement Model

Anthony R. Caggiula, Eric C. Donny, Matthew I. Palmatier, Xiu Liu, Nadia Chaudhri, and Alan F. Sved

Introduction

The utility of an animal model is predicated on its ability to incorporate essential features of the human phenomenon it is modeling in a way that permits systematic investigation of those features. For this reason, investigators who study the neurobiological mechanisms of addictive drugs such as opiates and stimulants are making extensive use of self-administration models as a way to more closely mimic the manner in which drugs of abuse are experienced by humans (Bozarth, Murray, & Wise, 1989; Caggiula, Donny, White, Chaudhri, Booth, Gharib, Hoffman, Perkins, & Sved, 2001; Carroll, Krattiger, Gieske, & Sadoff, 1990; Corrigall & Coen, 1989; Donny, Caggiula, Knopf, & Brown, 1995; Johanson, 1981; Roberts, 1992; Shaham & Stewart, 1995). A basic tenet of the self-administration model is that a drug, acting as a primary reinforcer, will increase the future occurrence of a response if its administration is contingent on that response (Meisch, 1993). Nicotine, like other drugs of abuse, is self-administered by a variety of animal species (Corrigall & Coen, 1989; Goldberg, Spealman, & Goldberg, 1981; Henningfield & Goldberg, 1983; Rose & Corrigall, 1997). Nicotine self-administration is dose- and schedule-dependent (Corrigall & Coen, 1989; Donny, Caggiula, Mielke, Jacobs, Rose, & Sved, 1998; Donny, Caggiula, Rowell, Gharib, Maldovan, Booth, Mielke, Hoffman, & McCallum, 2000; Shoaib, Schindler, & Goldberg, 1997), extinguishes when nicotine is removed (Corrigall & Coen, 1989; Taylor & Jentsch, 2001), and is dependent on nicotine delivery being response-contingent (Donny et al., 1998). Models of nicotine self-administration are being used to investigate the behavioral, environmental, and neurophysiological underpinnings of nicotine reinforcement (e.g., Caggiula et al., 2001; Corrigall, 1992; Picciotto, Zoli, Rimondini, Lena, Marubio, Pich, Fuxe, & Changeux, 1998) and to aid in the development of novel pharmacotherapies for smoking cessation.

A.R. Caggiula
Department of Psychology, 3131 Sennott Square, 210 South Bouquet Street, University of Pittsburgh, Pittsburgh, PA 15260, USA
e-mail: Tonypsy@pitt.edu

R.A. Bevins, A.R. Caggiula (eds.), *The Motivational Impact of Nicotine and its Role in Tobacco Use*, DOI: 10.1007/978-0-387-78748-0_6, © Springer Science+Business Media, LLC 2009

Table 6.1 Dual-reinforcement model

	Response-dependent Nicotine (Contingent)	Response-independent Nicotine (Non-contingent)
Primary Reinforcement	*Can* maintain operant behavior in the absence of non-nicotine stimuli	*Cannot* maintain operant behavior in the absence of non-nicotine stimuli
	Can establish concurrent *neutral* environmental stimuli as conditioned reinforcers*	*Cannot* establish concurrent *neutral* environmental stimuli as conditioned reinforcers*
Reinforcement Enhancement	*Can* elevate behavior maintained by reinforcing stimuli **	*Can* elevate behavior maintained by reinforcing stimuli **

*Pavlovian conditioning can theoretically be established when a neutral stimulus is temporally paired with discrete infusions of either self-administered or experimenter-administered (non-contingent) nicotine. We have opted to focus on the former because it is a better model of conditioning that may occur when humans smoke cigarettes.

**This applies to stimuli that are unconditioned reinforcers or that have been established as conditioned reinforcers through prior pairing with nicotine or some other unconditioned reinforcer.

However, there is mounting evidence that a simple, primary reinforcement model of nicotine self-administration fails to fully explain existing data from both the animal self-administration and human smoking literatures. We have recently proposed a "dual-reinforcement" model (Chaudhri, Caggiula, Donny, Palmatier, Liu, & Sved, 2006b; Donny, Chaudhri, Caggiula, Evans-Martin, Booth, Gharib, Clements, & Sved, 2003) that is designed to more fully capture the relationship between nicotine and self-administration in animals and smoking in humans. This model incorporates a large body of evidence that emphasizes the importance of non-nicotine stimuli that accompany nicotine delivery and contribute to the overall level of reinforcement afforded to the behavior. The model addresses the nature of the relationship between such stimuli and nicotine, and it postulates that the resulting behavior is a function of nicotine acting as both a primary reinforcer and an enhancer of the incentive motivational and reinforcing effects of accompanying stimuli. We will first briefly discuss the importance of non-nicotine stimuli in self-administration and smoking. We will then outline our model describing the two ways in which nicotine interacts with those stimuli and discuss the research conducted to test the major tenets of the model (Table 6.1).

Role of Non-Nicotine Stimuli in Self-Administration and Smoking

Smokers do not just self-administer nicotine, they take the drug within a context of multiple environmental stimuli, including the sight, smell and taste of cigarette smoke, the oropharyngeal consequences of smoking, and external contextual stimuli that are associated with the behavior. There is a substantial literature showing increases in craving or desire to smoke when smokers are exposed to smoking cues, such as a lit cigarette resting in an ashtray (Conklin & Tiffany, 2001; Sayette,

Martin, Wertz, Shiffman, & Perrott, 2001). Furthermore, research from several laboratories, most notably that of Rose and his colleagues, has demonstrated that the administration of non-nicotine smoking stimuli can increase subjective reports of liking and satisfaction, and decrease craving and withdrawal in dependent smokers (reviewed in Caggiula et al., 2001).For example, smoking a denicotinized cigarette increased satisfaction in briefly deprived smokers, while intravenous nicotine alone had no effect. Both nicotine and cues were necessary for complete reduction of craving (Rose, Behm, Westman, & Johnson, 2000). Furthermore, daily smokers will continue to smoke nicotine-free cigarettes over an 11-day period with only small decreases in the number of cigarettes smoked and in the motivation to smoke (as measured by a progressive ratio schedule of reinforcement; Donny, Houtsmuller, & Stitzer, 2007). These studies suggest that non-nicotine stimuli are extremely important in both motivating and maintaining smoking behavior.

It is now widely accepted that environmental stimuli associated with drug delivery can influence self-administration in animals of several drugs of abuse (Arroyo, Markou, Robbins, & Everitt, 1998; de Wit & Stewart, 1981; Goldberg et al., 1981; Markou, Weiss, Gold, Caine, Schulteis, & Koob, 1993; Robinson & Berridge, 1993; Schenk & Partridge, 2001), including nicotine (Balfour, Wright, Benwell, & Birrell, 2000; Di Chiara, 2000; Donny, Caggiula, Mielke, Booth, Gharib, Hoffman, Maldovan, Shupenko, & McCallum, 1999; Donny, Caggiula, Rose, Jacobs, Mielke, & Sved, 2000; Rose & Corrigall, 1997) and contribute to drug dependence and relapse in humans (Childress, 1992; Juliano, Donny, Houtsmuller, & Stitzer, 2006; Margolin, 1992; O'Brien, Childress, Ehrman, & Robbins, 1998). In a direct test of the hypothesis that environmental stimuli accompanying nicotine delivery become an important part of the stimulus complex that sustains nicotine self-administration, we conducted a series of experiments in male rats in which nicotine infusions and environmental stimuli were independently manipulated (Caggiula, Donny, Chaudhri, Perkins, Evans-Martin, & Sved, 2002a; Caggiula et al., 2001; Caggiula, Donny, White, Chaudhri, Booth, Gharib, Hoffman, Perkins, & Sved, 2002b). A compound visual stimulus (VS; the onset of a 1-sec cue light and the offset of a chamber light for 1-min) that accompanied lever pressing and nicotine infusions was found to be at least as important as nicotine in the rapid acquisition of self-administration, in the degree to which withdrawing nicotine extinguished the behavior, and in the reacquisition of lever pressing after extinction (Caggiula et al., 2002a; Caggiula et al., 2001, 2002b). These studies also demonstrated that the effectiveness of this stimulus in promoting self-administration was dependent on it being contingently related to the rat's responding and/or nicotine infusions, since the VS presented non-contingently did not enhance self-administration (Donny et al., 2003). A critical feature of this work must be emphasized, namely, the relationship between the VS and nicotine was synergistic; response rates generated by the combination of VS and nicotine were more than twice the sum of response rates produced by either the VS or nicotine alone (e.g., Fig. 6.1 upper panel). These results illustrate the importance of environmental stimuli in the acquisition of nicotine self-administration and indicate that such stimuli can combine with nicotine to potentiate the behavior (Caggiula et al., 2002a; Caggiula et al., 2001, 2002b).

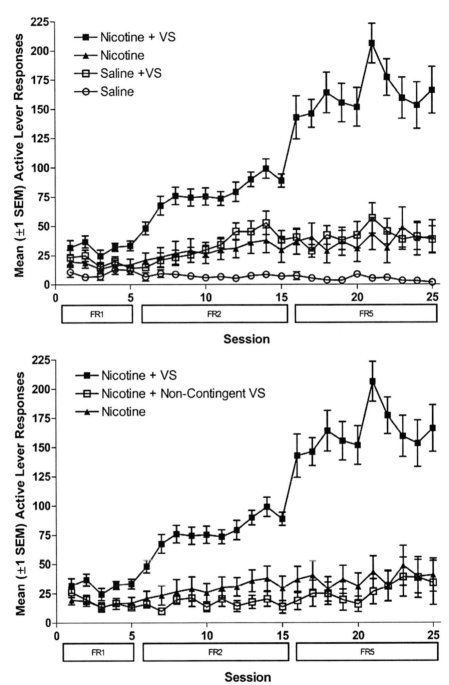

Fig. 6.1 Mean (+SE) response on the active lever for nicotine + visual stimulus (NIC+VS) peaks at more than twice the sum of NIC alone plus VS alone. For clarity the lower panel reproduces the NIC and NIC + VS data of the upper panel shows that non-contingent VS exposure (controlled by rats in the NIC+VS group through yoking) does not synergize with contingent NIC. N=8–12/group. Data derived from Donny et al. (2003)

Dual Reinforcing Effects of Nicotine

The above findings that environmental stimuli play a critical role in nicotine self-administration raise the important question: what is the nature of the synergism between these stimuli and nicotine? One possible answer is that the VS, acting as a neutral stimulus, develops conditioned reinforcing properties over time by virtue of its close temporal association with nicotine, acting as a primary reinforcer. While Pavlovian conditioning is an important part of our dual-reinforcement model (and will be addressed later), it is not a viable explanation for the synergism initially seen between nicotine and the VS. The VS is not a neutral stimulus but rather an unconditioned reinforcer. Rats exhibited response rates on the active lever for contingent VS—without nicotine—that were significantly higher than control values (non-contingent VS presentations or inactive lever responses). This finding is consistent with a wealth of data from an older literature on sensory reinforcement (Fowler, 1971; Harrington, 1963). In fact, the VS-alone and nicotine-alone often support similar rates of operant behavior (e.g., Fig. 6. 1; see also Palmatier, Evans-Martin, Hoffman, Caggiula, Chaudhri, Donny, Liu, Booth, Gharib, Craven, & Sved, 2006), suggesting that they are of similar strength as unconditioned reinforcers. Elemental conditioning models (e.g., Rescorla & Wagner, 1972) predict little or no change in the behavior evoked by a putative conditioned stimulus (in this case the VS) paired with nicotine, an equally salient unconditioned stimulus. Thus, the increased responding is probably not based on associative learning. A more likely explanation for the synergism emerged from our experiments manipulating the contingency between both reinforcers and the animal's behavior (Caggiula, Donny, White, Chaudhri,, Gharib, Booth, Sved, 2001; Donny et al., 2003).

To address this issue, we asked whether the enhancement of operant behavior, seen when both the VS and nicotine infusions are contingent on the rat's lever pressing, could occur when the VS was contingent on the animal's behavior with response-independent nicotine administration (i.e., either controlled by another rat in a yoked design or continuously infused). The results of the first study and multiple replications (Chaudhri et al., 2006b; Donny et al., 2003) were that response-independent nicotine infusions were as effective as contigent nicotine infusions in enhancing bar pressing for the VS to levels that were statistically indistinguishable from contingent nicotine (Fig. 6.2). This effect of nicotine occurred in naive rats during acquisition without previous association between nicotine and the VS, across a range of nicotine doses, and on both fixed-ratio (FR) and progressive-ratio (PR) reinforcement schedules (Chaudhri, Caggiula, Donny, Booth, Gharib, Craven, Palmatier, Liu, & Sved, 2007). The enhancement of bar pressing for the VS produced by non-contingent nicotine was also obtained by continuously infused nicotine (Fig. 6.2), but not by non-contingent food presentation (Donny et al., 2003), suggesting that not all primary reinforcers produce the enhancing effect. The enhanced lever pressing for the VS was equally attenuated and reinstated by the removal and subsequent replacement of contingent and non-contingent nicotine (Fig. 6.2). These data suggest that nicotine can enhance the reinforcing properties of other stimuli by a mechanism that does not require a discrete temporal relationship

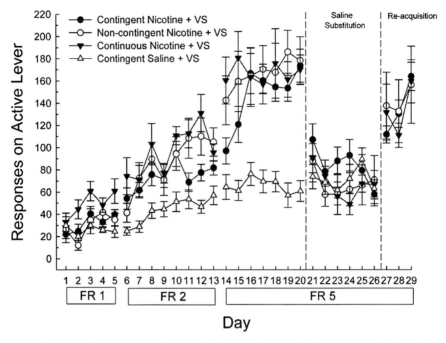

Fig. 6.2 Effects of response-contingent, yoked, or continuous nicotine or responding for visual stimulus (VS). Acquisition data (days1–20) were followed by 6 days in which saline was substituted for nicotine (days 21–26) and then 3 days in which nicotine was replaced (days 27–29). Results are mean + SEM of data obtained from —seven to nine animals per group (From Donny et al., 2003. Copyright © 2003 by Springer. Reprinted with permission)

with either the stimuli or the behavior. The demonstration that nicotine produces only modest primary reinforcing effects, but potent enhancement of the reinforcing effects of other stimuli, may help to resolve a long-standing paradox regarding how a drug with relatively modest primary reinforcing properties can support the establishment and maintenance of such a persistent behavior (i.e., smoking; Rose & Corrigall, 1997).

Predictions of the Dual-Reinforcement Model: Reinforcing Strength of the Nonpharmacological Stimulus

The dual reinforcement model makes important predictions about the relationship between the reinforcing value of nonpharmacological stimuli and the reinforcement-enhancing effects of nicotine. Specifically, nicotine should have a more pronounced enhancing effect on more reinforcing stimuli when compared to stimuli with little incentive value. Ultimately, if the stimulus is neither an unconditioned nor conditioned reinforcer (i.e., neutral), this enhancing effect of nicotine should be absent. We have used two approaches to test this hypothesis.

In the first approach (Chaudhri, Caggiula, Donny, Booth, Gharib, Craven, Palmatier, Liu, & Sved, 2006a) we compared the effects of contingent and non-contingent intravenous nicotine on the *same stimulus* that was rendered more or less reinforcing by prior Pavlovian conditioning. A weakly reinforcing light-tone stimulus was established as a conditioned reinforcer by repeated pairings with sucrose. A control group received equal exposure to the stimulus and sucrose in a temporally unpaired manner. Subsequently, both groups lever pressed for the stimulus with contingent nicotine, non-contingent nicotine, or non-contingent saline on FR and PR reinforcement schedules. Repeated pairing with sucrose established the light-tone stimulus as a robust conditioned reinforcer, as evidenced by more active-lever responding in the paired group (Fig. 6.3, upper panel). As predicted, contingent and non-contingent nicotine elevated responding equally for this conditioned stimulus. In contrast, for the less reinforcing (sucrose-unpaired) version of the same stimulus, contingent nicotine more effectively elevated behavior compared to non-contingent nicotine on both reinforcement schedules (Fig. 6.3, lower panel;see Chaudhri et al., 2006a for complete data). These data are consistent with other reports that nicotine can enhance responding for a stimulus that has been established as a conditioned reinforcer by prior association with a non-nicotine primary reinforcer (Olausson, Jentsch, & Taylor, 2004a, 2004b).

In the second approach (Palmatier, Matteson, Black, Liu, Caggiula, & Sved, 2007c), we compared the effects of subcutaneous non-contingent nicotine injections on *two stimuli* that differed in their unconditioned reinforcing effects. Across daily 1-h sessions, rats responded at higher rates for the House-Light off stimulus (5-s extinction of a house light + 83 dB tone) than for the Lever-Light on stimulus (5-s onset of a stimulus light + the same tone), confirming that the former was more reinforcing. After responses stabilized, rats in each group were randomly assigned to one of two drug conditions; nicotine or saline injections were given 5-min before each of the remaining test sessions. Saline injections did not affect responding for either stimulus. The House-Light off group showed increased responding following nicotine administration, whereas response rates for the Lever-Light on group were unchanged by nicotine (Fig. 6.4). Both studies strongly support our prediction that the relative reinforcing value of non-pharmacological stimuli determines the degree to which nicotine exerts its reinforcement enhancing effects.

Predictions of the Dual-Reinforcement Model: Behavioral Dissociation

Up to this point, we inferred that self-administered nicotine possesses both primary reinforcing and reinforcement-enhancing effects by comparing self-administered (contingent) with response-independent (non-contingent) nicotine using a standard self-administration model with only one active lever delivering the reinforcer(s). A different model was needed to determine whether rats can behaviorally distinguish between these two effects of nicotine and, ultimately, whether they are mediated by the same or different mechanisms. For this purpose, we adopted a concurrent

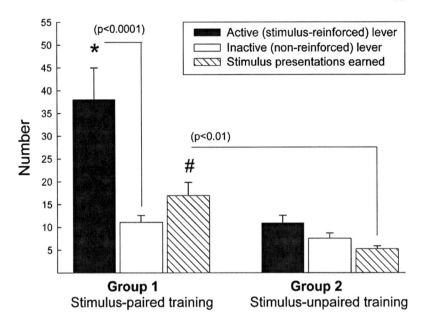

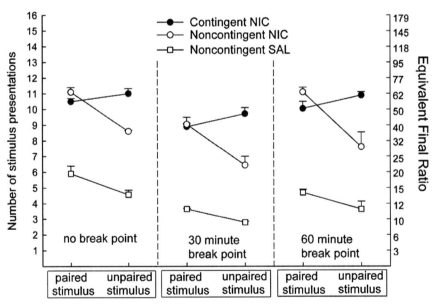

Fig. 6.3 Upper panel shows responses on the active lever, inactive lever, and number of stimulus presentations (mean + SEM) during a 30-minute test for conditioned reinforcement by rats trained previously with a stimulus that was paired with sucrose ($n = 41$), or the same stimulus that was explicitly unpaired with sucrose ($n = 25$). Lower panel shows interaction between stimulus-training condition (sucrose-paired vs. sucrose-unpaired) and drug contingency (contingent nicotine (NIC) vs. non-contingent NIC). Data from non-contingent SAL + stimulus conditions are also shown for comparison. Panels represent data from either the entire 180-minute test session (no break point),

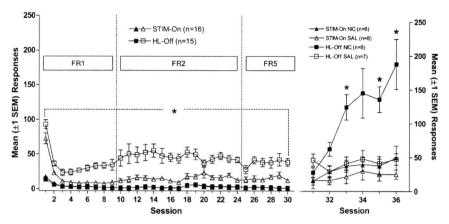

Fig. 6.4 *Left panel* shows the mean (±1 SEM) number of active- and inactive-lever responses made during the stimulus comparison phase. Active-lever responses were significantly higher in the House-Light off than the Lever-Light on condition. *Right panel* illustrates the mean (±1 SEM) active-lever responses made during nicotine/saline testing sessions. Active-lever responding in House-Light NIC condition was significantly greater than the House-Light Saline condition. The number of reinforcements earned in this study was previously reported in *Palmatier* et al. *(2007c)*

reinforcement paradigm (Palmatier et al., 2006). For the key group (two-Lever), pressing one lever delivered the same VS we used in earlier studies and pressing the other lever delivered infusions of nicotine. For comparison, another group (NIC+VS) received standard self-administration training; one lever controlled both the VS and nicotine. Control groups received either nicotine infusions (NIC-Only) or VS presentations (VS-Only) for pressing the active lever. Nicotine alone and VS alone maintained relatively modest levels of responding (Fig. 6.5). When these two reinforcers were combined (NIC+VS), response rates were substantially higher, as shown previously. For the two-Lever group, response rates on the nicotine lever were relatively low, matching the response rates of rats receiving nicotine alone (NIC-Only). However, responding on the VS lever was potently enhanced in this group, equaling the response rates for rats receiving both reinforcers for making a single response (NIC+VS). Moreover, responding in the concurrent reinforcement paradigm is truly under the independent control of each reinforcer; when the outcome associated with each lever is reversed, response rates on each lever change to match the reinforcement earned (Palmatier et al., unpublished). These data indicate that the reinforcement enhancing effects of nicotine are very potent even when only moderate quantities of the drug are self-administered. Moreover, they provide

Fig. 6.3 (Continued) or after a 30 minute or 60 minute break point was imposed. Data are mean (* SEM) stimulus presentations earned on the last 2 days of the progressive ratio schedule. All interactions are significant at p<0.05 (From Chaudhri et al., 2006a. Copyright © 2006 by Springer. Reprinted with permission)

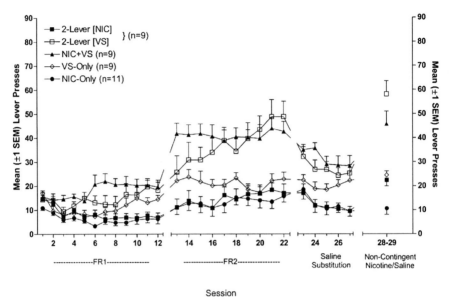

Fig. 6.5 Mean (+1 SEM) active lever responding for rats in the visual stimulus (VS)-Only, Nicotine (NIC)-Only, NIC+VS, and two-Lever groups. For the two-Lever group, responding on the infusion lever (■) is depicted separately from responding on the VS lever (□). Time-out responding is excluded. For the two-Lever group, responding for the VS lever exceeded responding in the VS-Only group for FR2 sessions and did not differ from VS+NIC rats. Saline substitution abolished, and NIC replacement reinstated the difference between two-Lever VS and VS-Only responding. See Palmatier et al., 2006 for details of procedures and statistical analyses. (From Palmatier et al., 2006. Copyright © 2005 by Springer. Reprinted with permission)

the first demonstration that the reinforcement enhancing and primary reinforcing effects of nicotine can be dissociated behaviorally.

Predictions of the Dual-Reinforcement Model: Pharmacological Dissociation

Previous research has utilized the standard (single active lever) self-administration paradigm in studying the effects of pharmacological probes on nicotine reinforcement for the purpose of inferring the underlying neurobiological mechanisms. For example, mice lacking the β2 subunit of nicotinic acetylcholine receptors (nAChR) self-administer much less nicotine than wild-type controls (Picciotto et al., 1998), suggesting that nicotinic receptors containing this subunit (e.g., α4β2) are critical to nicotine-derived reinforcement. Although this approach has been useful for describing the neurobiological systems that participate in nicotine's actions, it is unable to dissociate primary reinforcement from the reinforcement-enhancing functions of nicotine. For example, the difference observed between β2 knock-outs and wild-type controls could have been based on a difference in the primary reinforcing and/or reinforcement enhancing actions of nicotine. By contrast, the concurrent reinforcement paradigm enables us to ask specific questions about the neurobiological basis of these two effects of nicotine.

In a recent study (Palmatier, Evans-Martin, Hoffman, Caggiula, Chaudhri, Donny, Liu, & Sved, 2005) we sought to investigate the usefulness of this concurrent reinforcement paradigm for testing potential pharmacotherapies for smoking. The clinical efficacy of nicotine replacement therapy may lie, in part, in its ability to maintain the reinforcement-enhancement normally resulting from the nicotine in tobacco; in the absence of these enhancing effects, abstinent smokers may experience a loss of reinforcement that contributes to the mood disruptions associated with nicotine withdrawal (Hughes, Hatsukami, Pickens, Krahn, Malin, & Luknic, 1984). If a novel compound that selectively targets the primary reinforcing effects of nicotine was identified, it might be useful in combination with nicotine replacement therapy to decrease the motivation to smoke without altering the mood-related effects of nicotine replacement. Recent studies suggest that metabotropic glutamate 5 receptors (mGluR5) may be a target system for such treatment. For example, the mGluR5 antagonist 2-methyl-6-(phenylethynyl)-pyridine(MPEP) decreases nicotine self-administration (Paterson, Semenova, Gasparini, & Markou, 2003; Tessari, Pilla, Andreoli, Hutcheson, & Heidbreder, 2004), but does not alter nicotine's ability to decrease intracranial self-stimulation thresholds (Harrison, Gasparini, & Markou, 2002). This latter effect of nicotine may be related to the enhanced responding for the VSinduced by nicotine in our laboratory. We found that MPEP decreased the primary reinforcing effects of nicotine, as reflected by reduced responding on the nicotine lever of the two-lever group, but did not alter the enhancing effects of nicotine, since responding on VS lever continued to be elevated above controls. The results suggest that mGluR5 antagonists may decrease the incentive value of nicotine, without affecting its ability to enhance responding for other reinforcers.

Predictions of the Dual-Reinforcement Model: Role of Conditioning

There are two critical predictions of the model that we have only recently begun to address. First, nicotine, acting as a primary reinforcer, can establish a concurrent neutral stimulus as a conditioned reinforcer through Pavlovian associations. Second, nicotine, acting as a reinforcement enhancer, can then magnify the incentive value of such a nicotine-associated, conditioned reinforcer.

Modern theories of tobacco dependence have placed increasing emphasis on the role of nicotine/tobacco associated stimuli or 'cues' for the pharmacological effect of nicotine (Rose & Levin, 1991). Many contend that the effects of nicotine become associated with various non-nicotine stimuli and these stimuli acquire conditional value or serve as cues for future nicotine delivery. As a result, the conditional stimuli for tobacco can alter behavior in a manner that maintains smoking or results in lapse/relapse after sustained abstinence. Thus, proximal stimuli normally associated with smoking, such as a lit cigarette, can induce reports of craving in smokers but not in non-smokers (Carter & Tiffany, 1999). Despite this increased emphasis on nicotine-related stimuli, there are no appropriately controlled experimental demonstrations that nicotine can associatively increase the reinforcing value of other discrete non-nicotine stimuli. This is not to say that there are no studies in which stimuli accompanying nicotine self-administration have likely taken on conditioned reinforcing properties (e.g., Cohen, Perrault, Griebel, & Soubrie, 2005; Goldberg et al., 1981). However, at least two critical controls have been missing from this literature and are required before the second hypothesis—nicotine can enhance the incentive value of a nicotine-established, conditioned reinforcer—can be systematically tested. One control relates to the fact that laboratory rats find some sensory stimuli intrinsically reinforcing and this may be true of the cues used in some nicotine self-administration models. There is a substantial literature on "sensory reinforcement" (Fowler, 1971) that our recent findings on the reinforcing capabilities of the VS have confirmed. Thus in any conditioning study, the putative conditioned reinforcer must be tested for reinforcing properties independent of any association with nicotine. Second, an explicitly unpaired control group, in which animals are exposed to the same number of nicotine infusions and stimulus presentations as the conditioning group, is required to show that the putative conditioned reinforcer becomes reinforcing because of its specific, temporal association with nicotine and not simply because of the animal's past experience with the stimulus and the drug in the same context.

A study we recently completed (Palmatier, Donny, Liu, Matteson, Caggiula, & Sved, 2007a) employed the acquisition of a novel response technique to investigate whether nicotine could establish a conditioned reinforcer. Experimentally naïve rats (no prior operant training) were randomly assigned to one of three groups: Paired, Unpaired, or conditional stimulus (CS)-Only. Paired rats self-administered nicotine along with a putative conditional stimulus (CS; 15-s illumination of a stimulus light) via nose-poke. For CS-Only rats, nose-poke resulted in CS presentation with a saline infusion. For Unpaired rats, CS presentations and nicotine infusions were equated to the paired group but each event was passively received and separated by a minimum of 70 s (nose pokes were not possible). After conditioning, all rats were tested for acquisition of a novel response (lever pressing) reinforced by the CS. Responding by the paired rats was significantly higher than Unpaired or CS-Only rats, which did not differ from each other, thus confirming the prediction that the stimulus light became a nicotine-related conditioned reinforcer.

Paired rats were then assigned to one of the three self-administration conditions; NIC+CS (nicotine infusions accompanied CS), NC-NIC/CS, and NC-SAL/CS. For the latter two groups, lever pressing resulted in CS presentations but nicotine or saline infusions were yoked (therefore non-contingent; NC) to the NIC+CS group. The remaining rats (CS-Only and Unpaired) also received nicotine infusions yoked to the NIC+CS group during a second phase of the novel response test. When the CS had acquired value (i.e., previously paired with nicotine), non-contingent nicotine increased responding and CS presentations earned relative to the same (paired) CS with non-contingent saline, or to the other, unpaired control conditions. Thus, non-contingent infusions of nicotine may have enhanced the reinforcing strength of the

CS and/or retarded the development of extinction. For Paired NIC+CS rats, there was further acquisition of the lever press response, or acquisition of an association between contingent nicotine and the CS. This study demonstrates that nicotine can conditionally increase the motivational valence of non-nicotine stimuli. Moreover, once this conditioned value has accrued, the reinforcement enhancing effects of nicotine can sustain or promote more responding for the stimulus (also see Donny et al., 2003; Bevins and Palmatier, 2004).

Nature and Temporal Dynamics of Nicotine's Reinforcement-Enhancing Effects

Data presented to this point confirm a central prediction from the dual-reinforcement model, namely, that nicotine enhances responding for both unconditioned reinforcing stimuli (e.g., the VS in earlier studies) and a nicotine-established, conditioned reinforcing stimulus. The latter finding is consistent with research from other laboratories showing that nicotine also increases responding for conditioned reinforcing stimuli established by other primary reinforcers, such as water (Brunzell, Chang, Schneider, Olausson, Taylor, & Picciotto, 2006; Olausson et al., 2004a, 2004b). The convergence of these findings might suggest that nicotine is capable of equally enhancing all reinforcers, a conclusion that is at odds with our own finding, described earlier, that the magnitude of nicotine's enhancing effects depends on the reinforcing strength of the non-nicotine stimulus. More importantly, the conclusion is implausible as applied to smoking, since it is unlikely that nicotine equally enhances proximal conditioned stimuli such as the sight and taste of the cigarette; more remote contextual conditioned or unconditioned stimuli such as the settings within which smoking occurs or other co-abused drugs like alcohol; and remote, weakly reinforcing, conditioned or unconditioned stimuli. Translating these concerns into the present model, we can ask if the reinforcement-enhancing effects of nicotine are identical for unconditioned and conditioned reinforcing stimuli in terms of the magnitude of the effect and its temporal dynamics?

Two lines of investigation bear on this question. In the first, the enhancing effects of repeated nicotine exposure on a water-associated conditioned reinforcer persisted for an extended period after termination of nicotine treatment (Olausson et al., 2004a, 2004b). This persistence contrasts with a finding from our laboratory (Palmatier, Liu, Caggiula, Donny, Booth, Gahrib, Craven, & Sved, 2007b), in which we used the concurrent reinforcement paradigm to estimate the time course of nicotine's enhancing effects on an unconditioned reinforcing stimulus (VS) after nicotine withdrawal (saline substitution) or pharmacological antagonism of nAChRs by mecamylamine. For the Two-Lever group, acute mecamylamine challenge (or saline substitution) immediately and totally reduced the reinforcement enhancing effects of nicotine. In contrast, responding on the nicotine-lever decreased gradually over the seven days of testing, as would be expected of extinction learning. At least two, non-mutually exclusive hypotheses can be proposed to account for the discrepancy between the persistent effects reported by others (Brunzell et al., 2006;

Olausson et al., 2004a, 2004b) and the short time frame of our enhancing effects. First, the duration of nicotine's enhancing effects may depend on the strength of the reinforcing stimulus; the stimulus is likely to have been stronger (i.e., more reinforcing) in the Olausson et al., (2004a, 2004b) and Brunzell et al., (2006) studies than the VS in our experiment. Second, the difference may relate to a difference in the enhancing effects of nicotine on a conditioned (Brunzell et al., 2006; Olausson et al., 2004a, 2004b) versus an unconditioned (Palmatier et al., 2006; Palmatier et al., 2007c) reinforcer. We have not yet determined whether nicotine's enhancing effects on a nicotine-related conditioned reinforcer persist after termination of treatment and whether this temporal dimension is influenced by the strength of that conditioned reinforcer. Experiments designed to make such a determination by manipulating the nicotine-CS conditioning process are currently underway.

Significance of the Dual-Reinforcement Model

The research reviewed above indicates that the primary reinforcing actions of nicotine are not sufficient to explain the high rates of self-administration exhibited by laboratory animals or cigarette smoking by humans. Two additional factors must be considered, namely the conditioned and unconditioned reinforcing stimuli that accompany nicotine intake and the capacity of nicotine to enhance the reinforcing effects of such stimuli. Initial studies from our laboratory suggest that this reinforcement-enhancing effect of nicotine may be dissociable from its primary reinforcing component.

The dual-reinforcement model may have relevance at both the pre-clinical animal research level, in pursuit of neurobiological mechanisms of nicotine reinforcement, and at the level of understanding nicotine's role in smoking. For the former, reinforcement-enhancing effects are not unique to nicotine; they have also been shown for psychostimulants such as cocaine and amphetamine (Chaudhri et al., 2006b; Phillips & Fibiger, 1990; Taylor & Jentsch, 2001). This fact may be relevant in understanding the actions of an effective pharmacotherapy for smoking cessation, sustained release of bupropion (Jorenby, Leischow, Nides, Rennard, Johnston, Hughes, Smith, Muramoto, Daughton, Doan, Fiore, & Baker, 1999). Bupropion antagonizes nAChRs, but can also increase extracellular dopamine and norepinephrine (NE; Li, Perry, & Wong, 2002), suggesting that while reduced nAChR action may decrease the primary reinforcing effects of nicotine, other pharmacological actions of bupropion may lead to a reinforcement-enhancing effect. Indeed, we (Mays, Levin, Bak, Palmatier, Liu, Caggiula, Donny, Craven, & Sved, 2007) have found that bupropion pretreatment dose-dependently increased responding for a moderately reinforcing sensory stimulus and, like nicotine, this effect sensitized over repeated daily tests. Moreover, the enhancing effects of nicotine, but not bupropion, were blocked by mecamylamine, whereas the enhancing effects of bupropion, but not nicotine, were blocked by prazosin, an α-NE antagonist. Propranolol, a β-NE antagonist, had no detectable effects on responding for either. The results of this study indicate that bupropion has reinforcement-enhancing effects similar to nicotine. Furthermore, the reinforcement-enhancing effects of bupropion and nicotine are pharmacologically dissociable. The emerging pattern suggests that bupropion may 'replace' a reinforcement enhancing effect of nicotine. For example, in nicotine self-administration studies with rodents bupropion can increase (Rauhut, Neugebauer, Dwoskin, & Bardo, 2003) responding for intravenous nicotine infusions that are accompanied by non-nicotine stimuli. Also, acute treatment with bupropion increased ad lib smoking as well as ratings of positive mood and euphoria in people who were not intending to quit (Cousins, Stamat, & de Wit, 2001). While human studies have not investigated the impact of bupropion with and without non-nicotine reinforcers, the 'replacement' hypothesis outlined here argues that bupropion would eliminate some of the negative impact of quitting by sustaining and/or promoting other forms of reinforcement.

At the human level, recent evidence suggests that nicotine can modulate hedonic tone and reactivity to external rewards (Dawkins, Powell, West, Powell, & Pickering, 2006). This study reported that abstinent smokers ". . . expect to derive less enjoyment from a range of ordinary events and activities . . . " and " . . . showed virtually no reward responsivity . . ." Both effects were reversed by nicotine delivered via lozenges. Other data suggested that these positive effects of nicotine on hedonic tone were distinct from its effects on the ". . . general symptoms of nicotine withdrawal,"

Summary and Conclusions

Models of intravenous nicotine self-administration in laboratory animals are being used to investigate the behavioral and neurobiological consequences of nicotine reinforcement, and to aid in the development of novel pharmacotherapies for smoking cessation. Central to these models is the principle of primary reinforcement, which posits that response-contingent presentation of a primary reinforcer, nicotine, engenders robust operant behavior, whereas response-independent drug delivery does not. This dictum of nicotine as a primary reinforcer has been widely used to explain why people smoke tobacco—smoking results in the rapid delivery of nicotine to the brain, setting up a cascade of neurobiological processes that strengthen subsequent smoking behavior. However, there is mounting evidence that the primary reinforcement model of nicotine self-administration fails to fully explain existing data from both the animal self-administration and human smoking literatures. We have recently proposed a "dual reinforcement" model to more fully capture the relationship between nicotine and self-administration, including smoking. Briefly, the "dual reinforcement" model posits that nicotine acts as both a primary reinforcer and a reinforcement enhancer. The latter action of nicotine had originally been uncovered by showing that a reinforcing VS, which accompanies nicotine delivery, synergizes with nicotine in the acquisition and maintenance of self-administration, and that this synergism can be reproduced by combining operant responding for the reinforcing stimulus with non-contingent (response-independent) nicotine. Thus, self-administration (and smoking) is sustained by three actions: (1) nicotine, acting as a primary reinforcer, can sustain behavior that leads to its delivery; (2) nicotine, acting as a primary reinforcer, can establish neutral environmental stimuli as conditioned reinforcers through Pavlovian associations; and (3) nicotine, acting as a reinforcement enhancer, can magnify the incentive value of accompanying stimuli, be they conditioned or unconditioned reinforcers.

Acknowledgments We thank Sheri Booth, Maysa Gharib, Laure Craven, Kara Mays, Gina Matteson, Kasia Bak, Melissa Levin, and Emily Kraus for their assistance in conducting the research and performing analyses. Research conducted in our laboratory followed the NIH Guide for the Care and Use of Laboratory Animals and was approved by the Institutional Animal Care and Use Committee (Assurance #: A3187-01). This research was supported by NIH grants DA-10464, DA-12655, DA-17288, and DA-19278 and by a Howard Hughes Predoctoral Research Fellowship awarded to N. Chaudhri.

References

Arroyo, M., Markou, A., Robbins, T. W., & Everitt, B. J. (1998). Acquisition, maintenance and reinstatement of intravenous cocaine self-administration under a second-order schedule of reinforcement in rats: effects of conditioned cues and continuous access to cocaine. *Psychopharmacology (Berl)*, *140*(3), 331–344.

Balfour, D. J., Wright, A. E., Benwell, M. E., & Birrell, C. E. (2000). The putative role of extra-synaptic mesolimbic dopamine in the neurobiology of nicotine dependence. *Behavioural Brain Research*, *113*(1–2), 73–83.

Bevins, R. A. & Palmatier, M. I. (2004) Extending the role of associative learning processes in nicotine addiction. *Behavioral and Cognitive Neuroscience Review*, *3*, 143–158

Bozarth, M. A., Murray, A., & Wise, R. A. (1989). Influence of housing conditions on the acquisition of intravenous heroin and cocaine self-administration in rats. *Pharmacology, Biochemistry, and Behavior*, *33*(4), 903–907.

Brunzell, D. H., Chang, J. R., Schneider, B., Olausson, P., Taylor, J. R., & Picciotto, M. R. (2006). beta2-Subunit-containing nicotinic acetylcholine receptors are involved in nicotine-induced increases in conditioned reinforcement but not progressive ratio responding for food in C57BL/6 mice. *Psychopharmacology (Berl)*, *184*(3–4), 328–338.

Caggiula, A. R., Donny, E. C., Chaudhri, N., Perkins, K. A., Evans-Martin, F. F., & Sved, A. F. (2002a). Importance of nonpharmacological factors in nicotine self-administration. *Physiology Behavior*, *77*(4–5), 683–687.

Caggiula, A. R., Donny, E. C., White, A. R., Chaudhri, N., Booth, S., Gharib, M. A., Hoffman, A., Perkins, K. A., & Sved, A. F. (2001). Cue dependency of nicotine self-administration and smoking. *Pharmacology, Biochemistry, and Behavior*, *70*(4), 515–530.

Caggiula, A. R., Donny, E. C., White, A. R., Chaudhri, N., Booth, S., Gharib, M. A., Hoffman, A., Perkins, K. A., & Sved, A. F. (2002b). Environmental stimuli promote the acquisition of nicotine self-administration in rats. *Psychopharmacology (Berl)*, *163*(2), 230–237.

Caggiula, A. R., Donny, E. C., White, A. R., Chaudhri, N., Gharib, M., Booth, S., Sved, A. F. (2001). *Non-contingent nicotine enhances responding maintained by behaviorally contingent environmental cues*. Paper presented at the Society for Neuroscience.

Carroll, M. E., Krattiger, K. L., Gieske, D., & Sadoff, D. A. (1990). Cocaine-base smoking in rhesus monkeys: reinforcing and physiological effects. *Psychopharmacology (Berl)*, *102*(4), 443–450.

Carter, B. L., & Tiffany, S. T. (1999). Meta-analysis of cue-reactivity in addiction research. *Addiction*, *94*(3), 327–340.

Chaudhri, N., Caggiula, A. R., Donny, E. C., Booth, S., Gharib, M., Craven, L., et al. (2006a). Operant responding for conditioned and unconditioned reinforcers in rats is differentially enhanced by the primary reinforcing and reinforcement-enhancing effects of nicotine. *Psychopharmacology (Berl), 189*(1), 27–36.

Chaudhri, N., Caggiula, A. R., Donny, E. C., Booth, S., Gharib, M., Craven, L., et al. (2007). Self-administered and noncontingent nicotine enhance reinforced operant responding in rats: Impact of nicotine dose and reinforcement schedule. *Psychopharmacology (Berl), 190*(3), 353–362.

Chaudhri, N., Caggiula, A. R., Donny, E. C., Palmatier, M. I., Liu, X., & Sved, A. F. (2006b). Complex interactions between nicotine and nonpharmacological stimuli reveal multiple roles for nicotine in reinforcement. *Psychopharmacology (Berl), 184*(3–4), 353–366.

Childress, A. R., Ehrman, R., Rohsenow, D. J., Robbins, S. J., O'Brien, C. P. (1992). Classically conditioned factors in drug dependence. In J. H. Lowinson, Ruiz, P., Millman, R. B (Ed.), *Substance abuse: A comprehensive textbook* (pp. 55–69). Baltimore: Williams and Wilkins.

Cohen, C., Perrault, G., Griebel, G., & Soubrie, P. (2005). Nicotine-associated cues maintain nicotine-seeking behavior in rats several weeks after nicotine withdrawal: Reversal by the cannabinoid (CB1) receptor antagonist, rimonabant (SR141716). *Neuropsychopharmacology, 30*(1), 145–155.

Conklin, C. A., & Tiffany, S. T. (2001). The impact of imagining personalized versus standardized urge scenarios on cigarette craving and autonomic reactivity. *Experimental and Clinical Psychopharmacology, 9*(4), 399–408.

Corrigall, W. A. (1992). A rodent model for nicotine self-administration. In A. Boulton, Baker, G., Wu, P. (Ed.), *Neuromethods: Animal models of drug addiction* (Vol. 24, pp. 315–344). Totowa: The Humana Press.

Corrigall, W. A., & Coen, K. M. (1989). Nicotine maintains robust self-administration in rats on a limited-access schedule. *Psychopharmacology (Berl), 99*(4), 473–478.

Cousins, M. S., Stamat, H. M., & de Wit, H. (2001). Acute doses of d-amphetamine and bupropion increase cigarette smoking. *Psychopharmacology (Berl), 157*(3), 243–253.

Dawkins, L., Powell, J. H., West, R., Powell, J., & Pickering, A. (2006). A double-blind placebo controlled experimental study of nicotine: I–effects on incentive motivation. *Psychopharmacology (Berl), 189*(3), 355–367.

de Wit, H., & Stewart, J. (1981). Reinstatement of cocaine-reinforced responding in the rat. *Psychopharmacology (Berl), 75*(2), 134–143.

Di Chiara, G. (2000). Behavioural pharmacology and neurobiology of nicotine rewrd and dependence. In F. Clementi, Fomasari, D., Gotti, C. (Ed.), *Handbook of experimental pharmacology: neuronal nicotinic receptors*. Berlin: Springer-Verlag.

Donny, E. C., Caggiula, A. R., Knopf, S., & Brown, C. (1995). Nicotine self-administration in rats. *Psychopharmacology (Berl), 122*(4), 390–394.

Donny, E. C., Caggiula, A. R., Mielke, M. M., Booth, S., Gharib, M. A., Hoffman, A., Maldovan, V., Shupenko, C., & McCallum, S. E. (1999). Nicotine self-administration in rats on a progressive ratio schedule of reinforcement. *Psychopharmacology (Berl), 147*(2), 135–142.

Donny, E. C., Caggiula, A. R., Mielke, M. M., Jacobs, K. S., Rose, C., & Sved, A. F. (1998). Acquisition of nicotine self-administration in rats: the effects of dose, feeding schedule, and drug contingency. *Psychopharmacology (Berl), 136*(1), 83–90.

Donny, E. C., Caggiula, A. R., Rose, C., Jacobs, K. S., Mielke, M. M., & Sved, A. F. (2000). Differential effects of response-contingent and response-independent nicotine in rats. *European Journal of Pharmacology, 402*(3), 231–240.

Donny, E. C., Caggiula, A. R., Rowell, P. P., Gharib, M. A., Maldovan, V., Booth, S., Mielke, M. M., Hoffman, A., & McCallum, S. (2000). Nicotine self-administration in rats: estrous cycle effects, sex differences and nicotinic receptor binding. *Psychopharmacology (Berl), 151*(4), 392–405.

Donny, E. C., Chaudhri, N., Caggiula, A. R., Evans-Martin, F. F., Booth, S., Gharib, M. A., et al. (2003). Operant responding for a visual reinforcer in rats is enhanced by noncontingent nicotine: implications for nicotine self-administration and reinforcement. *Psychopharmacology (Berl)*, *169*(1), 68–76.

Donny, E. C., Houtsmuller, E., & Stitzer, M. L. (2007). Smoking in the absence of nicotine: behavioral, subjective and physiological effects over 11 days. *Addiction*, *102*(2), 324–334.

Fowler, H. (1971). Implications of sensory reinforcement. In R. Glaser (Ed.), *The Nature of Reinforcement. A Symposium of The Learning Research and Development Center* (pp. 151–195). New York: Academic Press.

Goldberg, S. R., Spealman, R. D., & Goldberg, D. M. (1981). Persistent behavior at high rates maintained by intravenous self-administration of nicotine. *Science*, *214*(4520), 573–575.

Harrington, G. M. (1963). Stimulus intensity, stimulus satiation, and optimum stimulation with light-contingent bar-press. *Psychological Reports*, *13* (107–111).

Harrison, A. A., Gasparini, F., & Markou, A. (2002). Nicotine potentiation of brain stimulation reward reversed by DH beta E and SCH 23390, but not by eticlopride, LY 314582 or MPEP in rats. *Psychopharmacology (Berl)*, *160*(1), 56–66.

Henningfield, J. E., & Goldberg, S. R. (1983). Control of behavior by intravenous nicotine injections in human subjects. *Pharmacology, Biochemistry, and Behavior*, *19*(6), 1021–1026.

Hughes, J. R., Hatsukami, D. K., Pickens, R. W., Krahn, D., Malin, S., & Luknic, A. (1984). Effect of nicotine on the tobacco withdrawal syndrome. *Psychopharmacology (Berl)*, *83*(1), 82–87.

Johanson, C. E., & Schuster, C. R. (1981). Animal models of drug self-administration. *Advances in Substance Abuse*, *2*(219–97).

Jorenby, D. E., Leischow, S. J., Nides, M. A., Rennard, S. I., Johnston, J. A., Hughes, A. R., et al. (1999). A controlled trial of sustained-release bupropion, a nicotine patch, or both for smoking cessation. *The New England Journal of Medicine*, *340*(9), 685–691.

Juliano, L. M., Donny, E. C., Houtsmuller, E. J., & Stitzer, M. L. (2006). Experimental evidence for a causal relationship between smoking lapse and relapse. *Journal of Abnormal Psychology*, *115*(1), 166–173.

Li, S. X., Perry, K. W., & Wong, D. T. (2002). Influence of fluoxetine on the ability of bupropion to modulate extracellular dopamine and norepinephrine concentrations in three mesocorticolimbic areas of rats. *Neuropharmacology*, *42*, 181–190.

Margolin, A., Avants, S. K. (1992). Cue-reactivity and cocaine addiction. . In T. R. Kosten, Kleber, H. D. (Ed.), *Clinicians guide to cocaine addiction* (Vol. 109–27). New York: Guilford Press.

Markou, A., Weiss, F., Gold, L. H., Caine, S. B., Schulteis, G., & Koob, G. F. (1993). Animal models of drug craving. *Psychopharmacology (Berl)*, *112*(2–3), 163–182.

Mays, K. L., Levin, M. E., Bak, K. M., Palmatier, M. I., Liu, X., Caggiula, A. R., et al. (2007). *Nicotine and bupropion have similar effects on responding for reinforcing non-drug stimuli.* Paper presented at the Society for Research on Nicotine and Tobacco, Austin, TX.

Meisch, R. A., Lemaire, G. A. (1993). Drug self-administration. In F. van Haaren (Ed.), *Methods in behavioral pharmacology* (pp. 257–300). BV: Elsevier Science Publications.

O'Brien, C. P., Childress, A. R., Ehrman, R., & Robbins, S. J. (1998). Conditioning factors in drug abuse: can they explain compulsion? *J Psychopharmacol*, *12*(1), 15–22.

Olausson, P., Jentsch, J. D., & Taylor, J. R. (2004a). Nicotine enhances responding with conditioned reinforcement. *Psychopharmacology (Berl)*, *171*(2), 173–178.

Olausson, P., Jentsch, J. D., & Taylor, J. R. (2004b). Repeated nicotine exposure enhances responding with conditioned reinforcement. *Psychopharmacology (Berl)*, *173*(1–2), 98–104.

Palmatier, M. I., Donny, E. C., Liu, X., Matteson, G. L., Caggiula, A. R., & Sved, A. F. (2007a). *Conditioned reinforcement established with self-administered nicotine: Motivational effects of stimuli associated with different unit nicotine doses.* Paper presented at the Society for Neuroscience, San Diego.

Palmatier, M. I., Evans-Martin, F. F., Hoffman, A., Caggiula, A. R., Chaudhri, N., Donny, E. C., et al. (2006). Dissociating the primary reinforcing and reinforcement-enhancing effects of nicotine using a rat self-administration paradigm with concurrently available drug and environmental reinforcers. *Psychopharmacology (Berl)*, *184*(3–4), 391–400.

Palmatier, M. I., Evans-Martin, F. F., Hoffman, A., Caggiula, A. R., Chaudhri, N., Donny, E. C., et al. (2005). *Self-administered nicotine enhances responding for a concurrently available visual reinforcer.* Paper presented at the Society for Neuroscience, Washington, D.C.

Palmatier, M. I., Liu, X., Caggiula, A. R., Donny, E. C., Booth, S., Gahrib, M., Craven, L., & Sved, A. F. (2007b). The Role of Nicotinic Acetylcholine Receptors in the Primary Reinforcing and Reinforcement-Enhancing Effects of Nicotine. *Neuropsychopharmacology, 32,* 1098–1108.

Palmatier, M. I., Matteson, G. L., Black, J. J., Liu, X., Caggiula, A. R., & Sved, A. F. (2007c). The reinforcement enhancing effects of nicotine depend on the incentive value of non-drug reinforcers and increase with repeated drug injections. *Drug and Alcohol Dependence, 89*(1), 52–9.

Paterson, N. E., Semenova, S., Gasparini, F., & Markou, A. (2003). The mGluR5 antagonist MPEP decreased nicotine self-administration in rats and mice. *Psychopharmacology (Berl), 167*(3), 257–264.

Phillips, A. G., & Fibiger, H. C. (1990). Role of reward and enhancement of conditioned reward in persistence of responding for cocaine. *Behavioural Pharmacology, 1*(4), 269–282.

Picciotto, M. R., Zoli, M., Rimondini, R., Lena, C., Marubio, L. M., Pich, E. M., et al. (1998). Acetylcholine receptors containing the beta2 subunit are involved in the reinforcing properties of nicotine. *Nature, 391*(6663), 173–177.

Rauhut, A. S., Neugebauer, N., Dwoskin, L. P., & Bardo, M. T. (2003). Effect of bupropion on nicotine self-administration in rats. *Psychopharmacology (Berl), 169*(1), 1–9.

Rescorla, R. A., & Wagner, A. R. (1972). A theory of Pavlovian conditioning: Variations in the effectiveness of reinforcement and non-reinforcement. In A. H. Black (Ed.), *Classical Conditioning II: Current Research and Theory* (pp. 64–99). New York: Appleton Century Crofts.

Roberts, D. C. S., & Richardson, N. R. (1992). Self-administration of psychomotor stimulants using progressive ratio schedules of reinforcement. In A. Boulton, Baker, G., Wu, P. H. (Ed.), *Neuromethods: animal models of drug addiction* (pp. 233–269). Clifton: Humana Press.

Robinson, T. E., & Berridge, K. C. (1993). The neural basis of drug craving: an incentive-sensitization theory of addiction. *Brain Research. Brain Research Reviews, 18*(3), 247–291.

Rose, J. E., Behm, F. M., Westman, E. C., & Johnson, M. (2000). Dissociating nicotine and nonnicotine components of cigarette smoking. *Pharmacology, Biochemistry, and Behavior, 67*(1), 71–81.

Rose, J. E., & Corrigall, W. A. (1997). Nicotine self-administration in animals and humans: similarities and differences. *Psychopharmacology (Berl), 130*(1), 28–40.

Rose, J. E., & Levin, E. D. (1991). Inter-relationships between conditioned and primary reinforcement in the maintenance of cigarette smoking. *British Journal of Addiction, 86*(5), 605–609.

Sayette, M. A., Martin, C. S., Wertz, J. M., Shiffman, S., & Perrott, M. A. (2001). A multidimensional analysis of cue-elicited craving in heavy smokers and tobacco chippers. *Addiction, 96*(10), 1419–1432.

Schenk, S., & Partridge, B. (2001). Influence of a conditioned light stimulus on cocaine self-administration in rats. *Psychopharmacology (Berl), 154*(4), 390–396.

Shaham, Y., & Stewart, J. (1995). Stress reinstates heroin-seeking in drug-free animals: an effect mimicking heroin, not withdrawal. *Psychopharmacology (Berl), 119*(3), 334–341.

Shoaib, M., Schindler, C. W., & Goldberg, S. R. (1997). Nicotine self-administration in rats: strain and nicotine pre-exposure effects on acquisition. *Psychopharmacology (Berl), 129*(1), 35–43.

Taylor, J. R., & Jentsch, J. D. (2001). Repeated intermittent administration of psychomotor stimulant drugs alters the acquisition of Pavlovian approach behavior in rats: differential effects of cocaine, d-amphetamine and 3,4- methylenedioxymethamphetamine ("Ecstasy"). *Biological Psychiatry, 50*(2), 137–143.

Tessari, M., Pilla, M., Andreoli, M., Hutcheson, D. M., & Heidbreder, C. A. (2004). Antagonism at metabotropic glutamate 5 receptors inhibits nicotine- and cocaine-taking behaviours and prevents nicotine-triggered relapse to nicotine-seeking. *European Journal of Pharmacology, 499*(1–2), 121–133.

Chapter 7
Altering the Motivational Function of Nicotine through Conditioning Processes

Rick A. Bevins

Introduction

The collection of chapters in this 55th Nebraska Symposium on Motivation Volume clearly highlights that effective strategies for reducing compulsive tobacco use will require a multi-faceted approach in which genetic, neurobiological, individual, and cultural factors are considered. It is difficult, if not impossible, to predict where the next important breakthrough will come from (Bevins & Bardo, 2004; Dethier, 1966; Laidler, 1998). Accordingly, further research that extends and challenges current theory and practice at each of these levels of analysis is needed. The continuing focus of our research program, and the topic of the present chapter, is on the role of Pavlovian conditioning processes involving nicotine. Theoretical and empirical approaches to nicotine dependence that include Pavlovian conditioning processes have lead to important advances in our understanding and treatment of chronic tobacco use (e.g., see Rose, Chapter 8 and Tiffany, Warthen, & Goedecker, Chapter 10 in current Volume). These approaches conceptualize the drug as an unconditioned stimulus (US) or reinforcer. That is, the pharmacological effects of the drug (e.g., reward, analgesia, psychomotor stimulation) enter into an association with stimuli that reliably co-occur with these effects (e.g., paraphernalia, situational cues). Later exposure to these conditioned stimuli (CSs) can evoke conditioned responses (CRs) that increase the chances an individual will seek drug.

Recently, we have suggested that the interoceptive stimulus effects of nicotine might also serve as a CS for other appetitive non-drug outcomes (i.e., USs) and/or a stimulus that occasions whether other CS–US associations will or will not occur (i.e., an occasion setter or facilitator; see Bevins & Palmatier, 2004). We have further suggested that such an associative learning history could impact the tenacity of nicotine addiction—e.g., shorten the time between experimentation and dependence, increase the difficulty of quitting, make sustaining abstinence more difficult, etc. At the current time these suggestions are speculative. With this in

R.A. Bevins
Department of Psychology, 238 Burnett Hall, University of Nebraska-Lincoln, Lincoln, NE 68588-0308, USA

R.A. Bevins, A.R. Caggiula (eds.), *The Motivational Impact of Nicotine and its Role in Tobacco Use*, DOI: 10.1007/978-0-387-78748-0_7, © Springer Science+Business Media, LLC 2009

mind, the present chapter will review the research in this area, as well as high-light some historical precursors and suggest some possible future directions for research. In doing so, hopefully the reader will gain an appreciation on how this approach might lead to further insight into how Pavlovian conditioning processes can alter the motivational function of nicotine in a manner that contributes to chronic tobacco use.

Nicotine as a Reinforcer

Most of the research examining the impact of conditioning processes with nicotine has conceptualized nicotine as a reinforcer. For the current discussion we mean rein-forcer in the same sense as used by Pavlov (1927) and Skinner (1938). According to Pavlov (1927), reinforcer was used interchangeably with unconditioned stimulus, which is shown by an example . "Tactile stimulation of the skin is used as a condi-tioned stimulus for acid. The conditioned stimulus is allowed to act for a period of 3 min and is then *reinforced*, being still continued so as to overlap the action of the acid" [p. 93 (italics added)]. According to this framework, exteroceptive cues that occur in close temporal and spatial relation with tobacco use have the potential to function as conditional stimuli and enter into an association with nicotine (i.e., the reinforcer or US). As a result of this conditioning, a CS acquires the ability to evoke or modify a response. The nature of this CR tends to be more readily predicted from a behavior systems/evolutionary approach to associative learning (cf. Domjan, 2005; Timberlake, 1994). In general terms, stimuli paired with an appetitive US tend to produce approach and search related CRs along with more US-specific behaviors. In contrast, stimuli paired with an aversive US will come to evoke avoid-ance and/or anti-predator behaviors. Translated to smoking, stimuli such as throat irritation and smell of cigarette smoke, sight of the cigarette, lighter and ashtray, smoking/work break areas, and/or smoking companions reliably co-occur with the physiological effects of the nicotine US. In smokers, these stimuli come to control changes in reported cravings and urges, as well as a variety of changes in more physiological measures such as heart rate and galvanic skin response (e.g., Geier, Mucha, & Pauli, 2000; Lazev, Herzog, & Brandon, 1999; Pritchard, Robinson, Guy, Davis, & Stiles, 1996; Rose & Levin, 1991; see Tiffany et al., Chapter 10, in this Volume).

To study the necessary and sufficient conditions for acquisition and expression of nicotine conditioned responding, researchers have developed several preclinical animal models (see Bevins & Palmatier, 2004 for a review). Perhaps the two most widely studied tasks are locomotor conditioning (Bevins, Besheer, & Pickett, 2001; Bevins & Palmatier, 2003; Bevins, Eurek, & Besheer, 2005; Palmatier & Bevins, 2002; Walter & Kuschinsky, 1989) and place conditioning (Grabus, Martin, Brown, & Damaj, 2006; Le Foll & Goldberg, 2005; Shoaib, Stolerman, & Kumar, 1994; see Brunzell & Picciotto, Chapter 3, in this Volume). As an example, in the locomotor conditioning task rats (and less often mice) receive a distinct environment (i.e., a context CS) paired with the psychomotor effect of nicotine. After repeated pairings of the context CS with the nicotine US, the context CS, in the absence of nicotine (i.e., CS-alone test) evokes an increase in activity relative to controls that receive equal exposure to the nicotine and the context in an unpaired fashion. Although a detailed review of this research is tangential to the goal of the present article, we know that acquisition of conditioned hyperactivity is sensitive to nicotine dose (US magnitude), temporal relation between the CS and US (interstimulus interval), and presentation of other excitatory CSs (Bevins et al., 2001; Bevins & Palmatier, 2004; Bevins et al., 2005). Notably, Pavlov (1927) reported that acquisition of conditioned salivation was affected by similar behavioral factors.

For Skinner (1938), "The operation of reinforcement is defined as the presentation of a certain kind of stimulus in a temporal relation with either a stimulus or response. A reinforcing stimulus is defined as such by its power to produce the resulting change" (p. 62). This definition encompasses that of Pavlov's stimulus–reinforcer relations and extends it to include behavior–reinforcer relations. Current behavioral researchers, albeit not exclusively, tend to use the term reinforcer or reinforcement to refer to the latter relation. As discussed in detail by Caggiula and colleagues in this Volume (Chapter 6) the direct positive reinforcing effects of nicotine, in conjunction with its reinforcer enhancing properties, are important for acquisition and maintenance of tobacco use (see also Chapter 5 by Markou and colleagues that provides a thoughtful discussion of how the removal or avoidance of a withdrawal state (negative reinforcement) also contributes to continued tobacco use).

An instrumental response (e.g., lever press) followed by intravenous (IV) nicotine can maintain and/or increase the frequency of that response (Corrigall & Coen, 1989; Donny, Caggiula, Mielke, Jacobs, Rose, & Sved, 1998). This preclinical self-administration model is one of the most widely used to study the reinforcing effects of abused drugs, including nicotine. In our laboratory, we have recently established nicotine self-administration in rats. Briefly, rats were surgically prepared with an IV catheter following a lever press autoshaping protocol with sucrose designed to engender a high operant level on both levers before starting the self-administration phase. The initiation of daily 1 h self-administration session was signaled by onset of the houselights and insertion of both levers. If the rat pressed the active lever, the levers were immediately withdrawn and nicotine was infused across 1 s; illumination of the cue lights above each lever signaled the infusion. After a 60-s timeout, the levers were reinserted. Notably, the house light remained on during the timeout. Inactive lever presses were recorded, but did not have any programmed consequence. Rats were started on 0.06 mg base/kg/infusion of nicotine and then switched to 0.03 mg base/kg/infusion. Figure 7.1 shows the active and inactive responses for each rat across the acquisition phase. All rats pressed more on the active than the inactive lever by the end of training with the 0.06 mg/kg dose of nicotine. This difference was enhanced when the dose was dropped to 0.03 mg/kg nicotine suggesting that rats were sensitive to the dose of nicotine in this protocol (Fig. 7.1). This point was further supported by each rat's behavior during a subsequent extinction phase where saline replaced nicotine as the infused solution; all remaining procedural details remained the same. That is, all rats increased presses

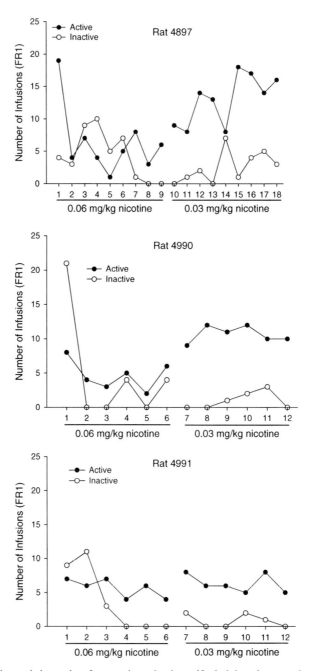

Fig. 7.1 Each panel shows data for a rat in a nicotine self-administration experiment conducted by Jennifer Murray in my laboratory. The main narrative includes a description of the procedures. All rats readily self-administered nicotine as indicated by more responding on the active (nicotine) than inactive lever

on the inactive lever on the first day of extinction (3 to 23, 0 to 10, and 0 to 3 for rats 4897, 4990, and 4991, respectively; data not shown). Additionally, active lever responding on average decreased across repeated extinction sessions.

Nicotine as a Discriminative Stimulus

As described in the previous section, nicotine is clearly able to function as reinforcer. This conceptualization and its theoretical extensions have lead to many important advances in our understanding of the addictive qualities of nicotine involved in tobacco addiction. Also contributing to our understanding of tobacco use and addiction is the research on the discriminative stimulus (S^D) effect of nicotine. That is, the pharmacological action of nicotine on the nervous system has perceptible interoceptive effects that can gain stimulus control over instrumental responding. Studying nicotine as a S^D has provided important insight into behavioral and neuropharmacological processes underlying the subjective effects of nicotine (e.g., Damaj, Creasy, Grove, Rosecrans, & Martin, 1994; Damaj, Creasy, Welch, Rosecrans, Aceto, & Martin, 1995; Perkins, DiMarco, Grobe, Scierka, & Stiller, 1994; Stolerman, 1989; see Perkins, Chapter 9, in this Volume).

Of interest for the present discussion is the two-lever operant drug discrimination task widely used by behavioral pharmacologists to study the S^D effects of nicotine in rodents (Fig. 7.2A). In this example, on sessions (days) when nicotine is administered presses on the right lever will be reinforced with a food pellet after a fixed-ratio (FR) 25 schedule is completed. At the same time, nicotine occasions nonreinforcement (i.e., extinction) of left lever presses. On saline sessions, the schedules are reversed. Left lever presses are reinforced on an FR25 and right lever presses are under extinction. With sufficient training, nicotine functions as a S^D/S^Δ as evidenced by better than 80% responding on the drug-appropriate lever before any reinforcer is delivered—right lever for nicotine sessions and left lever for saline sessions.

In contrast to neuropharmacological processes, potential behavioral (conditioning) processes involved in this discrimination have not been well studied. As described in the previous paragraph, the interoceptive effects of nicotine simultaneously function to occasion responding (S^D) as well as inhibit responding (S^Δ). Figure 7.2B diagrams some of the additional associative structures that could be of empirical and theoretical interest. For simplicity sake this diagram just shows a nicotine session and does not include the instrumental response (i.e., only stimuli are diagramed). Notably, the S^D and S^Δ function of nicotine are associated with different stimuli such as spatial location of the right versus left lever. Thus, on nicotine sessions exteroceptive and proprioceptive stimuli affiliated with the right lever are paired with food; stimuli associated with the left lever are not. Further, the interoceptive stimulus effects of nicotine are paired with intermittent access to food. From a broadly defined conditioning perspective, a glance at these potential associative structures described in Fig. 7.2B prompts several important questions. For example, does nicotine function as a contextual stimulus and acquire conditioned reinforcing value by being paired with food pellets? If so, does this contribute to

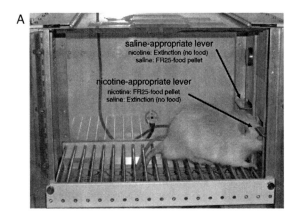

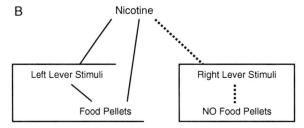

Fig. 7.2 Panel A shows a typical conditioning chamber set up to conduct two-lever operant drug discrimination. The text associated with each *arrow* describes the response contingency in force under a prototypical drug discrimination experiment using nicotine and saline as the injected solutions to be discriminated. **Panel B** shows hypothetical stimulus associations that are imbedded within the response contingencies of an operant drug discrimination study. Although only a nicotine session is shown for simplicity sake, it is clear that there are many direct and higher-order associations possible (see narrative for more detail)

discrimination performance? Alternatively, perhaps nicotine functions as a negative and/or positive facilitator (occasion setter) that disambiguates the stimulus relation between the lever stimuli and availability of food. On this latter point, observations of a well-trained rat will reveal that it engages in many food-related behaviors such as gnawing, licking, and/or nosing the lever while performing the instrumentally trained response (Bevins, 2001; Peterson, Ackil, Frommer, & Hearst, 1972; see also Kintsch & Witte, 1962). They also display goal-tracking behavior such as orienting and moving to the food trough or dipper (Bevins, 2001; Farwell & Ayres, 1979). Such behaviors indicate acquisition of a lever CS–food US association and suggest that the pharmacological effects of nicotine are likely occasioning that the lever stimuli will be paired with food.

The discussion in the previous paragraph is not meant to imply that the response–reinforcer relation is not an important variable in operant drug discrimination with nicotine or any other drug. Indeed, the schedule of reinforcement has been shown to alter acquisition and generalization in a two-lever drug discrimination task with nicotine (e.g., Stolerman, 1989). Rather, this discussion is meant to highlight that there are many relatively complex stimulus–stimulus and stimulus–reinforcer (i.e., Pavlovian) relations embedded in the task that could also affect the functioning of nicotine as an interoceptive stimulus. In fact, Pavlovian relations co-vary with the response–reinforcer relations and might as readily account for changes in the discriminative qualities of nicotine with changes in the reinforcement schedule. Given the importance of Pavlovian conditioning processes in nicotine addiction prescribed by theorists and researchers (e.g., Bevins & Palmatier, 2004; Conklin & Tiffany, 2002; Geier et al., 2000; Henningfield, Schuh, & Jarvik, 1995; Lazev et al., 1999; Rose & Levin, 1991; see Tiffany et al., Chapter 10, in this Volume), there is surprisingly little research investigating the interoceptive stimulus effects of nicotine from this theoretical perspective.

Interoceptive Pavlovian Conditioning: A Historical Framework

There has been a long history in the Pavlovian conditioning field of studying interoceptive stimuli as CSs. The early research was interested in stimulation of the viscera (stomach, intestine) or brain as the CS (Bykov, 1957; Doty, 1961; Loucks, 1938). For example, Bykov prepared a dog surgically so that water flowed in and then out of the stomach (i.e., the interoceptive CS). This irrigation of the stomach, which produced very little salivation alone, was then paired with access to meat powder and bread US. As described by Bykov (1957), "After several such combinations we found that if water was allowed to flow into the stomach 20 seconds in advance of the reinforcement, the irrigation alone caused the dog to start licking its lips and turning its head to the food box while there was a copious salivary secretion" (p. 249). This example is especially notable given our interest in Pavlovian appetitive conditioning using interoceptive stimuli produced by drug states (see later). That is, Bykov's dog displayed food-related CRs to the interoceptive CS that included licking lips and salivation (Pavlov, 1927), as well as sign/goal tracking (i.e., turning toward food box).

The study of interoceptive stimuli was later extended to the peripheral administration of ligands (e.g., Cook, Davidson, Davis, & Kelleher, 1960). Of particular relevance to the present discussion is the extension of this research to the pharmacological effects of abused drugs. This type of research can be categorized as either drug–drug conditioning or drug–non-drug US conditioning. A recent example of drug–drug conditioning comes from Shepard Siegel's laboratory (e.g., Kim, Siegel, & Patenall, 1999; Sokolowska, Siegel, & Kim, 2002) investigating the ability of the early pharmacological effects of morphine (early onset cues) to serve as a CS for its later, more profound, analgesic effects in rats (for similar research with ethanol see Greeley, Lê, Poulos, & Cappell, 1984). Other drug–drug conditioning research has used one drug as the CS for the later delivery of a different drug (e.g., Revusky, Davey, & Zagorski, 1989). In drug–non-drug US conditioning, the drug state serves as the CS for delivery of a non-pharmacological US. A well-controlled example of this under studied area was conducted by Bormann and Overton (1993). In that conditioned suppression experiment rats had an IP injection of morphine repeatedly paired with a foot-shock US. Relative to controls, the morphine CS came to evoke a conditioned fear response as measured by drink suppression. Turner and Altshuler (1976) reported a similar result in rats using amphetamine as the CS and a decrease in lever pressing as the measure of conditioned fear.

Nicotine as an Interoceptive CS

Until recent research from our laboratory (see also Troisi, 2006), there has been very little research directly assessing the role of nicotine as a CS. A notable exception to this statement is a study in humans by Clements, Glautier, Stolerman, White, and Taylor (1996). Clements and colleagues, inspired by some of the early drug–drug conditioning research with rats, sought to test whether nicotine could function as a CS for an ethanol US. In that study, one set of smokers received eight conditioning sessions. On half the sessions, a subcutaneous (SC) injection of nicotine (0.6 mg) into the upper arm was followed by a drink containing 9.4% alcohol. For the remaining sessions, a saline injection was followed by a placebo drink that used the same base as in the nicotine sessions (i.e., red angostura). Measures of conditioning included skin conductance, inter-beat interval of the heart, as well as mood/urge ratings. In summarizing their results Clements et al. (1996) concluded that "the study provided inconclusive evidence for the ability of one drug to act as a CS for the presentation of another in human subjects" (p. 94).

In retrospect, the lack of evidence for conditioning to the nicotine CS was not surprising for several reasons. For example, Clements and colleagues acknowledged the route and dose of nicotine may not have been sufficiently salient, or the proper temporal dynamics, to function as a CS. This point is especially notable given that the participants were smokers. That is, from a Pavlovian conditioning perspective, the CS effects of nicotine likely already have a rich conditioning history that might make it difficult to see any effect of a few conditioning trials in the laboratory. As an example, the individuals in this study smoked an average of 15.3 cigarettes per day. Although the duration of smoking is not reported, it is probably an underestimate to say that the participants with a mean age of 27 (range = 21–44) years were smoking at this rate for at least 9 years (i.e., since they were 18 years old). If so, the average number of cigarettes consumed by an individual is estimated at just over 50,000. Thus, in this example there were *at least* 50,000 potential conditioning trials in which the interoceptive stimulus effects of nicotine could have been paired with other appetitive stimuli (e.g., alcohol, food, socialization, work break, peer acceptance, etc.). The four conditioning trials used by Clements et al. (1996) seem few in comparison to an individual's experience before entering the experiment.

We do not mean to imply that the CS effects of a drug cannot be studied in the laboratory situation with human participants. Rather, experiments will simply need to take such history into account. Indeed, in a more recent and cleverly designed study Alessi, Roll, Reilly, and Johanson (2002) clearly demonstrated the feasibility of studying a drug state as CS capable of entering into an association with a reward.

Briefly, human participants had a non-preferred drug (typically diazepam) paired with increased pay during a subsequent computer task. The monetary outcome (US) induced a preference for the interoceptive effects of diazepam (CS). Or, in the word of the authors "drug (diazepam) may have acquired the properties of a conditioned reinforcer as a result of its association with money" (p. 81).

More recently, we have developed a preclinical animal model to study the ability of the pharmacological effects of nicotine to serve as an interoceptive contextual CS for a non-drug appetitive US (i.e., sucrose) in rats (Besheer, Palmatier, Metschke, & Bevins, 2004; Bevins and Palmatier, 2004; Bevins, Penrod, & Reichel, 2007; Murray & Bevins, 2007a, 2007b; Reichel, Linkugel, & Bevins, 2007; Wilkinson, Murray, Li, Wiltgen, Penrod, Berg, & Bevins, 2006). In this Pavlovian appetitive conditioning task, rats received a SC injection of nicotine (i.e., the CS) paired with intermittent access to liquid sucrose (i.e., the US) across a 20-min session. Intermixed with these nicotine sessions were saline sessions in which rats were injected with saline, placed into the same conditioning chambers, but sucrose was withheld (Fig. 7.3A for procedural schematic). Relative to saline (no drug), nicotine evokes differential approach and head entry into the dipper receptacle (Fig. 7.3B). This increase in behaviors directed at the location where the reinforcer has occurred in the past has been referred to as 'goal tracking' (Boakes, 1977; Farwell & Ayres, 1979) and is a widely used measure of Pavlovian conditioning (e.g., Bouton & Sunsay, 2003; Delamater, 1995; Rescorla, 2006).

Ongoing research in the laboratory has focused on neuropharmacological and behavioral processes underlying nicotine's ability to function as an interoceptive context CS in this appetitive drug discrimination procedure. For instance, Wilkinson et al. (2006) found that the magnitude of the goal-tracking CR increased with the number of nicotine CS–sucrose US pairings and that this more robust CR was more resistant to extinction (i.e., more nicotine CS presentations without sucrose to decrease the CR toward control). The CR magnitude also increased with higher concentrations of sucrose (unpublished data). A nicotine dose as low as 0.1 mg/kg can serve as a CS using a fading-dose procedure (Bevins & Palmatier, 2004) or as the dose used from the initiation of training (Murray & Bevins, 2007a, 2007b). Although acquisition rate is similar with lower (0.1 and 0.2 mg/kg) and higher (0.4 mg/kg) doses of nicotine, resistance to extinction increased with nicotine CS dose (Murray & Bevins, 2007b). Importantly, nicotine's ability to evoke this appetitive CR does not reflect state-dependent learning (Bevins et al., 2007).

Besheer et al. (2004) established that the CS effects of nicotine were blocked by pretreatment with the central and peripheral nicotinic acetylcholine receptor (nAChR) antagonist mecamylamine, but not the mostly peripheral nAChR antagonist hexamethonium, suggesting a role of central nervous system (CNS) receptors. Additional neuropharmacological research published or in progress in our laboratory has implicated the $\alpha4\beta2^*$ nAChR, the dopamine and norepinephrine transporter, the glutamatergic N-methyl D-aspartate (NMDA) receptor, and the cannabinoid CB1 receptor in the CS effects of nicotine. Dopamine D1, D2, and D3 receptors, as well as the metabotropic glutamate receptor subtype 5 receptor and the $\alpha7^*$ nAChR appear to have minimal role in nicotine's ability to

A. Typical Acquisition Protocol

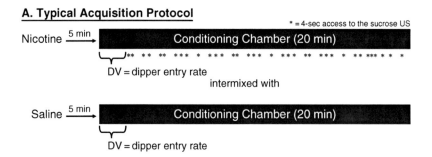

B. Acquisition of the Discrimination

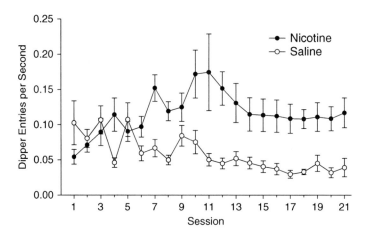

Fig. 7.3 **Panel A** shows a schematic of a typical protocol used to train the interoceptive stimulus effects of nicotine as an excitatory conditioned stimuli (CS). In brief, nicotine sessions are intermixed with saline session. On nicotine sessions, rats receive intermittent access to sucrose in a dipper receptacle; sucrose is withheld on saline sessions. **Panel B** shows acquisition of conditioned responding (i.e., dipper entries before first sucrose delivery or equivalent time in saline sessions) to the nicotine CS. In this study conducted by Jill Rosno in my laboratory, the nicotine CS dose was (0.4 mg base/kg, SC) and the unconditioned stimulus (US) was 26% sucrose. In a given nicotine session, There were 36 separate 4-s deliveries of the sucrose US

function as a CS (Murray & Bevins, 2007a; unpublished data from experiments in progress; see Chapters 2, 3, and 4 of present Volume (Placzek & Dani; Brunzell & Picciotto; Dwoskin, Pivavarchyk, Joyce, Neugebauer, Zheng, Zhang, Bardo, & Crooks, respectively) for a discussion of nAChRs). In sum, the specificity exemplified by the agonist and antagonist research just described, along with the consistency of the behavioral manipulations with past learning research highlights the utility of this Pavlovian drug discrimination task for studying the underlying behavioral and neural processes of the interoceptive conditional stimulus effects of nicotine.

In more "standard" Pavlovian discrimination tasks, auditory and visual stimuli are often used as CSs. These type of discrete stimuli—versus situational or static apparatus cues—can be readily turned on and off during a conditioning session. Further, several presentations can be programmed in each session allowing one to track acquisition of conditioned responding trial-by-trial. To date, all our published research on the CS effects of nicotine has used SC injections of nicotine. As such, our empirical efforts have employed manipulations comparable to those used with exteroceptive contextual or static apparatus cues. Recent advances in our laboratory, however, have extended this conceptualization of the CS effects of nicotine to include more discrete stimulus properties. Those advances are based on pairing a low dose of nicotine infused IV with brief access to sucrose in long daily sessions. More specifically, food restricted male Sprague Dawley rats were dipper trained for 3 days and then surgically prepared with IV catheters. Acquisition training followed the surgical recovery period. For acquisition, rats received ten IV infusions of nicotine (0.01 mg base/kg) in a 2-h session. Each 1-s nicotine infusion (i.e., the CS) was followed 30 s later by 4-s access to 26% (w/v) sucrose (i.e., the US); nicotine infusions were separated by an average of 11 min. This protocol was repeated daily for 12 days. The last day of acquisition was followed 24 h later by the first of seven extinction sessions in which the nicotine CS was still infused, but the sucrose US was withheld.

Figure 7.4 shows the results from this study examining the ability of IV nicotine to function as a CS. The main dependent measure is number of dipper entries in the 30 s following the nicotine infusion (CS period) minus number of entries in the 30 s before the infusion (pre-CS period). A positive value indicates an increase in dipper entries; 0 indicates no change. Nicotine readily acquired control of conditioned responding (i.e., goal tracking). Further, this conditioned responding decreased

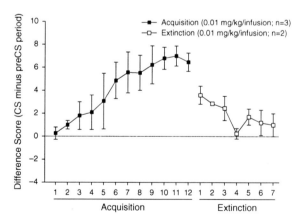

Fig. 7.4 This figure shows results of an experiment conducted by Jennifer Murray in my laboratory using a 1-s intravenous administration of 0.01 mg base/kg nicotine as the conditioned stimuli (CS); 4-sec access to the sucrose unconditioned stimulus (US) followed 30 s later. Intravenous nicotine acquired control over conditioned responding and this conditioning was susceptible to extinction

systematically across sessions when sucrose was withheld (i.e., extinction). These findings are notable for several reasons. First, they demonstrate that a dose of nicotine on the lower end of the self-administration dose-effect curve has sufficient stimulus properties to function as a CS. Second, after acquisition training, dipper entries increased after each nicotine infusion (trial-by-trial data not shown) suggesting that IV nicotine can be used in a manner more similar to a discrete cue. Finally, in the extinction phase nicotine infusions continued, but there was a progressive decrease in dipper entries across sessions. Because nicotine was infused to the same extent in acquisition and extinction, a psychomotor stimulant account of the increased dipper entries in the acquisition phase is untenable. That is, a psychomotor account predicts that the pattern of responding should not change in the extinction phase; this obviously did not occur. Accordingly, the increase in dipper entries in acquisition reflects a conditioned association between nicotine and sucrose. Indeed, we recently conducted an unpaired control group in which nicotine and sucrose occurred in the same session, but their presentations were separated by at least 4 min. This unpaired control did not display an increase in dipper entries immediately following nicotine infusion (data not shown). This result indicates that temporal contiguity between the nicotine and sucrose is required; a conclusion consistent with the extinction results and the implication of conditioning processes (Pavlov, 1927; Wasserman & Miller, 1997).

Nicotine as an Interoceptive Occasion Setter

The research examining the ability of nicotine to function as a CS assumes that the interoceptive effects of nicotine enter into a direct association with the sucrose US. Differential control of a goal-tracking CR by nicotine provides evidence for this conditioned association (see later discussion). A natural extension of this associative analysis is that the nicotine drug state should also be able to serve as a positive or negative occasion setter (i.e., also termed 'facilitator' or 'modulator' in the Pavlovian conditioning literature). A positive occasion setter is a stimulus that sets the occasion upon which each presentation of a CS will be paired with the US; a negative occasion setter indicates that presentations of the CS will not be reinforced (see Schmajuk & Holland (1998) and Swartzentruber (1995) for reviews). Research from our laboratory has shown that nicotine can function in both capacities (Bevins, Wilkinson, Palmatier, Siebert, & Wiltgen, 2006; Palmatier, Peterson, Wilkinson, & Bevins, 2004; Palmatier, Wilkinson, & Bevins, 2005; Palmatier & Bevins, 2007). For example, as a positive drug feature (i.e., occasion setter) nicotine disambiguated the relation between a brief light cue and sucrose delivery. That is, the discrete light CS was paired with the sucrose US when nicotine was administered before the start of the session. In contrast, on saline sessions the same light CS was present, but access to sucrose was withheld. As a negative feature, the interoceptive effects of nicotine indicate that the light CS will not be followed by the sucrose US. Rather, the light CS will be paired with sucrose on saline (no drug) sessions.

Although we have not conducted nearly the amount of neuropharmacological research within this nicotine occasion setting task as with the CS task, the Pavlovian discrimination is quickly acquired, mediated by central nicotinic acetylcholine receptors, and is pharmacologically specific (Bevins et al., 2006; Palmatier et al., 2004; Palmatier et al., 2005). Rather, our empirical efforts in this area have focused more on the underlying behavioral processes mediating nicotine's ability to modulate responding. For the positive occasion setting research, this has entailed asking whether nicotine (or other drug states such as chlordiazepoxide) facilitate conditioned responding to a CS through simple excitatory processes such as a direct association with the US or, is it necessary to infer a non-associative or higher-order associative process to account for its modulatory control over conditioned responding. One account of occasion setting suggests that the discrete CS (e.g., light in our situation) acquires weak excitatory strength from being paired with the sucrose US on half the sessions. Although this excitation is not sufficient to evoke conditioned responding alone, when the CS is combined with the 'occasion setter' that has also been paired with the US on half the sessions, excitation passes some threshold and conditioned responding is observed (cf. Rescorla, 1986). Note that this explanation assumes that the CS and the occasion setter enter into separate excitatory associations with the US that will 'summate' when the two are presented together. This summation account predicts that nicotine will lose its ability to modulate (facilitate) responding to the CS after extensive presentation of the nicotine occasion setter without the sucrose US—i.e., procedural extinction.

We recently tested this account using nicotine as the occasion setter (Experiment 1 in Palmatier & Bevins, 2007). Briefly, nicotine was trained as a positive occasion setter as described earlier. In a subsequent phase, nicotine was presented repeatedly without the discrete CS or sucrose US. This phase was meant to decrease excitation controlled directly by nicotine. Then, the light was re-introduced. Even though there were as many nicotine extinction sessions as there were original nicotine training sessions, conditioned responding to the discrete CS was still facilitated by the nicotine. A similar pattern was observed when amphetamine or chlordiazepoxide functioned as the occasion setter (Palmatier & Bevins, 2007). Combined, this research strains any summation type account. Further, it suggests that the nicotine drug state is modulating responding to the CS via a higher order associative or non-associative process. Currently unpublished research from our laboratory has confirmed this assumption. That is, nicotine trained as an occasion setter for one discrete CS (e.g., light) was able to transfer its modulatory control to a completely separate and distinct CS (e.g., white noise) that has been separately trained with chlordiazepoxide as the occasion setter. Notably, the pharmacological effects of chlordiazepoxide do not substitute for a nicotine occasion setter in the absence of this associative training. Additionally, a novel drug state (amphetamine) did not prompt conditioned responding to either of the discrete CS indicating that training two Pavlovian occasion setting discriminations within subject does not merely result in a drug versus no drug discrimination where the default is to respond when in a drug state. Thus, we are left to conclude that transfer of modulatory control of conditioned responding between nicotine and chlordiazepoxide reflects a common underlying higher-order associative or non-associative processes that allows for generalization. That is, related conditioning histories allows for functional substitution (versus pharmacological substitution) by drug states (Palmatier, 2004; see Bonardi & Hall, 1994 for comparable results with exteroceptive stimuli).

Implications for the Motivational Function of Nicotine

We suggest that a more complete analysis of nicotine dependence will also include nicotine in the role of a CS. An explicit assumption in our research is that nicotine's ability to control a CR reflects an acquired excitatory association with the sucrose US (Bevins & Palmatier, 2004). Although the inferred nature of the association may vary with one's theoretical preference, this assumption of acquired excitation is held in some form by most Pavlovian conditioning theorists (Bouton 2002; Domjan, 2005; Konorski, 1948; Miller & Escobar, 2002; Pavlov, 1927; Pearce, 1987; Rescorla 1988; Timberlake, 1994; Wagner & Brandon, 2001) and is supported by the research described in this chapter. If nicotine acquires additional appetitive properties by virtue of its conditioning history, then not only are the stimulus properties of the drug changed as evidenced by its control of a CR, but its ability to function in other capacities (e.g., reward, reinforcer, US, etc.) might also be changed. Such changes in the motivational function of nicotine for the smoker could affect the trajectory of nicotine dependence and suggest modifications to current intervention strategies. In less technical and more speculative terms, if the "meaning" of nicotine is altered by an individual's experiences while using nicotine, these associated experiences could alter the progression to dependence, affect the tenacity of the addiction, change the difficulty of quitting, alter the likelihood of relapse, and/or change the magnitude and duration of the relapse. Although in our current research and in the present proposal we focus on positive or appetitive experiences which would change these addiction outcomes for the worse, there is a clear prediction that negative or aversive experiences could also change the trajectory for dependence (e.g., prevent further experimentation and hence development of dependence, decrease likelihood of relapse, etc.).

The research reviewed in this chapter clearly establishes that interoceptive effects of nicotine function as a CS that comes to evoke an appetitive CR. However, the possibility that the motivational impact of nicotine would change as a function of conditioning history has not been directly assessed. Widely studied phenomena such as second-order conditioning (Bevins, Delzer, & Bardo, 1996; Holland & Rescorla, 1975; Pavlov, 1927), counterconditioning (Brooks, Hale, Nelson, & Bouton, 1995; Lovibond & Dickinson, 1982; Pearce & Dickinson, 1975), and revaluation (Holland & Straub, 1979; Molina, Bannoura, Chotro, McKinzie, Arnold, & Spear, 1996; Yin & Knowlton, 2002) support the idea that a cue paired with a biologically relevant outcome will acquire additional appetitive or aversive properties depending on the nature of the US. Additionally, there are a few scattered but important published reports more directly related to this suggestion. Perhaps the most directly relevant is a very clever experiment by Molina et al. (1996). In that study, they reported that a tactile aversion conditioned by an ethanol US was reversed if ethanol was later paired with sucrose. That is, 10-day-old rat pups had a distinct tactile CS paired with intragastrically administered ethanol (2 g/kg, 16.8% v/v). Relative to unpaired controls, this conditioning history produced a clear aversion for the tactile CS. If rat pups had this same dose of ethanol subsequently paired with 10 min of a sucrose solution (15.3% w/v) infused through an intra-oral cannula then they did not display this tactile aversion. Merely exposing the pups to unpaired ethanol and sucrose or providing an alternative learning history was not sufficient to alter the previously acquired tactile aversion. In the authors' words, "after pups in the present experiments acquired an aversion to the texture as a consequence of its pairing with alcohol US properties, the pup's representation of these properties was changed (devalued) during Phase 2 by pairing the state of alcohol intoxication with an appetitive sucrose infusion" (p. 130). Notably, ongoing research in our laboratory indicates that an appetitive conditioning history with nicotine as a CS appears to enhance its rewarding US effects as measured in a place conditioning task.

We also suggest that a more complete analysis of nicotine dependence will include nicotine in the role of an occasion setter. As such, nicotine disambiguates when other stimuli will be paired with a US. Although functioning as an occasion setter does not preclude also serving as a CS, it will be of interest to determine if some conditions are more likely to encourage higher-order associations rather than direct associations with nicotine. The motivational impact of Pavlovian conditioning history where nicotine serves as an occasion setter was highlighted by the functional substitution research described earlier (Palmatier, 2004). In that research, a drug pharmacologically distinct from nicotine (i.e., chlordiazepoxide), facilitated conditioned responding to the CS (e.g., light) that was paired with sucrose only in the nicotine state. This substitution occurs only when chlordiazepoxide is trained as an occasion setter for a different CS (e.g., white noise). That is, transfer of motivational function was based on learning histories and not on an overlap in the pharmacological effects of the drugs. This functional substitution could have important implications for smoking relapse. Seemingly unrelated stimuli could prompt craving, urges, and/or drug seeking because they share a common conditioning history with nicotine.

Finally, better intervention and prevention programs for nicotine dependence will require a multi-faceted and translational approach in which genetic, neurobiological, individual, and cultural factors are considered. In the present chapter we have focused on interoceptive Pavlovian conditioning processes in which nicotine's motivational function could be altered by conditioning history. Such conditioning history could significantly affect nicotine addiction. Albeit speculative, alterations in nicotine's effects resulting from Pavlovian conditioning could speed the transition between experimentation and dependence, make quitting more difficult, and/or contribute to the high relapse rate. Clearly, more research is required to test these possibilities, as well as to better understand interoceptive Pavlovian conditioning processes with nicotine. This understanding will no doubt enhance the effectiveness of intervention and prevention programs for tobacco use.

Acknowledgments I want to thank all the individuals that have worked so hard over the years on the research discussed in this Chapter. The research and the uncountable discussions prompted by this work have shaped my thinking in important ways. The research and the preparation of this chapter were partially supported by DA018114.

References

Alessi, S. M., Roll, J. M., Reilly, M. P., & Johanson, C.-E. (2002). Establishment of a diazepam preference in human volunteers following differential-conditioning history of placebo versus diazepam choice. *Experimental and Clinical Psychopharmacology, 10,* 77–83.

Besheer, J., Palmatier, M. I., Metschke, D. M., & Bevins, R. A. (2004). Nicotine as a signal for the presence or absence of sucrose reward: A Pavlovian drug appetitive conditioning preparation in rats. *Psychopharmacology, 172,* 108–117.

Bevins, R. A., Delzer, T. A., & Bardo, M. T. (1996). Second-order conditioning detects unexpressed morphine-induced salt aversion. *Animal Learning & Behavior, 24,* 221–229.

Bevins, R. A. (2001). Should we essentially ignore the role of stimuli in a general account of operant selection *Behavioral & Brain Sciences, 24,* 528–529.

Bevins, R. A., Besheer, J., & Pickett, K. S. (2001). Nicotine-conditioned locomotor activity in rats: Dopaminergic and GABAergic influences on conditioned expression. *Pharmacology, Biochemistry and Behavior, 68,* 135–145.

Bevins, R. A., & Bardo, M. T. (2004). Introduction: Motivation, drug abuse, and 50 years of theoretical and empirical inquiry. In R. A. Bevins & M. T. Bardo (Eds.), *Motivational Factors in the Etiology of Drug Abuse, Volume 50 of the Nebraska Symposium on Motivation* (pp. ix–xv). Lincoln NE: University of Nebraska Press.

Bevins, R. A., & Palmatier, M. I. (2003). Nicotine-conditioned locomotor sensitization in rats: Assessment of the US-preexposure effect. *Behavioural Brain Research, 143,* 65–74.

Bevins, R. A., & Palmatier, M. I. (2004). Extending the role of associative learning processes in nicotine addiction. *Behavioral and Cognitive Neuroscience Reviews, 3,* 143–158.

Bevins, R. A., Eurek, S., & Besheer, J. (2005). Timing of conditioned response in a nicotine locomotor conditioning preparation: Manipulations of the temporal arrangement between context cues and drug administration. *Behavioural Brain Research, 159,* 135–143.

Bevins, R. A., Wilkinson, J. L., Palmatier, M. I., Siebert, H. L., & Wiltgen, S. M. (2006). Characterization of nicotine's ability to serve as a negative feature in a Pavlovian appetitive conditioning task in rats. *Psychopharmacology, 184,* 470–481.

Bevins, R. A., Penrod, R. D., & Reichel, C. M. (2007). Nicotine does not produce state-dependent effects on learning in a Pavlovian appetitive goal-tracking task with rats. *Behavioural Brain Research, 177,* 134–141.

Boakes, R. A. (1977). Performance on learning to associate a stimulus with positive reinforcement. In H. Davis & H. M. B. Hurwitz (Eds.) Operant-Pavlovian interactions (pp. 67–97). Hillsdale NJ: Erlbaum.

Bonardi, C., & Hall, G. (1994). Occasion-setting training renders stimuli more similar: Acquired equivalence between the targets of feature-positive discriminations. *Quarterly Journal of Experimental Psychology, 47B,* 63–81.

Bormann, N. M., & Overton, D. A. (1993). Morphine as a conditioned stimulus in a conditioned emotional response paradigm. *Psychopharmacology, 112,* 277–284.

Bouton, M. E. (2002). Context, ambiguity, and unlearning: Sources of relapse after behavioral extinction. *Biological Psychiatry, 52,* 976–986.

Bouton, M. E., & Sunsay, C. (2003). Importance of trial versus accumulating time across trials in partially reinforced appetitive conditioning. *Journal of Experimental Psychology: Animal Behavior Processes, 29,* 62–77.

Brooks, D. C., Hale, B., Nelson, J. B., & Bouton, M. E. (1995). Reinstatement after counterconditioning. *Animal Learning & Behavior, 23,* 383–390.

Bykov, K. M. (1957). *The cerebral cortex and the internal organs*. New York: Chemical Publishing Company.

Clements, K., Glautier, S., Stolerman, I. P., White, J.-A. W., & Taylor, C. (1996). Classical conditioning in humans: Nicotine as CS and alcohol as US. *Human Psychopharmacology, 11,* 85–95.

Conklin, C. A., & Tiffany, S. T. (2002). Applying extinction research and theory to cue-exposure addiction treatments. *Addiction, 97,* 155–167.

Cook, L., Davidson, A., Davis, D. J., Kelleher, R. T. (1960). Epinephrine, norepinephrine, and acetylcholine as conditioned stimuli for avoidance behavior. *Science, 131,* 990–991.

Corrigall, W. A., & Coen, K. M. (1989). Nicotine maintains robust self-administration in rats on a limited-access schedule. *Psychopharmacology, 99,* 473–478.

Dethier, V. G. (1966). Insects and the concept of motivation. In D. Levine (Ed.), *Nebraska Symposium on Motivation, 1966* (pp. 105–136). Lincoln NE: University of Nebraska Press.

Damaj, M. I., Creasy, K. R., Grove, A. D., Rosecrans, J. A., & Martin, B. R. (1994). Pharmacological effects of epibatidine optical enantiomers. *Brain Research, 664,* 34–40.

Damaj, M. I., Creasy, K. R., Welch, S. P., Rosecrans, J. A., Aceto, M. D., & Martin, B. R. (1995). Comparative pharmacology of nicotine and ABT-418, a new nicotinic agonist. *Psychopharmacology, 120,* 483–490.

Delamater, A. R. (1995). Outcome-selective effects of intertrial reinforcement in a Pavlovian appetitive conditioning paradigm with rats. *Animal Learning & Behavior, 23,* 31–39.

Domjan, M. (2005). Pavlovian conditioning: A functional perspective. *Annual Review of Psychology, 56,* 179–206.

Donny, E. C., Caggiula, A. R., Mielke, M. M., Jacobs, K. S., Rose, C., & Sved, A. F. (1998). Acquisition of nicotine self-administration in rats: the effects of dose, feeding schedule, and drug contingency. *Psychopharmacology, 136,* 83–90.

Doty, R. W. (1961). Conditioned reflexes formed and evoked by brain stimulation. In D. E. Sheer (Ed.), *Electrical stimulation of the brain: An interdisciplinary survey of neurobehavioral integrative systems* (pp. 397–412). Austin TX: University of Texas Press.

Farwell, B. J., & Ayres, J. J. B. (1979). Stimulus-reinforcer and response-reinforcer relations in the control of conditioned appetitive headpoking ("goal tracking") in rats. *Learning and Motivation, 10,* 295–312.

Geier, A., Mucha, R. F., & Pauli, P. (2000). Appetitive nature of drug cues confirmed with physiological measures in a model using pictures of smoking. *Psychopharmacology, 150,* 283–291.

Grabus, S. D., Martin, B. R., Brown, S. E., & Damaj, M. I. (2006). Nicotine place preference in the mouse: influences of prior handling, dose and strain and attenuation by nicotinic receptor antagonists. *Psychopharmacology, 184,* 456–463.

Greeley, J., Lê, D. A., Poulos, C. X., & Cappell, H. (1984). Alcohol is an effective cue in the conditioned control of tolerance to alcohol. *Psychopharmacology, 83,* 159–162.

Henningfield, J. E., Schuh, L. M., & Jarvik, M. E. (1995). Pathophysiology of tobacco dependence. In F. E. Bloom & D. J. Kupfer (Eds.), *Psychopharmacology: The fourth generation of progress* (pp. 1715–1729). New York: Raven Press.

Holland, P. C., & Rescorla, R. A. (1975). Second-order conditioning with food unconditioned stimulus. *Journal of Comparative and Physiological Psychology, 88,* 459–467.

Holland, P. C., & Straub, J. J. (1979). Differential effects of two ways of devaluing the unconditioned stimulus after Pavlovian appetitive conditioning. *Journal of Experimental Psychology: Animal Behavior Processes, 5,* 65–78

Kim, J. A., Siegel, S., & Patenall, V. R. A. (1999). Drug-onset cues as signals: Intraadministration associations and tolerance. *Journal of Experimental Psychology: Animal Behavior Processes, 25,* 491–504.

Kintsch, W. & Witte, R. S. (1962). Concurrent conditioning of bar press and salivation response. *Journal of Comparative and Physiological Psychology, 55,* 963–968.

Konorski, J. (1948). *Conditioned reflexes and neuron organization*. Cambridge: Cambridge University Press.

Laidler, K. J. (1998). *To light such a candle: Chapters in the history of science and technology.* Oxford: Oxford University Press.

Lazev, A. B., Herzog, T. A., & Brandon, T. H. (1999). Classical conditioning of environmental cues to cigarette smoking. *Experimental and Clinical Psychopharmacology, 7,* 56–63.

Le Foll, B., & Goldberg, S. R. (2005). Nicotine induces conditioned place preferences over a large range of doses in rats. *Psychopharmacology, 178,* 481–492.

Loucks, R. B. (1938). Studies of neural structures essential for learning. II: The conditioning of salivary and striped muscle responses to faradization of cortical sensory elements, and the action of sleep upon such mechanisms. *Journal of Comparative Psychology, 25,* 315–332.

Lovibond, P. F., & Dickinson, A. (1982). Counterconditioning of appetitive and defensive CRs in rabbits. *The Quarterly Journal of Experimental Psychology B: Comparative and Physiological Psychology, 34B,* 115–126.

Miller, R., & Escobar, M. (2002). Learning: Laws and models of basic conditioning. In H. Pashler & R. Gallistel (Eds.), *Steven's handbook of experimental psychology (3rd ed.), Vol.3: Learning, motivation, and emotion* (pp. 47–102). Hoboken NJ: John Wiley & Sons, Inc.

Molina, J. C., Bannoura, M. D., Chotro, M. G., McKinzie, D. L., Arnold, H. M., & Spear, N. E. (1996). Alcohol-mediated tactile conditioned aversions in infant rats: Devaluation of conditioning through alcohol-sucrose associations. *Neurobiology of Learning and Memory, 66,* 121–132.

Murray, J. E., & Bevins, R. A. (2007a). Behavioral and neuropharmacological characterization of a nicotine conditioned stimulus. *European Journal of Pharmacology, 561,* 91–104.

Murray, J. E., & Bevins, R. A. (2007b). The conditional stimulus effects of nicotine vary as a function of training dose. *Behavioural Pharmacology, 18,* 707–716.

Palmatier, M. I., & Bevins, R. A. (2002). Examination of GABAergic and dopaminergic compounds in the acquisition of nicotine-conditioned hyperactivity in rats. *Neuropsychobiology, 45,* 87–94.

Palmatier, M. I. (2004). Drug modulators in appetitive Pavlovian conditioning. Unpublished Dissertation, Department of Psychology, University of Nebraska-Lincoln.

Palmatier, M. I., Peterson, J. L., Wilkinson, J. L., & Bevins, R. A. (2004). Nicotine serves as a feature-positive modulator of Pavlovian appetitive conditioning in rats. *Behavioural Pharmacology, 15,* 183–194.

Palmatier, M. I., Wilkinson, J. L., & Bevins, R. A. (2005). Stimulus properties of nicotine, amphetamine, and chlordiazepoxide as positive features in a Pavlovian appetitive discrimination task in rats. *Neuropsychopharmacology, 30,* 731–741.

Palmatier, M. I., & Bevins, R. A. (2007). Facilitation by drug states does not depend on acquired excitatory strength. *Behavioural Brain Research, 176,* 292–301.

Pavlov, I. P. (1927). *Conditioned reflexes.* London: Oxford University Press.

Pearce, J. M., & Dickinson, A. (1975). Pavlovian counterconditioning: Changing the suppressive properties of shock by association with food. *Journal of Experimental Psychology: Animal Behavior Processes, 2,* 170–177.

Pearce, J. M. (1987). A model of stimulus generalisation for Pavlovian conditioning. *Psychological Review, 84,* 61–73.

Perkins, K. A., DiMarco, A., Grobe, J. E., Scierka, A., & Stiller, R. L. (1994). Nicotine discrimination in male and female smokers. *Psychopharmacology, 116,* 407–413.

Peterson G. B., Ackil, J. E., Frommer, G. P., & Hearst, E. S. (1972). Conditioned approach and contact behavior toward signals for food or brain-stimulation reinforcement. *Science, 177,* 1009–1011.

Pritchard, W. S., Robinson, J. H., Guy, T. D., Davis, R. A., & Stiles, M. F. (1996). Assessing the sensory role of nicotine in cigarette smoking. *Psychopharmacology, 127,* 55–62.

Reichel, C. M., Linkugel, J. D., & Bevins, R. A. (2007). Nicotine as a conditioned stimulus: Impact of ADHD medications. *Experimental and Clinical Psychopharmacology, 15,* 501–509.

Rescorla, R. A. (1986). Extinction of facilitation. *Journal of Experimental Psychology: Animal Behavior Processes, 12,* 16–24.

Rescorla, R. A. (1988). Behavioral studies of Pavlovian conditioning. *Annual Review of Neuroscience, 11,* 329–352.

Rescorla, R. A. (2006). Deepened extinction from compound stimuli presentation. *Journal of Experimental Psychology: Animal Behavior Processes, 32,* 135–144.

Revusky, S., Davey, V., & Zagorski, M. (1989). Heart rate conditioning with pentobarbital as a conditioned stimulus and amphetamine as an unconditioned stimulus. *Behavioral Neuroscience, 103,* 296–307.

Rose, J. E., & Levin, E. D. (1991). Inter-relationships between conditioned and primary reinforcement in the maintenance of cigarette smoking. *British Journal of Addiction, 86,* 605–609.

Schmajuk, N. A., & Holland, P. C. (1998). *Occasion setting: Associative learning and cognition in animals.* Washington DC: American Psychological Association.

Shoaib, M., Stolerman, I. P., & Kumar, R. C. (1994). Nicotine-induced place preferences following prior nicotine exposure in rats. *Psychopharmacology, 113,* 445–452.

Skinner, B. F. (1938). *The behavior of organisms.* New York: Appleton Century Crofts.

Sokolowska, M., Siegel, S., & Kim, J. A. (2002). Intraadministration associations: Conditional hyperalgesia elicited by morphine onset cues. *Journal of Experimental Psychology: Animal Behavior Processes, 28,* 309–320.

Stolerman, I. P. (1989). Discriminative stimulus effects of nicotine in rats trained under different schedules of reinforcement. *Psychopharmacology, 97,* 131–138.

Swartzentruber, D. E. (1995). Modulatory mechanisms in Pavlovian conditioning. *Animal Learning & Behavior, 23,* 123–143.

Timberlake, W. (1994). Behavior systems, associationism, and Pavlovian conditioning. *Psychonomic Bulletin & Review, 1,* 405–420.

Troisi, J. R. II (2006). Pavlovian-instrumental transfer of the discriminative stimulus effects of nicotine and ethanol in rats. *The Psychological Record, 56,* 499–512.

Turner, E. G., & Altshuler, H. L. (1976). Conditioned suppression of an operant response using d-amphetamine as the conditioned stimulus. *Psychopharmacology, 50,* 139–143.

Wagner, A. R., & Brandon, S. E. (2001). A componential model of Pavlovian conditioning. In R. R. Mower & S. B. Klein (Eds.), *Handbook of contemporary learning theories* (pp. 23–64). Mahwah, NJ: LEA.

Walter, S., & Kuschinsky, K. (1989). Conditioning of nicotine effects on motility and behaviour in rats. *Naunyn-Schmiedeberg's Archives of Pharmacology, 339,* 208–213.

Wasserman, E. A., & Miller, R. R. (1997). What's elementary about associative learning *Annual Review of Psychology, 48,* 573–607.

Wilkinson, J. L., Murray, J. E., Li, C., Wiltgen, S. M., Penrod, R. D., Berg, S. A., & Bevins, R. A. (2006). Interoceptive Pavlovian conditioning with nicotine as the conditional stimulus varies as a function of number of conditioning trials and unpaired sucrose deliveries. *Behavioural Pharmacology, 17,* 161–172.

Yin, H. H., & Knowlton, B. J. (2002). Reinforcer devaluation abolishes conditioned cue preference: Evidence for stimulus-stimulus associations. *Behavioral Neuroscience, 116,* 174–177.

Chapter 8
New Findings on Nicotine Addiction and Treatment

Jed E. Rose

Introduction

Over the last 10 years, we have witnessed a rapid expansion in both the scientific understanding of tobacco addiction and in the range of pharmacotherapies available for smoking cessation treatment. These recent developments will be reviewed below, emphasizing the link between basic research and the development of new treatments. This link is bidirectional: increased knowledge gained from basic animal and human laboratory research informs the development of new treatments; in addition, however, findings from treatment studies help us test and refine hypotheses about underlying mechanisms. We will consider three main areas of treatment research: (1) pre-cessation administration of therapeutic agents, including nicotine, varenicline, mecamylamine and bupropion; (2) development of nicotine vaccines; and (3) progress towards tailoring cessation treatments based on a smoker's genetic make-up.

Pre-cessation Administration of Pharmacologic Agents

Pre-cessation use of Nicotine Replacement Therapy

Since the advent of nicotine replacement therapy (NRT) in the 1980 s, an assumption has often been made that its main mechanism of action was the alleviation of smoking withdrawal symptoms (e.g., Peters & Morgan, 2002). In that case, it has been a rational strategy to begin NRT upon quitting smoking. However, a different rationale for substitution therapy generally – and NRT specifically – is to attenuate the reinforcing effects of the abused substance, in this case cigarettes (Henningfield & Jasinski, 1988). By using NRT to establish a level of nicotine in the smoker's blood

J.E. Rose
Center for Nicotine and Smoking Cessation Research, Duke University Medical Center, 2424 Erwin Road, Suite 210, Durham, NC 27705, USA
e-mail: rose0003@mc.duke.edu

R.A Bevins, A.R. Caggiula (eds.), *The Motivational Impact of Nicotine and its Role in Tobacco Use*, DOI: 10.1007/978-0-387-78748-0_8, © Springer Science+Business Media, LLC 2009 (and brain), and continuing smoking for a prescribed period of days or weeks, cigarettes may be less reinforcing (Levin et al., 1994). This reduction of reinforcement may be due to either satiation or tolerance: satiation refers to the reduction in the motivation to obtain additional positive or negative reinforcement from smoking; tolerance refers to the attenuation of the effect of nicotine such as through receptor desensitization (temporary inactivation of nicotinic receptors after continuous exposure to nicotine). Either mechanism will result in a cigarette being less reinforcing if it is smoked when plasma nicotine levels are elevated, as compared to smoking after a period of deprivation.

It is therefore reasonable to hypothesize that administration of NRT during the weeks leading up to a target quit date might present the smoker with many occasions of smoking when reinforcement is attenuated. This in turn may both lessen a smoker's dependence on cigarettes and facilitate cessation. Indeed, several studies have now discovered this to be the case; there is a robust increase in abstinence rates after 2-week pre-cessation treatment with NRT, during which smokers use both NRT and cigarettes concurrently. For example, two published articles have reported a significant enhancement in quit rates after pre-cessation nicotine skin patch administration (Rose, Behm, Westman, & Kukovich, 2006; Schuurmans, Diacon, van Biljon, & Bolliger, 2004). In these studies, pre-quit nicotine patch administration approximately doubled abstinence rates. Moreover, a large-scale (n = 400) replication trial has recently replicated these findings, also finding a doubling in abstinence rates over conventional NRT (Rose, Herskovic, Behm, & Westman, 2007).

A similar trial using pre-cessation nicotine chewing gum also reported a trend for increased abstinence relative to conventional NRT (Herrera, Franco, Herrera, Partidas, Rolando & Fagerstrom, 1995). Although there is not sufficient information to determine whether pre-cessation nicotine chewing gum is as effective as pre-cessation skin patch treatment, an ad lib dosing regimen of nicotine gum might, in theory, not be as effective. The reason is that if subjects alternated between smoking and using gum, nicotine levels just prior to smoking a cigarette might not be adequate to attenuate its reinforcing effects. If on-demand nicotine formulations are used in a pre-cessation context, it will be important to compare ad lib dosing with fixed-time dosing (e.g., once/hr).

An additional line of evidence supporting the rationale behind pre-cessation NRT is the analysis of post-quit date "lapses" during conventional NRT. Smokers often lapse, that is, smoke a cigarette, while on "post-quit" nicotine patch treatment. We would expect that the reinforcing effects of these cigarettes would be reduced relative to placebo patch treatment. Indeed, in some clinical trials evaluating nicotine patch treatment subjective ratings of reward were lower in the active nicotine patch condition (Levin et al., 1994; Rose & Behm, 2004). If extinction of the reinforcing value of cigarettes depends on the number of "nonreinforced trials," one would predict that as the number of lapses increases, NRT should have a greater effect in terms of suppressing the progression to a full-blown relapse. A recent analysis of lapse episodes by Shiffman, Scharf, Shadel, Gwaltney, Dang, Paton, & Clark (2006) supports this conclusion: the odds ratio for success after (post-quit) NRT increased after the first lapse. Although lapses often led to relapse, lapses were more predictive of relapse in the placebo NRT condition. Thus, NRT may have helped reduce the resumption of smoking by attenuating the reinforcing effects of the cigarettes smoked during lapses (see also Shiffman, Ferguson, & Gwaltney, 2006, for alternative explanations).

This learning-theory analysis might also help explain why not all studies have reported a reduction in the rewarding effects of smoking during NRT. For example, Cardenas, Busto, MacDonald, & Corrigall (2002) found no difference between the subjective rewarding effect of smoking two test cigarettes after wearing active vs. placebo nicotine patches in an acute laboratory study; however, a critical difference between that study and the clinical trials reporting an attenuation of smoking reward by concurrent NRT is that the clinical trials allowed subjects to learn, over time, that cigarette-related sensory cues were less rewarding.

Sensory cues, such as taste, aroma, and airway sensations accompanying inhalation provide much of the immediate rewarding effect of smoking (Rose, 2006; Rose, Westman, Behm, Johnson, & Goldberg, 1999). The rewarding value of these cues may be enhanced by the pharmacologic effects of nicotine, operating through multiple processes. One of these processes does not rely on contingency, or pairing, of cues and nicotine (Palmatier, Matteson, Black, Liu, Caggiula, Craven, & Sved, 2007), and is thus a nonassociative facilitation of reward value by nicotine.

However, in addition to this nonassociative effect, it is likely that, over many years of pairing cigarette cues with nicotine administration, these cues also become conditioned reinforcers through Pavlovian conditioning (Rose & Levin, 1991). Thus, in order to devalue these cues, it may be necessary to present numerous learning trials in which the cues are not reinforced. A clinical trial extending over days or weeks, in which frequent smoking episodes occur during NRT, may thus provide the best opportunity to observe an attenuation of cigarette reward.

The rate of ad lib smoking might also influence whether a reduction in cigarette reward rating occurs during NRT. If smokers reduce their rate of smoking, then each cigarette will be smoked after a longer period of deprivation; this factor would tend to increase reward ratings and could offset the reduction in reward due to NRT. Hence, if rates of smoking decline during NRT but reward ratings remain constant, it does not necessarily mean that NRT had no effect on reward. An effective procedure for revealing the effect of NRT on cigarette reward might be to pace smoking behavior; by maintaining a constant rate of smoking, the diminished rewarding effects of each cigarette might be more clearly shown without being offset by a possible increase in cigarette deprivation resulting from cigarettes being spaced farther apart.

It is somewhat surprising that only 2 weeks, and possibly less time, is needed to have a discernible impact on ratings of cigarette reward, given that the behavior of smoking has years of previous conditioning. However, this may be an example of the "overtraining extinction effect" (Ishida & Papini, 2007), analogous to the "overtraining reversal effect" (Orona, Foster, Lambert, & Gabriel, 1982; Valles, Rocha, & Nation, 2006), according to which overlearning can in some situations facilitate subsequent extinction. One explanation for this effect is that extended training results in such a strong and specific expectation of reinforcement that it is especially surprising when reinforcement does not occur. This increased salience of omitted reinforcement may promote more rapid extinction.

Another factor that bodes well for a smoking cessation therapy based on extinguishing the rewarding properties of cigarettes is that, unlike laboratory-based cue-extinction approaches, extinction will take place in the diverse contexts of a smoker's life. Thus, there is less likelihood of the "renewal effect" (Bouton & Swartzentruber, 1991), according to which extinction disappears and the previously reinforced response returns when the context in which extinction occurs is changed.

In a complementary approach to pre-cessation NRT, nicotine reinforcement of smoking can also be reduced using denicotinized cigarettes. Denicotinized cigarettes have been shown to promote extinction of smoking behavior (Donny, Houtsmuller, & Stitzer, 2007; Rose & Behm, 2004), and in principle these cigarettes can be used with or without concurrent NRT. However, in one published study, concurrent NRT enhanced compliance with use of denicotinized cigarettes; subjects reported smoking significantly fewer nicotine containing cigarettes in the active NRT condition (Rose, Behm et al, 2006). Possibly NRT prevented nicotine withdrawal symptoms that might otherwise have driven subjects to smoke nicotine containing cigarettes; alternatively, the attenuation of the rewarding effects of nicotine cigarettes by NRT reduced the temptation to smoke them instead of the denicotinized cigarettes. In any case, use of denicotinized cigarettes in conjunction with NRT during the weeks leading up to a quit date provides a compelling approach. Nicotine delivery is dissociated from the act of smoking in two ways: first, smoking denicotinized cigarettes is not reinforced by nicotine delivery; and second, nicotine is provided at times when smoking does not occur. Although it may be argued that the continuous delivery of nicotine from a skin patch does at times accompany cigarettes, nonetheless the behavioral contingency is broken between the act of smoking and nicotine delivery: the nicotine level in the bloodstream (and brain) is not changed from pre- to post-smoking.

The use of denicotinized cigarettes during pre-cessation NRT has another potential advantage in terms of allaying concerns about receiving excessive nicotine from cigarettes in addition to receiving nicotine from a skin patch. Although studies have not found any acute danger associated with smoking cigarettes while wearing nicotine patches, concerns nevertheless remain in the minds of many smokers and clinicians alike. These concerns would likely be reduced if denicotinized cigarettes were used during pre-cessation nicotine patch treatment. Further clinical trials will be needed to evaluate the potential efficacy of this approach.

The discussion thus far has assumed that the relevant association to be broken is the association between the act of smoking and receipt of nicotine reinforcement. However, one should also consider the role of other learned associations. For example, there is an association between environmental cues and the act of smoking; this association may be weakened as subjects smoke fewer cigarettes per day leading up to the target quit date. In fact, in studies we have conducted thus far, the reduction in cigarettes per day and craving during the 2 weeks of pre-cessation NRT were better predictors of subsequent smoking abstinence than was the reduction in ratings of the subjective rewarding properties of cigarettes (unpublished data). However, it is likely that an attenuation of reward leads to reduced smoking; as discussed above, if smokers space cigarettes farther apart, the rewarding effects of smoking may be maintained because each cigarette will be smoked after a greater degree of deprivation than when smoking occurs at the usual rate. Nonetheless, the reduced nicotine reward initially obtained from smoking while receiving NRT may be important in leading to a reduced frequency of smoking, and ultimately to a weakening of the association between environmental stimuli and smoking behavior.

It may be difficult in practice to disentangle the effects of weakening the association between external environmental cues and smoking behavior from the effects of weakening the association between smoking and obtaining a rewarding effect. As mentioned above, studies controlling the frequency of smoking during the pre-quit NRT treatment might be informative. If the frequency of smoking is held constant (e.g., by appropriate instructions), then one could test the hypothesis that the therapeutic effect of pre-cessation NRT depends on weakening the stimulus–response association between environmental cues and smoking behavior. According to this hypothesis, one would predict that no enhancement in quit rates will be observed if the rate of smoking is maintained at baseline levels. In contrast, if breaking the association between smoking behavior and obtaining a rewarding effect from nicotine is the critical element in enhancing quit rates, then the usual therapeutic effect should be obtained even when rates of smoking leading up to the target quit date are held constant. The therapeutic effect of pre-cessation NRT might actually be enhanced because the number of "extinction" trials would be greater than when subjects decrease their smoking rates during the pre-cessation period.

Varenicline

Cigarette reward may be attenuated not only by administering nicotine itself prior to a quit-smoking date, but also by administration of other nicotinic agents. One such agent is varenicline, a nicotinic receptor partial agonist. Varenicline activates – but also blocks – nicotinic receptors of the $\alpha 4\beta 2$ subtype (Coe et al., 2005), and in addition it may act on other subtypes of nicotinic receptors (Mihalak, Carroll, & Luetje, 2006). Varenicline has received FDA approval as a smoking cessation pharmacotherapy; treatment guidelines recommend initiating treatment 1 week before a target quit date (Lam & Patel, 2007). Although the usual rationale provided is that this period is required to attain therapeutic blood levels of varenicline, the discussion in the previous section suggests that it may be important for the patient to experience an attenuation of the rewarding effects of cigarettes for some time while on varenicline treatment. Whether quit rates could be further improved by prolonging the pre-cessation treatment period beyond 1 week has not been determined.

It is also not yet known how varenicline treatment would compare with NRT when NRT is initiated before the target quit-smoking date. The odds ratio of success for varenicline relative to placebo is approximately 4:1 (Oncken et al., 2006), which is similar to the estimated effect of pre-cessation NRT (abstinence rates twice that of conventional NRT, which in turn doubles abstinence rates relative to placebo).

Unfortunately, a clinical trial directly comparing varenicline and pre-cessation NRT would be very costly, potentially requiring well over a thousand participants to achieve adequate statistical power to detect what may be a small difference in efficacy.

Pre-cessation Mecamylamine Treatment

Might there be other strategies for clearly augmenting success rates beyond pre-cessation NRT? We think there is such a strategy: administering a nicotinic receptor antagonist concurrently with NRT. In a large-scale Phase III clinical trial, the nicotinic receptor antagonist mecamylamine, used in combination with pre-cessation NRT, was found to be more efficacious than pre-cessation NRT alone (Rose, 2006). It may be noted that not all trials have been sufficiently powered to detect the modest increment in abstinence rates obtained when mecamylamine is added to pre-quit NRT (Glover et al., 2007). However, given that the comparison condition of pre-cessation (plus post-cessation) NRT is possibly twice as effective as standard NRT, it is significant that combined pre-cessation nicotine + pre-cessation mecamylamine treatment surpassed this highly active "control" condition.

Pre-cessation Bupropion Treatment

Bupropion is another approved smoking cessation treatment, and like varenicline, it is recommended that treatment be initiated at least 1 week before the target quit date (Martinez-Raga, Keaney, Sutherland, Perez-Galvez, & Strang, 2003). Again, the rationale often given is that this period is needed to achieve therapeutic drug levels. However, a behavioral extinction effect may also be operative, whereby bupropion could attenuate nicotine reinforcement. This attenuation of nicotine reinforcement might result from two mechanisms (Damaj et al., 2004): first, bupropion has been shown to block nicotinic receptors, and thus its effects might to some extent resemble those of varenicline or mecamylamine; second, bupropion has dopaminergic and possibly noradrenergic stimulant effects that could substitute for the psychological stimulant or reward-enhancing effect (Mays et al., 2007) that is sought by some smokers, thereby inducing partial satiation. The role of extinction in pre-cessation bupropion treatment could be evaluated by studies that vary the duration of pre-cessation treatment or the number of cigarettes smoked during this period.

Nicotine Vaccine

We turn now to nicotine vaccines, which several companies are attempting to develop as smoking cessation treatments. The idea behind a nicotine vaccine is simple: if nicotine can be intercepted before reaching the brain, its reinforcing effects should be attenuated. This, in turn, should facilitate smoking cessation, analogous to the treatments discussed above for reducing nicotine reinforcement. Nicotine is not an antigen; by itself it is not thought to elicit an antibody reaction; however, by conjugating nicotine with various molecules that are recognized by the immune system as "foreign," an antibody response can be elicited (LeSage et al., 2006).

Although the strategy behind a nicotine vaccine appears straightforward, one puzzle is that the amount of antibody likely to be present in the blood stream is relatively small compared to the dose of nicotine inhaled from a cigarette. That is, animal studies have reported an antibody concentration on the order of 1 μM (Heading, 2007). In a human smoker, this antibody concentration, assuming a plasma volume of 2.75 l, is only sufficient to bind approximately 445 μg nicotine, less than the dose delivered in five puffs of a typical cigarette. It is puzzling that a nicotine antibody in such concentrations would be effective, for if an antibody has extremely high affinity for nicotine (e.g., an equilibrium binding constant of less than 50 nM), then the antibody would quickly become saturated with nicotine from the first few puffs of smoke. In that case nicotine inhaled from subsequent puffs of cigarette smoke will simply "bypass" the saturated antibody and reach the brain just as quickly as it would without vaccination.

A possible resolution to this puzzle is that nicotine antibodies might have only moderate affinity for nicotine, thereby avoiding saturation of antibody binding sites. In this case, the nicotine in arterial blood will partition between an antibody-bound and an unbound (free) fraction. The reduction in free nicotine concentration will reduce the rate at which nicotine crosses the blood–brain barrier. Then, as the nicotine bound to the antibody dissociates and slowly enters the brain, antibody molecules will be freed up to bind to additional nicotine; the same process could be repeated for each puff (or cigarette). Ultimately, significant amounts of nicotine may reach the brain; however, by reducing the rate with which nicotine enters the brain, reinforcement for smoking may be attenuated.

The feasibility of nicotine vaccines has been supported in Phase II clinical trials (e.g., Hatsukami et al., 2005). In addition, the rationale is indirectly supported by recent studies of the kinetics of nicotine inhaled into the lungs. In a recent study of lung-to-brain nicotine in our laboratory, the radiotracer C-11 nicotine was added to the tobacco of a cigarette. After inhalation of a single puff of smoke, the radioactive tracer was detected in the lung, and subsequently in the brain. We found that brain nicotine levels peaked approximately 1–2 minutes after inhalation (Rose et al., 2006) – much longer than the 7-seconds frequently quoted based on early speculations (Russell & Feyerabend, 1978). The reason for this delay is that nicotine distributes into lung tissue and some time is required for it to be eliminated into the bloodstream (Brewer, Roberts, & Rowell, 2004; Rose, Lokitz et al., 2006). The slower-than-expected kinetics is good news for the potential efficacy of nicotine vaccines, because it allows more time for the vaccine to bind a portion of the nicotine before it reaches the brain. Indeed, perhaps individual differences in lung retention of nicotine could be used to predict which smokers will respond favorably to vaccine therapy. Future research is needed to evaluate this possibility.

Tailoring Smoking Cessation Treatment Based on Genetics

It has been known for some time that quit-smoking success has a substantial heritable component, on the order of 50% (Xian, Scherrer, Madden, Lyons, Tsuang, True, & Eisen, 2003). However, until now the specific genetic underpinnings of this component have not been identified. Recently, a genome-wide association study has identified genetic variants associated with quit-smoking success. In this study, conducted as a collaboration between our research center and the laboratory of Dr. George Uhl at the National Institute on Drug Abuse (NIDA), many genes were found to contribute to quitting outcome (Uhl, Liu, Drgon, Johnson, Walther, & Rose, 2007). Each gene had a small influence, but cumulatively accounted for a substantial fraction of the variance in clinical outcome.

This genetic information can be applied to both research and treatment settings. In clinical research, using genotype as a covariate in clinical trials will increase the power to detect the effects of pharmacotherapy or other treatments. In clinical practice, genetic information might have the following applications: (1) more intensive treatment can be given to smokers who have a high genetic liability for relapse; (2) treatment can be tailored further by ascertaining which smokers are likely to respond more favorably to specific treatments such as NRT, varenicline or bupropion. Some preliminary findings in this regard have been reported using a candidate gene approach (Lerman et al., 2006), and genome-wide information should prove even more useful; and (3) information about the protein products of the genes identified may lead to novel interventions. For example, several genes identified as predictors of quitting outcome involved cell adhesion molecules (e.g., cadherin 13) that may be involved in synapse formation and memory-like processes (Uhl et al., 2007). This finding is in accord with the view that cigarette addiction involves learning and memory processes such as reinforcement of cues and behavior; quitting smoking involves cue extinction, a form of learning, and also involves learning new behaviors and coping techniques to substitute for smoking. Additional targets for smoking cessation treatment development will hopefully be identified from a better understanding of these genetic mechanisms.

Conclusion

We have reviewed several recent innovative smoking treatment approaches and the potential mechanisms underlying their efficacy. We have seen that learning theory, receptor mechanisms, pharmacokinetics, and genetic influences all have demonstrable implications for treatment development. If the next 10 years of research prove as fruitful as the previous ones, we can anticipate a growing armamentarium of ever more successful treatments to combat cigarette addiction.

Acknowledgments This work was supported by an unrestricted grant on adult smoking cessation provided by Philip Morris USA, Inc. The author appreciates helpful suggestions on an earlier draft of this manuscript from Frederique Behm and Alexey Mukhin, M.D., Ph.D.

Financial Disclosure

The author receives patent royalties based on sales of some nicotine patches, and also owns patent rights to combination agonist–antagonist treatments.

References

Bouton, M. E., & Swartzentruber D. (1991). Sources of relapse after extinction in pavlovian and instrumental learning. *Clinical Psychology Review, 11*, 123–140.

Brewer, B. G., Roberts, A. M., & Rowell, P. P. (2004). Short-term distribution of nicotine in the rat lung. *Drug and Alcohol Dependence, 75*, 193–198.

Cardenas, L., Busto, U. E., MacDonald, A., & Corrigall, W. A. (2002). Nicotine patches and the subjective effects of cigarette smoking: A pilot study. *Canadian Journal of Clinical Pharmacology, 9*, 175–182.

Coe, J. W., Brooks, P. R., Vetelino, M. G., Wirtz, M. C., Arnold, E. P., Huang, J., et al. (2005). Varenicline: An alpha4beta2 nicotinic receptor partial agonist for smoking cessation. *Journal of Medicinal Chemistry, 48*, 3474–3477.

Damaj, M. I., Carroll, F. I., Eaton, J. B., Navarro, H. A., Blough, B. E., Mirza, S., et al. (2004). Enantioselective effects of hydroxy metabolites of bupropion on behavior and on function of monoamine transporters and nicotinic receptors. *Molecular Pharmacology, 66*, 675–682.

Donny, E. C., Houtsmuller, E., & Stitzer, M. L. (2007). Smoking in the absence of nicotine: Behavioral, subjective and physiological effects over 11 days. *Addiction, 102*, 324–334.

Glover, E. D., Laflin, M. T., Schuh, K. J., Schuh, L. M., Nides, M., Christen, A. G., et al. (2007). A randomized, controlled trial to assess the efficacy and safety of a transdermal delivery system of nicotine/mecamylamine in cigarette smokers. *Addiction, 102*, 795–802.

Hatsukami, D. K., Rennard, S., Jorenby, D., Fiore, M., Koopmeiners, J., de Vos, A., et al. (2005). Safety and immunogenicity of a nicotine conjugate vaccine in current smokers. *Clinical Pharmacology & Therapeutics, 78*, 456–467.

Heading, C. E. (2007). Drug evaluation: Cyt-002-nicqb, a therapeutic vaccine for the treatment of nicotine addiction. *Current Opinion in Investigational Drugs, 8*, 71–77.

Henningfield, J. E., & Jasinski, D. R. (1988). Pharmacologic basis for nicotine replacement. In O. F. Pomerleau & C. S. Pomerleau (Eds.), *Nicotine replacement: A critical evaluation* (pp. 35–61). New York: Alan R. Liss, Inc.

Herrera, N., Franco, R., Herrera, L., Partidas, A., Rolando, R., & Fagerstrom, K. O. (1995). Nicotine gum, 2 and 4 mg, for nicotine dependence. A double-blind placebo-controlled trial within a behavior modification support program. *Chest, 108*, 447–451.

Ishida, M., & Papini, M. R. (2007). Massed trial overtraining effects on extinction and reversal performance in turtles (geoclemys reevesii). *The Quarterly Journal of Experimental Psychology Section B, 50*, 1–16.

Lam, S., & Patel, P. N. (2007). Varenicline: A selective alpha4beta2 nicotinic acetylcholine receptor partial agonist approved for smoking cessation. *Cardiology in Review, 15*, 154–161.

Lerman, C., Jepson, C., Wileyto, E. P., Epstein, L. H., Rukstalis, M., Patterson, F., et al. (2006). Role of functional genetic variation in the dopamine d2 receptor (drd2) in response to bupropion and nicotine replacement therapy for tobacco dependence: Results of two randomized clinical trials. *Neuropsychopharmacology, 31*, 231–242.

LeSage, M. G., Keyler, D. E., Hieda, Y., Collins, G., Burroughs, D., Le, C., et al. (2006). Effects of a nicotine conjugate vaccine on the acquisition and maintenance of nicotine self-administration in rats. *Psychopharmacology (Berl), 184*, 409–416.

Levin, E. D., Westman, E. C., Stein, R. M., Carnahan, E., Sanchez, M., Herman, S., et al. (1994). Nicotine skin patch treatment increases abstinence, decreases withdrawal symptoms and attenuates rewarding effects of smoking. *Journal of Clinical Psychopharmacolog, 14*, 41–49.

Martinez-Raga, J., Keaney, F., Sutherland, G., Perez-Galvez, B., & Strang, J. (2003). Treatment of nicotine dependence with bupropion sr: Review of its efficacy, safety and pharmacological profile. *Addiction Biology, 8*, 13–21.

Mays, K. L., Levin, M. E., Bak, K. M., Palmatier, M. I., Liu, X., Caggiula, A. R.,et al. (2007). Nicotine and bupropion have similar effects on responding for reinforcing non-drug stimuli. *Presented at the 13th annual meeting of the Society for Research on Nicotine and Tobacco, February 21–24, Austin, Texas.*

Mihalak, K. B., Carroll, F. I., & Luetje, C. W. (2006). Varenicline is a partial agonist at alpha4beta2 and a full agonist at alpha7 neuronal nicotinic receptors. *Molecular Pharmacology, 70*, 801–805.

Oncken, C., Gonzales, D., Nides, M., Rennard, S., Watsky, E., Billing, C. B., et al. (2006). Efficacy and safety of the novel selective nicotinic acetylcholine receptor partial agonist, varenicline, for smoking cessation. *Archives of Internal Medicine, 166*, 1571–1577.

Orona, E., Foster, K., Lambert, R. W., & Gabriel, M. (1982). Cingulate cortical and anterior thalamic neuronal correlates of the overtraining reversal effect in rabbits. *Behavioural Brain Research, 4*, 133–154.

Palmatier, M. I., Matteson, G. L., Black, J. J., Liu, X., Caggiula, A. R., Craven, L., et al. (2007). The reinforcement enhancing effects of nicotine depend on the incentive value of non-drug reinforcers and increase with repeated drug injections. *Drug and Alcohol Dependence, 89*, 52–59.

Peters, M. J., & Morgan, L. C. (2002). The pharmacotherapy of smoking cessation. *Medical Journal of Australia, 176*, 486–490.

Rose, J. E. (2006). Nicotine and nonnicotine factors in cigarette addiction. *Psychopharmacology (Berl), 184*, 274–285.

Rose, J. E., & Behm, F. M. (2004). Extinguishing the rewarding value of smoke cues: Pharmacological and behavioral treatments. *Nicotine & Tobacco Research, 6*, 523–532.

Rose, J. E., & Levin, E. D. (1991). Inter-relationships between conditioned and primary reinforcement in the maintenance of cigarette smoking. *British Journal of Addiction, 86*, 605–609.

Rose, J. E., Westman, E. C., Behm, F. M., Johnson, M. P., & Goldberg, J. S. (1999). Blockade of smoking satisfaction using the peripheral nicotinic antagonist trimethaphan. *Pharmacology, Biochemistry and Behavior, 62*, 165–172.

Rose, J. E., Behm, F. M., Westman, E. C., & Kukovich, P. (2006). Pre-cessation treatment with nicotine skin patch facilitates smoking cessation. *Nicotine & Tobacco Research, 8*, 89–101.

Rose, J. E., Lokitz, S. J., Garg, S., Turkington, T. G., Minton, R. C., Smith, H. C., et al. (2006). Highly dependent cigarette smokers show slower brain uptake of nicotine than less dependent smokers. *Presented at the 35th annual meeting of the Society for Neuroscience, Atlanta, Georgia, October 14–18, 2006.*

Rose, J. E., Herskovic, J. E., Behm, F. M., & Westman, E. C. (2007). Pre-cessation treatment with nicotine patch. Significantly increases abstinence rates relative to conventional treatment. *Presented at the 13th annual meeting of the Society for Research on Nicotine and Tobacco, February 21–24, Austin, Texas.*

Russell, M. A. H., & Feyerabend, C. (1978). Cigarette smoking: A dependence on high-nicotine boli. *Drug Metabolism Reviews, 8*, 29–57.

Schuurmans, M. M., Diacon, A. H., van Biljon, X., & Bolliger, C. T. (2004). Effect of pre-treatment with nicotine patch on withdrawal symptoms and abstinence rates in smokers subsequently quitting with the nicotine patch: A randomized controlled trial. *Addiction, 99*, 634–640.

Shiffman, S., Ferguson, S. G., & Gwaltney, C. J. (2006). Immediate hedonic response to smoking lapses: Relationship to smoking relapse, and effects of nicotine replacement therapy. *Psychopharmacology (Berl), 184*, 608–618.

Shiffman, S., Scharf, D. M., Shadel, W. G., Gwaltney, C. J., Dang, Q., Paton, S. M., et al. (2006). Analyzing milestones in smoking cessation: Illustration in a nicotine patch trial in adult smokers. *Journal of Consulting and Clinical Psychology, 74*, 276–285.

Uhl, G. R., Liu, Q.-R., Drgon, T., Johnson, C., Walther, D., & Rose, J. E. (2007). Molecular genetics of nicotine dependence and abstinence: Whole genome association using 520,000 SNPs. *BMC Genetics, 8*, 1–11.

Valles, R., Rocha, A., & Nation, J. R. (2006). The effects of acquisition training schedule on extinction and reinstatement of cocaine self-administration in male rats. *Experimental and Clinical Psychopharmacology, 14*, 245–253.

Xian, H., Scherrer, J. F., Madden, P. A., Lyons, M. J., Tsuang, M., True, W. R., et al. (2003). The heritability of failed smoking cessation and nicotine withdrawal in twins who smoked and attempted to quit. *Nicotine & Tobacco Research, 5*, 245–254.

Chapter 9
Sex Differences in Nicotine Reinforcement and Reward: Influences on the Persistence of Tobacco Smoking

Kenneth A. Perkins

Introduction

Current treatments for smoking cessation show limited efficacy, despite the development of new medications, with none producing long-term quit rates of more than 30% in formal clinical trials (Piasecki & Baker, 2001). In an effort to improve cessation, research over the past decade has paid more attention to genetic or other individual differences in smoking persistence and response to treatments (e.g., pharmacogenetics; Munafo, Shields, Berrettini, Patterson, & Lerman, 2005). The focus of this chapter will be on differences in smoking persistence and response to medication as a function of perhaps the most prominent of all individual differences, a smoker's sex. As will be discussed in detail, findings from our laboratory and elsewhere indicate that, compared to the smoking behavior of men, the smoking behavior of women is influenced less by nicotine and more by non-nicotine factors. These results have implications for clinical research and may help explain why women have greater difficulty quitting in general (e.g., Borrelli, Papandonatos, Spring, Hitsman, & Niaura, 2004; Fortmann & Killen, 1994; Scharf & Shiffman, 2004) and with nicotine replacement therapy in particular (Cepeda-Benito, Reynoso, & Erath, 2004; Perkins & Scott, in press Wetter, Kenford, Smith, Fiore, Jorenby, & Baker, 1999). They also suggest other directions for clinical research aimed at improving cessation outcome in women smokers.

Note that it is almost certainly the case that men and women do not differ on most effects of nicotine, such as its physiological, cognitive, or psychomotor effects (Benowitz & Hatsukami, 1998). Rather, the research literature indicates that men and women differ in sensitivity to a relatively specific but very important area of responses to nicotine, that of nicotine's reinforcing and rewarding effects. Reinforcement pertains to self-administration of the drug as assessed by several procedures (ad libitum, or ad lib, consumption, fixed or variable ratio schedule of

K.A. Perkins
Western Psychiatric Institute and Clinic, University of Pittsburgh School of Medicine, 3811 O'Hara Street, Pittsburgh, PA 15213, USA
e-mail: perkinska@upmc.edu

R.A. Bevins, A.R. Caggiula (eds.), *The Motivational Impact of Nicotine and its Role in Tobacco Use*, DOI: 10.1007/978-0-387-78748-0_9, © Springer Science+Business Media, LLC 2009

reinforcement, progressive ratio, choice of active versus placebo substance, etc.). Reward is less precisely defined but refers to the hedonic value of the substance, typically assessed in humans via self-reported "liking," "satisfying," "good drug effects," etc. (Everitt & Robbins, 2005). (Animal studies necessarily employ behavioral indices such as conditioned place preference or perhaps intracranial self-stimulation; see Lerman, Perkins & Gould, in press).

By reinforcement and reward, we are *not* referring to craving, withdrawal, mood, or other characteristics of the drug user's subjective or behavioral state. The latter responses can be distinguished from the former in that the latter can be assessed in the absence of drug availability or indeed any history of drug use at all, while assessment of the former can only be done in the context of substance use. While craving, withdrawal, and mood may, or may not, relate to drug reinforcement and reward, they are certainly not the same thing as reinforcement or reward and should be kept distinct. Thus, while reliable sex differences in these various smoking-related subjective states may exist, such potential differences do not directly bear on the central thesis of this chapter, that men and women differ in the degree to which nicotine versus non-nicotine factors influence smoking reinforcement and reward.

Clinical Implications of Sex Differences in Factors Promoting Smoking Persistence

Identification of consistent sex differences in the factors that maintain smoking persistence or in responses to particular treatments has potentially important implications for clinical practice. First, if women have greater overall difficulty quitting smoking, this sex difference indicates the presence of a very large subpopulation of smokers (nearly half) requiring greater help to quit. Most controlled studies on a variety of treatments do tend to show poorer clinical outcome in women versus men attempting to quit (e.g., Borrelli et al., 2004; Fortmann & Killen, 1994; Scharf & Shiffman, 2004; Wetter et al., 1999). Examining population-based data on current versus former smokers over the age of 34, we observe that the "quit ratio," the ratio of former smokers to ever smokers, is lower in women versus men (55.2% versus 59.2%, respectively, based on 2002 national data presented in Rodu & Cole, 2007). This difference translates to about a million fewer women who have quit smoking, compared to the number one would expect if women quit at the same rate as men. Second, poorer response to certain treatments in women versus men would highlight the inadequacy of these treatments, further indicating a need for improved therapies. Moreover, sex differences in response to particular treatments may reveal important differences between men and women in basic mechanisms that maintain smoking and suggest new directions for research on the etiology of dependence as well as on treatment development.

Even if there were no sex differences in smoking persistence and treatment response, increases in quitting success among women due to improved treatments would arguably have greater public health benefit than the same degree of increase in quitting success among men. Smoking consistently produces greater risks in the primary smoking-related illnesses among women than men, including lung cancer (International Early Lung Cancer Action Program Investigators, 2006), myocardial infarction (MI, or heart attack; Prescott, Hippe, Schnohr, Ole Hein, & Vestbo, 1998), and deterioration in lung function due to smoking (Dransfield, Davis, Gerald, & Bailey, 2006), perhaps explaining women's greater risk of chronic obstructive pulmonary disease (COPD). These diseases constitute the three most common causes of premature morbidity and mortality due to smoking, accounting for the vast majority of the 440,000 deaths annually in the US (Centers for Disease Control and Prevention, 2005). Furthermore, smoking in women induces health risks not observed in men, such as risks to fetal development in pregnant women who smoke, including infant mortality from several causes and decreased infant lung function (DiFranza, Aligne, & Weitzman, 2004). Maternal smoking, perhaps more than paternal smoking, is also associated with increased risk of the offspring becoming a smoker (Buka, Shenassa, & Niaura, 2003). Thus, developing treatments that improve the quit rates in women smokers would have a larger impact in reducing the total adverse health toll due to smoking than the same improvement in quit rates among men, although treatments that are more effective with all smokers are sorely needed.

Possible Sources of Sex Differences in Smoking Reinforcement

Before reviewing evidence of sex differences in smoking reinforcement and reward, it is instructive to consider the possible sources of such differences. For the most part, any consistent individual difference in drug response is likely due to pharmacokinetic or pharmacodynamic factors, although other sources of sex differences in drug response are possible.

Pharmacokinetic

A difference between groups in response to nicotine administration could be due to pharmacokinetic differences, such that one group has slower or faster absorption or clearance of the drug compared to others. Thus, a smaller reinforcing effect of nicotine in women versus men could be due to women simply having lower blood levels of the drug following administration of a given dose. Recent research does suggest that women may have faster clearance rates of nicotine than men, by about 10%, especially if they also use oral contraceptives (Benowitz, Lessov-Schlaggar, Swan, & Jacob, 2006). However, this difference is unlikely to account for sex differences in the acutely reinforcing effects of nicotine intake for at least two reasons. First, the half-life of nicotine clearance is about 2 hours, while the reinforcing effects of nicotine are usually measured over briefer periods of time (e.g., minutes). Second, different nicotine blood levels between men and women following dose administration would result in different magnitudes of response on *all* measures of nicotine effects. So, in addition to lower reinforcing effects of nicotine, women would also demonstrate lower heart rate, psychomotor, mood, and all other responses to nicotine. Such broad-based sex differences in effects of nicotine have not been seen in studies of controlled nicotine administration (e.g., Benowitz & Hatsukami, 1998; Perkins, Gerlach, Broge et al., 2001).

Pharmacodynamic

Differences in the reinforcing effects of nicotine could also be due to pharmacodynamic factors, or differences in tissue sensitivity to a given blood level of nicotine. Controlling for pharmacokinetic factors, people may differ in how sensitive their brain receptors, or other sites of drug action, are to the drug. Because different drug effects typically result from actions of the drug at different brain or body sites, differential sensitivity to nicotine between sites could explain the selective sex difference in sensitivity to nicotine's reinforcing and rewarding effects in the face of virtually no differences in other effects of nicotine, as noted previously. Differences in pharmacodynamic effects of drug are determined by manipulating the drug dose and keeping all other aspects the same (e.g., method of administration, expectations for drug). Considerable evidence, outlined later in this chapter, suggests that women are less sensitive than men to pharmacodynamic effects of nicotine related to reinforcement and reward.

Non-pharmacological

A third, frequently overlooked, explanation for individual differences in drug reinforcement could stem from differences in sensitivity to *non*-pharmacological factors involved in drug use. Drug use of all kinds involves behavioral rituals and accompanying environmental stimuli that can become conditioned to the pharmacological influences of the drug. In tobacco smoking, for example, pulling out a cigarette and lighting it is followed by the sight of a lit cigarette and the olfactory/taste sensations from inhaling the smoke. Such stimuli are often referred to as "cues", or discriminative stimuli for nicotine via cigarette smoking. Less obvious cues also include environmental contextual factors, such as familiar smoking settings (e.g., favorite bar, being with a smoking friend; see Conklin, 2006). Along with cues, which can be viewed as non-verbal information about drug availability, the non-pharmacological factors can include other aspects of drug use, including verbal information about drug availability (i.e., being told about the drug content of a substance) that elicits expectancies for certain drug effects (Perkins, Sayette, Conklin, & Caggiula, 2003).

Consequently, even if men and women did not differ in pharmacokinetic or pharmacodynamic factors, differential responsivity to the conditioned stimuli accompanying nicotine intake via smoking could result in sex differences in reinforcement and reward. Non-pharmacological aspects could include stimuli other than verbal or non-verbal information about drug availability, such as social modeling influences (e.g., watching someone else smoke) or unconditioned effects of substance use (e.g., smoke effects on peripheral sensations). Non-pharmacological influences are examined by manipulating those influences while keeping constant nicotine dosing (i.e., pharmacodynamics). Less research has examined sex differences in non-pharmacological factors in tobacco smoking, but some research suggests that women are more sensitive than men to certain non-pharmacological effects of smoking (e.g., Perkins et al., 2001). Those findings will also be discussed.

Gender

Finally, a fourth potential explanation for sex differences in nicotine reinforcement and reward concerns the influence of "gender," or constraints on behavior due to cultural expectations about sex roles. Gender influences are likely responsible for the fact that tobacco use in a given society is almost always adopted first by men, then by women. Such influences are probably important in explaining why smoking prevalence remains much lower among women than men in most developing nations (Lopez, Collishaw, & Piha, 1994). However, virtually no controlled laboratory research has examined "gender" influences on smoking reinforcement and reward, and this chapter will therefore not address this possibility. It is worth noting that such influences may be indirectly examined by assessing cross-species consistency in nicotine's reinforcing effects, as sex differences observed in both humans and non-humans would suggest a lack of culturally-specific influences.

Reduced Sensitivity to Nicotine Reinforcement and Reward in Women Versus Men

Beginning in the mid-1980s, we conducted research on a wide variety of acute effects of nicotine per se, administered via nasal spray in order to mimic rapid uptake of nicotine as with tobacco inhalation but in more controlled fashion. We first examined the effects of nicotine on energy balance (resting metabolism, food intake, etc.) to understand the influence of nicotine on body weight regulation (see Perkins, 1993). We then explored the acute effects of nicotine on physiological, psychomotor, and self-reported mood responses to characterize acute and chronic tolerance to nicotine, believed to be a key feature of dependence (USDHHS, 1988). We routinely compared effects between men and women because of reports suggesting that women were *more* sensitive than men to nicotine (e.g., Silverstein, Feld, & Kozlowski, 1980; Grunberg, Winders, & Wewers, 1991). However, sex differences were almost never apparent in any of this research. Only when we began to study nicotine reinforcement and reward in the early 1990 s did we start to observe consistent and robust sex differences, with women less sensitive than men to manipulations of nicotine dose exposure, indicating reduced pharmacodynamic effects of nicotine. This research on reinforcement and reward generally followed two approaches in assessing sensitivity to nicotine: (1) the direct effects of nicotine on self-administration behavior and reward ratings, and (2) the influence of nicotine dose pre-treatment on subsequent self-administration of nicotine or smoking behavior.

Direct Effects of Nicotine on Self-administration Behavior and Reward Ratings

Sex differences in nicotine reinforcement are perhaps most directly shown by differences in the degree to which nicotine influences self-administration behavior. Since the 1980s, research has shown that humans will self-administer nicotine via novel forms (i.e., other than tobacco smoking), such as via intravenous infusion (Henningfield & Goldberg, 1983). These findings contributed to the view that nicotine was the key psychoactive ingredient in tobacco that made tobacco dependence-producing (USDHHS, 1988).

Ad Lib Self-administration of Nicotine Nasal Spray

The clearest demonstration from our laboratory that nicotine is reinforcing in humans came from a relatively early quasi-clinical study using our experimental nicotine nasal spray and a placebo spray (Perkins et al., 1996). Smokers wanting to quit right away were recruited and received group-based counseling before their quit day. They were then randomized to receive either the nicotine or the placebo spray to use ad lib during their first week after quitting. Subjects returned to the clinic every day during this first week after quitting to provide biochemical validation of abstinence via expired-air CO and to exchange their spray bottle from the prior day for a new one, which allowed us to measure the amount of spray used in the prior 24 hours. Although participants were smokers wanting to quit, the main goal of the study was not to see if nicotine spray aided abstinence but rather to determine whether nicotine nasal spray would be self-administered by humans; smokers wanting to quit provided an appropriate sample with which to study this question over an extended period (i.e., 4 full days in the natural environment, rather than a few hours in the laboratory). At that time, only a few studies had demonstrated nicotine reinforcement in humans, and no prior study had demonstrated nicotine reinforcement via nasal spray. Only subjects who maintained smoking abstinence throughout the week of spray access were included in analyses because spray use in those who continued smoking would be difficult to interpret. Note also that the active spray provided small, "puff" sized doses of nicotine per spray, just 1.5 μg/kg (or about 0.1 mg, versus 0.5 mg in the commercially available Nicotrol[R] spray marketed as an NRT for smoking cessation).

As shown in the left-hand side of Fig. 9.1, self-administration behavior was similar between the nicotine and placebo spray groups on day 2 (i.e., the day after their quit day), the first full day of spray access, but was maintained across days only in the nicotine group and not in the placebo group. When we examined spray self-administration as a function of sex, we were very surprised to see that nicotine spray use was twice that of placebo spray use among men, but spray use was similar

SPRAY USE

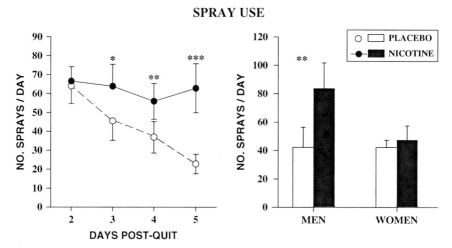

Fig. 9.1 *Left*: Mean ± SEM number of sprays self-administered across each of the 4 days of access by participants randomized to nicotine (*n* = 17) versus placebo (*n* = 18) spray who maintained continuous abstinence during the quit week. *Right*: Mean ± SEM number of sprays self-administered daily by continuously abstinent men versus women randomized to nicotine versus placebo spray. * $p < 0.05$, ** $p < 0.01$, and*** $p < 0.001$ for differences between the groups. Reprinted with permission from Figs. 1 and 2 in Perkins, Grobe, D'Amico, Fonte, Wilson, & Stiller (1996) Low-dose nicotine nasal spray use and effects during initial smoking cessation. *Experimental and Clinical Psychopharmacology, 4*, 157–165, published by the American Psychological Association

between nicotine and placebo among women, as shown in the right-hand side of Fig. 9.1. Because subjects were abstinent smokers, this nicotine self-administration may be an example of negative reinforcement, to relieve the aversive symptoms of tobacco withdrawal, rather than positive reinforcement. Nevertheless, these findings demonstrate that nicotine per se is reinforcing under these conditions, but only in men and not in women.

Nicotine Versus Placebo Spray Choice

We have since used a choice procedure to examine factors that influence nicotine self-administration, including sex differences. In this choice procedure (Perkins, Grobe, Weiss, Fonte, & Caggiula, 1996), subjects are presented in blind fashion with two identically-appearing substances (e.g., nasal sprays, cigarettes) that vary in drug content and are labeled in a way to distinguish them from each other (e.g., "spray A" or "spray B"). They are then instructed to self-administer a set number of substance "uses" (sprays, puffs, etc.) but are free to choose how many will come from the two substances—all from one, all from the other, or a mix of the two. The proportion of choices from the substance with active drug indicates the relative reinforcing value of the drug. In a study of nicotine (2.5 μg/kg per spray) versus placebo nasal spray choice, we found that choice of nicotine spray was greater in smokers versus nonsmokers, as expected (Perkins, Sanders, D'Amico, & Wilson, 1997). Moreover, nicotine choice tended to be greater in male versus female smokers, as well as nonsignificantly greater in male versus female *non*smokers. This latter, unexpected observation suggested that the sex difference in the relative reinforcing effects of nicotine was apparent from virtually the very first experience with the drug and did not require chronic exposure to it, as in dependent smokers.

These results are a bit difficult to interpret because nicotine spray choice was not above 50% (i.e., above chance levels, to show absolute reinforcement) for most nonsmokers, suggesting that greater nicotine choice in men may reflect less aversiveness rather than greater absolute reinforcement per se. (See Perkins, 2004 for more on how procedural details can influence the specific choice behavior obtained.) Yet, the findings are consistent with the studies of nicotine reinforcement in smokers.

Reinforcing and Rewarding Effects of Nicotine Dose via Cigarettes

To ascertain whether the prior findings with nicotine via spray generalize to the most important form of nicotine use, cigarette smoking, we examined sex differences in the influence of nicotine on the rewarding and reinforcing effects of cigarette smoking (Perkins, Jacobs, Sanders, & Caggiula, 2002). Male and female smokers were given controlled exposure in blind fashion to a "moderate" nicotine cigarette (actually their preferred brand, yield at least 0.7 mg nicotine) and "low" nicotine cigarette (0.1 mg), with each presented on a different day (i.e., only one brand available at a time). They then rated the administered cigarette for its reward value ("liking") and other characteristics, and were given access to additional puffs on a progressive ratio schedule to determine reinforcement. Interactions of sex by dose were observed on most of these measures, as dose effects typically were not significant for women but were for men, as shown in Fig. 9.2. These results indicated that the prior sex differences in nicotine reinforcement, whether by ad lib self-administration in the natural environment or in the choice procedure within the laboratory, were not specific to the nasal spray form of administration but were present with cigarette smoking reinforcement as well.

Influence of Nicotine Pre-treatment on Subsequent Nicotine or Smoking Reinforcement

Other evidence for sex differences in sensitivity to nicotine dose manipulations comes from studies that examined self-administration behavior, of either nasal spray or smoking, following pre-treatment with different doses of nicotine. Theoretically, the greater the dose of nicotine pre-treatment, the less subsequent nicotine self-administration behavior the smokers should engage in, if regulation of nicotine intake is an important factor driving their behavior, as is emphasized in defining dependence (e.g., USDHHS, 1988).

Smoking Reward and Perception

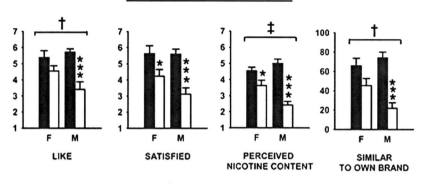

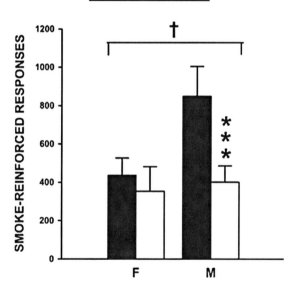

Fig. 9.2 Means ± SEM ratings for smoking reward ("liking," "satisfied") and perception ("perceived nicotine content," "similar to own brand,"; *top*) and responses on a progressive ratio procedure (smoking reinforcement, *bottom*) in men ($n = 17$) and women ($n = 13$) as a function of nicotine dose in cigarettes presented in blind fashion on separate days. ("Moderate" dose was subject's preferred brand, yield ≥ 0.7 mg; "low" was 0.1 mg brand.) *Horizontal brackets* indicate a significant dose by sex interaction. + $p < 0.05$, ++ $p < 0.01$. *Asterisks* as in Fig. 9.1. Reprinted from Figs. 1 and 2 in Perkins, Jacobs, Sanders, & Caggiula (2002) Sex differences in the subjective and reinforcing effects of cigarette nicotine dose. *Psychopharmacology, 163*, 194–201. With kind permission from Springer Science and Business Media

Ad lib Smoking Following Nicotine Spray Pre-treatment

In the first such study from our laboratory (Perkins, Grobe, Stiller, Fonte, & Goettler, 1992), smokers abstinent overnight participated in three sessions, in which nicotine by nasal spray (0, 15, or 30 μg/kg, comparable to about 0, 0.5, or 1 cigarette) was administered every 30 minutes for 2.5 hour. In between spray administrations, subjects were free to smoke their preferred brand in unblinded fashion, and the amount of ad lib smoking behavior was assessed. We hypothesized that the greater the pre-treatment dose of nicotine, the lesser is the subsequent smoking in an effort to regulate nicotine intake.

As shown in Fig. 9.3, we found that smoking behavior of men significantly declined as a function of nicotine pre-treatment in dose-dependent fashion, even with the intermediate dose (15 μg/kg), while the smoking behavior of women declined significantly only following the high dose (30 μg/kg) and not the intermediate dose. These results indicated that the smoking behavior of women was less sensitive to nicotine pre-treatment in that a larger pre-treatment dose was required in order to see a significant change in smoking behavior. The fact that nicotine pre-treatment was corrected for body weight ruled out typical body weight differences between men and women as an explanation for the differential sensitivity to the pre-treatment exposure. This study was the first from our laboratory clearly pointing to an important sex difference in nicotine reinforcement.

Nicotines Spray Choice Following Nicotine Patch Pre-treatment

We later examined this question using a different approach, pre-treating abstinent smokers with nicotine patch doses and observing the subsequent self-administration of nicotine spray, using the choice procedure described previously (Perkins, Fonte,

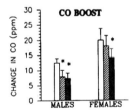 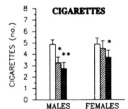 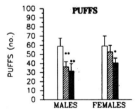

Fig. 9.3 Mean ± SEM carbon monoxide (CO) boost, and total number of cigarettes and puffs in male and female smokers ($n = 8$ each) across the 2.5 hour session as a function of administration of 0, 15, or 30 μg/kg nicotine via nasal spray every 30 minutes. * $p < 0.05$, ** $p < 0.01$ for difference from placebo. Reprinted from Perkins, Grobe, Stiller, Fonte, & Goettler (1992) Nasal spray nicotine replacement suppresses cigarette smoking desire and behavior. *Clinical Pharmacology & Therapeutics, 52,* 627–634, published by Mosby-Year Book, Inc

Meeker, White, & Wilson, 2001). Male and female smokers were pre-treated with 0 (double placebo), 14–21 mg (single active plus single placebo), or 28–42 mg (double active) nicotine via patches. (Whether or not single or double 14 mg patches versus the 21 mg patches were used was determined by subject's body weight in order to equate exposure between heavy and light smokers. As desired, differential dosing by patch based on body weight resulted in equal blood nicotine levels between men and women prior to the choice procedure.) After several hours of rest and other assessments to allow for absorption of nicotine from the patches, subjects chose between active (2.5 µg/kg) and placebo (0) nasal sprays. We hypothesized that nicotine choice would decrease as a function of increasing nicotine patch dose pre-treatment, again indicating nicotine regulation. Nicotine choice tended to decrease in men but was flat in women with increasing nicotine patch pre-treatment, suggesting that nicotine reinforcement was sensitive to the nicotine pre-treatment manipulation in men but not women. This sex difference was not significant, however, perhaps because of the small sample (eight men, eight women).

Other Relevant Findings

We have not conducted extensive research on potential mechanisms for the reduced sensitivity of women to the reinforcing effects of nicotine. However, in a program of research on the discriminative stimulus effects of nicotine by nasal spray, we sometimes, but not always, found that women were less sensitive than men to the influence of dose on these effects of nicotine (Perkins, 1999). Thus, if women are less sensitive to perceiving the interoceptive stimulus effects of nicotine (i.e., its effects in the brain), then it would seem logical that they might alter their self-administration behavior less in response to manipulations of nicotine dose.

On the other hand, little research with non-human species has examined sex differences in nicotine reinforcement, and at least one rat model of intravenous nicotine self-administration suggests that reinforcement may be at least as strong in female versus male rats (e.g., Chaudhri et al., 2005). It is worth noting that animal research indicates greater sensitivity of females to some effects of nicotine, such as anxiolytic effects (Cheeta, Irvine, Tucci, Sandhu, & File, 2001), but less sensitivity to other effects, such as analgesic effects (Damaj, 2001). Such varying patterns of differences may highlight the importance of the dependent measure of interest in considering sex differences in response to nicotine and other drugs, as we stated at the outset.

Sex Differences in Non-Pharmacological Influences of Smoking

All drugs of dependence contain non-pharmacological aspects of use that contribute to the reinforcing effects of the drug, particularly aspects such as the behavioral ritual (e.g., drug seeking and preparation) and sensory stimuli (e.g., sight and smell of cigarette smoke). It is sex differences in these aspects that account for a conundrum raised by the sex difference in nicotine reinforcement and reward described above. That is, if the sole sex difference in factors influencing smoking was that women were less sensitive than men to the reinforcing effects of nicotine, then it would almost certainly have to be the case that smoking prevalence is substantially lower in women than men. However, although prevalence has typically been lower in women than men, prevalence in the U.S. has declined over the past half century more slowly among women than men, such that it is now similar, about 19% versus 23%, respectively (Centers for Disease Control and Prevention, 2005). We believe that the reduced sensitivity of women to the reinforcing effects of nicotine is essentially countered by their *greater* sensitivity to reinforcement from *non-nicotine* effects of smoking. Such effects include, but probably are not limited to, conditioned reinforcement from environmental stimuli associated with smoking. Such stimuli can be viewed as providing information about drug availability, either in nonverbal form (e.g., drug cues) or verbal form (e.g., oral or written text conveying the drug contents of a substance). Thus, the greater sensitivity of women to non-nicotine effects of smoking balances their lower sensitivity to nicotine effects. Because both pharmacological and non-pharmacological aspects of smoking are intertwined when smokers smoke cigarettes, the sex differences in the relative contributions of these aspects to the behavior are obscured. Only when each aspect is isolated and manipulated is it possible to clearly see sex differences in factors promoting smoking.

Sex Differences in Sensitivity to Nonverbal Drug Information (Cues)

The most obvious cues for smoking are the immediate sensory stimuli of the sight and smell/taste of a lit cigarette. Such an in vivo cue has been widely used in research aimed at assessing self-report and physiological responses to smoking cues (Carter & Tiffany, 2001). Little research has systematically examined sex differences in reinforcement from such cues, but we have found in a few studies that their removal impacts smoking reward and reinforcement more in women than in men.

Smoking Reinforcement due to Lit Cigarette Cue

We tested the influence of a lit cigarette cue on smoking reinforcement in what may have been the first published study to explicitly examine smoking reinforcement (and not just self-report or physiological indices of craving) as a function of smoking-related cues (Perkins, Epstein, Grobe,& Fonte, 1994). Specifically, we compared responding on a simple computer task reinforced by cigarette puffs on four occasions in a 2 × 2 within-subjects design: in the presence versus absence of a lit cigarette cue, and following overnight smoking abstinence versus no abstinence. Puffs were available on five varying schedules of reinforcement, ranging from "easy" (VR4, or an average of four responses to earn one reinforcer) to "lean" (VR32, or an average of 32 responses to earn one reinforcer), with three intermediate schedules (VR8, VR12, and VR16). A comparison reinforcer of a small amount of money ($.02) was always available on a constant schedule (VR4). The presence of the cue increased smoke-reinforced responding but only under the leanest two schedules

(VR16, VR32), and not under the schedules that provided "easier" reinforcement of smoke puffs. Moreover, in post hoc analyses after publication, we found that this influence of the lit cigarette cue on the abstinent days tended to be greater in women (13.7 versus 50.6 responses for puffs under no cue versus cue, respectively, across the VR16 and VR32 schedules) than in men (45.9 versus 62.1, respectively).

Smoking Reward and Reinforcement after Blocking Smoking Cues

The prior study indicated the importance of an in vivo smoking cue (lit cigarette) to smoking reinforcement, but it was not clear whether this influence was due to the sight or the smell of the lit cigarette. Therefore, we examined further the notion of sex differences in responses to smoking cues in a study that sought to determine whether blocking the sight and/or the taste/smell of cigarette smoke would differentially influence smoking reward and reinforcement in women versus men (Perkins, Gerlach, Vender et al., 2001). Subjects participated in four sessions in a 2×2 within-subjects design involving: the blocking of the sight of a lit cigarette, blocking the taste/smell of a lit cigarette, blocking both, or blocking neither. Subjects, who were not abstinent before the session, smoked one of their preferred brand at baseline and waited one hour. They then took eight puffs via computer instructions on a "test" cigarette (actually another of their preferred brand but with markings covered over) under various blockade conditions. The sight of the cigarette was blocked by opaque goggles (versus the control procedure of clear goggles), while the taste/smell of the cigarette was blocked by nose clips placed so that they closed the nostrils (versus placed higher on the bridge of the nose).

As shown in Fig. 9.4, reward ratings of "liking" and "satisfying" of the puffs were significantly lower in women versus men due to the taste/smell blockade (sex by blockade interaction), regardless of the sight condition. Moreover, blocking of taste/smell, but not sight, significantly reduced subsequent ad lib smoking of the same "test" cigarette type in women but not in men. Thus, smoking reward and reinforcement were more sensitive to manipulations of cigarette smoke taste and smell in women than in men. These results highlighted the importance of olfactory and taste cues, which are often ignored in smoking research, but also showed the relative unimportance of the sight of a lit cigarette, a cue that is often given substantial attention in smoking research.

Sex Differences in Sensitivity to Verbal Drug Information (Expectancies)

In humans, information about the drug content of a substance can also be verbal. Verbal information is displayed in the environment in many different ways, particularly with legal drugs such as nicotine or alcohol. Packaging or advertisements contain text that can convey information about the drug content of the substance, and drug users can be given oral or written information about what is contained in the substance. As with any drug of abuse, information that cigarettes contain

"Like Puffs"

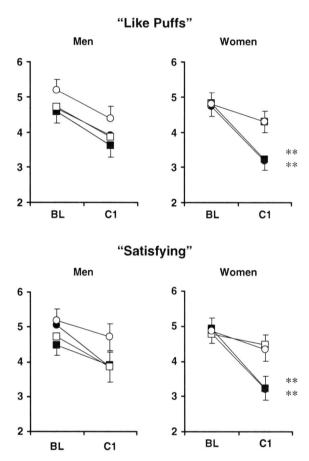

Fig. 9.4 Means ± SEM ratings for smoking reward ("like puffs," "satisfying") in men ($n = 21$) and women ($n = 30$) presented with their preferred brand unblinded at baseline (BL) and then 1 hour later blinded to brand while under olfactory/taste and/or visual blockade conditions (C1). ** $p < 0.01$ for difference from the no blockade condition in change from baseline rating. Reprinted from Perkins, Gerlach, Vender, Grobe, Meeker, & Hutchison (2001) Sex differences in the subjective and reinforcing effects of visual and olfactory cigarette smoke stimuli. *Nicotine & Tobacco Research, 3,* 141–150, published by the Society for Research on Nicotine and Tobacco (see the journal's website: http://www.informaworld.com)

nicotine creates "stimulus expectancies" for nicotine in the user, which in turn can influence (via "response expectancies") effects the user is likely to experience from nicotine cigarettes (see Perkins et al., 2003).

We first examined sex differences in the influence of verbal information about nicotine on responses to smoking by using the balanced-placebo design (BPD), a procedure used in alcohol research for decades. The BPD involves randomly assigning subjects to receive a substance containing actual drug or no drug, and half of those within each drug condition are told they are receiving actual drug or no drug, in a 2×2 between-subjects design (Perkins et al., 2003). Thus, half the subjects get drug information that is accurate (i.e., they are told and get actual drug, or are told and get a substance with no drug), while the other half get drug information that is inaccurate (i.e., they are told they are getting a substance containing drug but in fact get no drug, or are told they are getting a substance containing no drug but in fact get drug). We employed the BPD to assess the separate and combined effects of actual nicotine dose (via cigarette brands that were moderate or very low in nicotine) and expected nicotine dose (via instructions about the nicotine content of the cigarettes) in men and women (Perkins et al., 2004). Dose instructions had effects larger than actual dose on smoking reward (e.g., "liking") and perception (e.g., "how much nicotine"), but not on craving or withdrawal. Of more interest, women showed greater responses than men to the actual nicotine dose of cigarettes when the dose instructions were accurate, although they did not respond more to inaccurate instructions.

Although this result superficially seemed contrary to the findings noted previously, that women were less sensitive to nicotine dose manipulations, we hypothesized that the greater response of women to dose in this study was due to their greater sensitivity to the accurate dose *instructions* (i.e., the non-pharmacological influence of verbal information about drug). To test this notion, we subsequently repeated the study but with one major change: instead of half the subjects getting inaccurate information about dose, half the subjects got *no* information about dose (i.e., were kept blind to dose). Thus, this study (Perkins et al., 2006) tested the effects of actual nicotine dose in the presence versus the absence of accurate verbal information about dose. Aside from smoking reward ("liking"), we assessed reinforcement by the number of ad lib puffs smoked on that cigarette brand over 30 minutes and by the latency to the first puff. Women showed no effects of actual nicotine dose on smoking reward and reinforcement under blind conditions, consistent with the results of Perkins et al. (2002; Fig. 9.3), described previously, but showed strong dose effects when given accurate dose information. The interaction of dose by instructions (absence/presence) was significant in women for reward and both reinforcement measures. Men showed no dose effects under either instructional condition, except for a dose effect on smoking reward under blind conditions. These findings confirmed that women are more sensitive than men to the non-pharmacological influence of verbal information about nicotine dose.

Sex Differences in the Reinforcing Effects of Control over Smoking

The key to assessing drug reinforcement is that drug administration must be contingent upon a subject's response. Basic research has demonstrated that the effects of the same drug doses can differ when administered non-contingently (i.e., regardless of a subject's behavior) versus contingently (e.g., Dworkin, Mirkis, & Smith, 1995). This effect of the contingency of the drug administration is, by definition, non-pharmacological, as drug dosing (i.e., pharmacology) is kept identical between conditions; the only difference is whether drug is administered contingent or non-contingent on a subject response. To our knowledge, only one published study has examined this notion in humans, finding that cocaine produced greater cardiovascular effects, but similar subjective effects, when presented non-contingently versus contingently (Donny, Bigelow, & Walsh, 2006). No published human research has investigated the influence of contingency in nicotine administration, or individual differences in the influence of contingent versus non-contingent drug administration.

In an unpublished dissertation, Grobe (1999) examined the role of behavioral contingencies surrounding cigarette smoking in moderating acute responses to smoking using a design where smokers were matched in pairs based on smoking characteristics, age, and sex, and then randomly assigned to contingent versus non-contingent smoking groups. Because this study is not published, it will be presented here in detail. Participants were male and female dependent tobacco smokers who abstained from smoking overnight prior to the session. Subjects were 25.4 ± 0.7 (mean, SE) years of age, smoked for 9.1 ± 0.6 years, and had average smoking rates of 18.7 ± 0.8 cigarettes per day. A yoked procedure was developed to equate for dosing, pattern of drug intake, and other stimuli associated with tobacco administration. During the test session, each participant in the contingent group (n = 31) had control over tobacco intake. In contrast, each participant in the non-contingent group (n = 28) was yoked to the first group in that they smoked according to the pattern established by his or her matched counterpart in the contingent group. (The non-contingent group had three fewer participants than the contingent group, because three in the latter group could not be matched; however, all were included in analyses.)

Self-administration of tobacco smoke was controlled by computerized puffing instructions, to control puff duration. When a person in the contingent group wanted a puff of tobacco smoke, he or she pressed a button to initiate the puffing instructions. The computer recorded the timing of these button presses for puffs by those in the contingent group. This pattern was then presented to the matched subject in the noncontingent group to signal when he or she was to take a puff via the same puffing instructions. Subjects in the noncontingent group could not control the pattern of puffing. With this procedure, the contingent and noncontingent groups were equated on tobacco exposure, pattern of intake, and stimuli associated with drug delivery; control over exposure and pattern was confirmed by the similar CO increases between contingent (13.1 ± 1.1 ppm) versus noncontingent (11.0 ± 0.8 ppm) groups. Thus, the manipulation of controllability was not confounded by substantially different tobacco exposure. After 90 minutes of smoking either contingently or noncontingently, according to the assigned condition, subjects completed 0–100 visual-analog scale measures of subjective mood (depressed, angry, tense, etc.) and smoking reward ("smoking pleasure"), and a behavioral measure of the relative reinforcing values of the respective smoking contexts (i.e., reinforcement). Reinforcement was determined by responding on an operant task to gain access to continued smoking under their respective smoking context (i.e., contingent versus noncontingent) versus a modest amount of money as an alternative.

Compared to contingent smoking, non-contingent (yoked) smoking resulted in less smoking reward and reinforcement. These effects remained robust after controlling for actual smoke exposure (CO boost). Moreover, compared to contingent smoking, women found noncontingent smoking to be significantly less reinforcing (Fig. 9.5, top) and less effective in alleviating feelings of depressed mood (Fig. 9.5, bottom), perhaps in relief of tobacco withdrawal due to abstaining prior to the

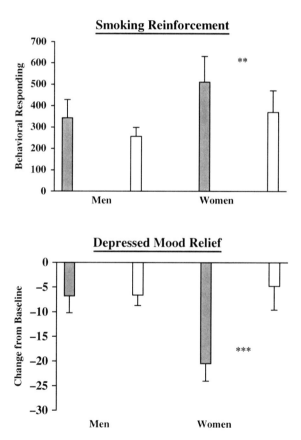

Fig. 9.5 Mean ± SEM responses for continued access to smoking (reinforcement, *top*) and decrease from pre-smoking baseline in 0–100 visual analog scale of "depressed" mood (*bottom*) in men and women who smoked in contingent (*filled bars*, $n = 31$) versus non-contingent (*open bars*, $n = 28$) fashion. ** $p < 0.01$, *** $p < 0.001$ for difference between contingent and non-contingent groups, by sex. From Grobe, J. E. (1999) *The importance of controllability over drug intake in moderating the effects of tobacco smoking*. Unpublished Ph.D. dissertation, University of Pittsburgh

session. In contrast, the men were not significantly affected by the contingency manipulation on these measures. A similar pattern was observed for self-report measures of irritableness and tension (not shown).

These results suggest that the greater influence in women versus men of non-pharmacological factors in cigarette smoking may extend beyond verbal and non-verbal information (cues) about drug content, discussed previously. The results also suggest that studies of acute responses to smoking need to take into consideration the extent to which the smoking is done contingently versus non-contingently (e.g., when done ad lib or when directed to do so by the experimenter) to determine their generalizability to the effects of smoking in the natural environment.

Other Relevant Findings

The studies we discussed in this section indicate that several non-nicotine aspects of smoking influence smoking reward and reinforcement more in women than in men. These factors include the smell or taste, but perhaps not the sight, of cigarette smoke; accurate verbal information about the nicotine content of a cigarette; and controllability over the pattern of ad lib smoking. Many other non-nicotine factors influence smoking reinforcement and reward, and their impact may differ between men and women. For example, one unpublished survey by the American Lung Association (Sept 1998) asked 1,001 smokers who had quit but relapsed why they relapsed. Many responses were given equally between men and women, but women were more likely than men to report that they "missed the comfort of something to hold" (37% versus 28%, respectively) or "missed having something to do with hands" (25% versus 17%, respectively). These observations suggest that the motor effects of smoking (i.e., smoking ritual), in addition to the sensory effects of smoking (e.g., taste and smell of smoke), may differentially influence smoking reinforcement and reward in women versus men. Formal controlled research of this notion is warranted and should be fairly easy to do.

Notably, the sex differences in non-nicotine influences on reinforcement may extend to non-human species, suggesting a difference that is not specific to "gender" (i.e., human sex roles, cultural factors). Chaudhri et al. (2005) assessed nicotine self-administration behavior in the absence or presence of a visual stimulus associated with each nicotine infusion (i.e., cue). In the absence of any cue, male and female rats responded comparably for nicotine (as determined by the difference in responses on the active versus inactive lever). However, when the cue was presented concurrent with nicotine infusion, responding increased and was significantly greater in females versus males. Removal of the cue produced a decrease in responding only among the females, such that responding for nicotine no longer differed between sexes. These findings are generally similar to the sex differences in the influence of non-nicotine factors on smoking reinforcement and reward in humans described previously. Given the limited attention paid to sex differences in nicotine reinforcement in human models, however, a great deal more programmatic research is needed to determine the reliability of such sex differences.

Clinical Implications

Aside from providing directions for the study of possible sex differences in the etiology of tobacco dependence, these results suggest that men and women may differ in their response to smoking cessation treatments. If women's smoking is less responsive to manipulations of nicotine per se, then they should benefit less from the most common medication for smoking cessation, nicotine replacement therapy (NRT), but be at no disadvantage when treated with non-NRT medications. By the same token, if women's smoking is more responsive to non-nicotine factors, then they should benefit more from treatment approaches that address these factors, such as counseling to cope with smoking cues. As will be discussed, considerable evidence supports the first point, that women have less success in quitting with NRT (particularly nicotine patch) and not with other medications. Little research has examined the second point.

Sex Differences in NRT Efficacy

Evidence has accumulated over the past two decades to show that NRT has less influence on long-term quit rates in women versus men (Perkins, 2001; Wetter et al., 1999). In a recent meta-analysis, we found that women have poorer quit rates than men at 6-month follow-up in controlled trials comparing nicotine versus placebo patch (see Perkins & Scott, in press). The odds ratio of abstinence due to nicotine versus placebo patch for men versus women was 1.45 (95% confidence interval of 1.04–2.02, $p = 0.03$). This analysis was a follow-up to a meta-analysis of 11 NRT patch trials concluding that the sex difference in long-term abstinence due to patch was modest and non-significant (Munafo, Bradburn, Bowes, & David, 2004). However, that meta-analysis contained only a fraction of the relevant trials testing patch effects in men and women. Although the authors of the earlier meta-analysis sought outcome data separated by sex from the investigators of some 30 relevant clinical trials, they were successful in obtaining such results for only 10 of them. Results from those 10 trials were added to the lone patch trial in the literature that had reported outcome results by sex, leaving 11 for analysis. (The fact that only one out of 30 relevant NRT patch trials published as of 2004 reported clinical outcome by sex, likely delayed by years a discovery that could lead to improved treatment of women for smoking cessation.) We found results for two additional trials plus another trial published after the Munafo et al., (2004) meta-analysis, and determined that the results from these 14 trials did point to a significant sex difference in NRT patch response (Perkins & Scott, in press).

The full clinical picture may not be so simple, however. Other research indicates that the sex difference in NRT response may vary as functions of: the NRT formulation, interactions of sex by dopamine genotype, or the intensity of the counseling accompanying NRT. First, West and colleagues (West et al., 2001) found small to moderate disadvantages of women versus men in 15-week abstinence rates due to NRT gum, patch, or nasal spray in an open label trial (i.e., no placebo control condition). However, women tended to do *better* than men on NRT inhaler, which is puffed like a cigarette but delivers nicotine via buccal absorption, similar to gum. The fact that the inhaler mimics some of the sensory-motor effects of smoking cigarettes (i.e., non-nicotine aspects of smoking) could help explain why women may gain better therapeutic response from that formulation. Thus, something about the formulation may moderate the sex difference in outcome due to NRT, and subsequent research could improve quit rates in women by enhancing features of NRT formulations that show better quit rates in women. Notably, women are less compliant than men with nicotine patch (Cooper et al., 2004) and perhaps with nicotine gum (Killen, Fortmann, Newman, & Varady, 1990), which could reflect, or help cause, their poorer clinical outcome with patch and gum. In any case, sex differences in compliance across formulation may be a place to start in examining this issue.

Second, a post hoc analysis of a large placebo-controlled NRT patch trial showed that women with at least one A1 allele of the DRD2 gene had a large therapeutic response (abstinent at 6 months) to active patch, while women homozygous for the A2 allele had no response (Yudkin, Munafo, Hey, Roberts, Welch, Johnstone et al., 2004). Results for men were the reverse (i.e., large therapeutic response in those homozygous for A2). Those of European descent tend to be homozygous for the A2 allele, perhaps helping to account for the poorer outcome of women versus men in many trials of the nicotine patch (Perkins & Scott, in press).

Third, a meta-analysis of 21 studies testing NRT of all types (Cepeda-Benito et al., 2004) found that NRT had no effect at 6 months in women given low-intensity behavioral counseling for cessation (OR = 1.03, CI = 0.62–1.68) but was effective in women given high-intensity counseling (OR = 1.90, CI = 1.58–2.30). The NRT was effective in men regardless of the intensity of counseling (OR's above 2). Note, however, that this observation was not replicated in our meta-analysis focusing on NRT patch trials, as counseling did not moderate the sex difference in patch efficacy (Perkins & Scott, in press). The difference between analyses could be due to the larger number of trials examined by Cepeda-Benito et al. (2004), or to variability in the influence of counseling as a function of NRT formulation. If counseling does in fact moderate the sex difference in NRT efficacy, clinical research could improve cessation rates in women by making use of intense counseling that enhances NRT response. Cepeda-Benito et al. (2004) also found that NRT was not effective in women at all at the one-year follow-up point but was effective in men, supporting the general notion that women are less responsive than men to the therapeutic efficacy of NRT.

Despite some differences in the relative contribution of nicotine versus non-nicotine factors to their smoking reinforcement and reward, most of the causes of smoking persistence in men and women likely are the same. The sex differences in clinical results discussed here are generalizations and do not necessarily apply to every single female or male smoker. Thus, the smoking of many women may be strongly influenced by nicotine dose, and NRT may be very beneficial in helping these women quit, while the smoking of many men may be sensitive to manipulations of non-nicotine factors, and NRT may have little effect in these men. Furthermore, the safety, low cost, and over-the-counter (OTC) availability of NRT still make it an important medication for all smokers, including women, to use when quitting. In fact, a critical problem with smoking cessation treatment in the general population is that physicians seldom recommend medication, and are only half as likely to recommend medication for women smokers compared to men who smoke (Steinberg, Akincigil, Delnevo, Crystal, & Carson, 2006). Nevertheless, clinical research suggests that women may be more likely than men to need additional help to quit, and NRT alone may have little benefit for most women smokers.

Sex Differences in Response to Other Medications

If women were also less successful than men with cessation medications other than NRT, then one would have to conclude that the sex differences in response to NRT are probably not relevant to the central issue of sex differences in the influence of nicotine on smoking reinforcement and reward. However, clinical evidence indicates that women are equally, or perhaps more, successful than men in studies of non-NRT medications. A meta-analysis of 12 clinical trials with bupropion versus placebo showed similar and highly significant effects of bupropion in women and men (OR's = 2.47 and 2.53, respectively; Scharf & Shiffman, 2004). Yet, women had poorer cessation rates overall (OR = 0.75, CI = 0.59–0.94 for cessation in women versus men), consistent with much other research that women generally have more difficulty quitting (e.g., Perkins, 2001; Wetter et al., 1999). Although less numerous, clinical trials of clonidine and naltrexone tend to show somewhat better outcome in women versus men (Perkins, 2001), although neither drug is clearly efficacious in placebo-controlled trials and thus has not been approved by the FDA for smoking cessation. Notably, clonidine's efficacy in women is more apparent in studies involving intense behavioral counseling, versus minimal counseling (Perkins, 2001), similar to NRT outcome with women in Cepeda-Benito et al., (2004). Thus, women do at least as well as men when trying to quit with non-nicotine medications, and so the specific deficit of women versus men in clinical outcome with NRT supports the idea that nicotine is a less important influence on smoking reinforcement and reward in women versus men.

Sex Differences in Treatments Aimed at Non-Nicotine Influences on Smoking

Standard behavioral counseling for smoking cessation often addresses coping with the influences of smoking cues on craving to smoke. Smokers are usually advised to avoid being in environments where smokers congregate (e.g., smoking areas outside buildings, smoking sections of restaurants) or to engage in cognitive and behavioral strategies to divert attention from the cues, such as by keeping busy with a distracting task or take a walk to escape the cues altogether (Perkins, Conklin,

& Levine, 2008). To our knowledge, no studies have tested sex differences in the effectiveness of these counseling steps. However, relapse risk is very high if quitting smokers are not able to avoid lapsing early in the quit attempt (whatever the cause), and this risk may be much greater in women than men (Borrelli et al., 2004). Thus, improving the ability of quitting smokers to successfully cope with urges to smoke early in a quit attempt, such as by reducing the influence of smoking cues, would greatly increase long-term abstinence, particularly in women.

Another approach in addressing sensory effects of smoking is to provide substitutes that simulate these effects. Standard counseling recommends strategies such as sucking on a straw or consuming carrot sticks or cinnamon sticks as substitutes for the motor effects of smoking. However, the sensory effects of smoking appear more important than the motor effects (Perkins, Gerlach, Vender et al. 2001; Perkins, Ciccocioppo, Conklin, Milanak, Grottenthaler, & Sayette, in press), suggesting that substitutes for the sensory effects may be more effective. Rose and colleagues developed several sensory substitutes that mimicked the throat irritating effects of nicotine-containing smoke, including citric aerosol (Rose & Hickman, 1987). Moreover, denicotinized cigarettes can be viewed as the ultimate in sensory substitutes, since they match almost all the effects of smoking other than nicotine intake (Pickworth et al. 1999). Yet, we are not aware of research that has specifically examined whether men and women differ in clinical response to these substitutes when attempting to quit. Together with the previously noted sex differences in efficacy with the NRT inhaler (West et al., 2001), the formulation whose method of use is most similar to smoking, development of sensory substitutes may be a fruitful area of research into improved cessation methods for women.

The greater influence in women of controllability over smoking may be addressed by behavioral treatments that remove control over smoking in the period prior to the quit date, such as the "scheduled reduction" approach of Cinciripini et al. (Cinciripini, Lapitsky, Seay, Wallfisch, Kitchens, & Van Vunakis, 1995), in which smokers smoke only after a specific amount of time has passed since the prior cigarette. This behavioral procedure has been shown to improve abstinence rates, although the mechanism for its efficacy is unclear. Smokers may learn to cope with urges to smoke that occur before the next "scheduled" cigarette. Alternatively, or in addition, the cues associated with access to smoking may narrow when the availability of each cigarette is determined strictly by time. In any case, such a procedure may aid abstinence more in women than in men.

Conclusions and Future Directions

Because women have greater difficulty quitting smoking and suffer higher risks of smoking-related morbidity and mortality, more effective smoking cessation treatments for women could have profound effects in improving public health. Although men and women smokers are more similar than they are different, we have found that smoking reinforcement and reward in women are influenced less by nicotine and more by non-nicotine factors, compared to reinforcement and reward in men.

Women self-administer nicotine to a lesser degree, and nicotine pre-treatment alters their subsequent smoking or nicotine self-administration to a lesser extent, relative to men. By contrast, smoking reinforcement and reward in women are influenced more by the presence of smoking cues, particularly olfactory/taste of cigarette smoke, and by accurate verbal information about the nicotine content of cigarettes, two factors that are independent of actual nicotine intake (i.e., are non-nicotine in nature). Women may also be more sensitive to the presence of control over the pattern of smoking. These differences may help explain why women benefit less than men from NRT medication, particularly the patch, when trying to quit.

Future research should determine the possible mechanisms for these sex differences. The obvious hormonal differences between women and men have been proposed as a reason women may be less sensitive to the reinforcing and rewarding effects of nicotine (e.g., Sofuoglu, Babb, & Hatsukami, 2001). Craving and withdrawal may vary in women as a function of menstrual cycle phase (Carpenter, Upadhyaya, LaRowe, Saladin, & Brady, 2006; Perkins et al., 2000), lending some support for this idea. Estradiol in animals and progesterone in humans may blunt responses to nicotine and other drugs (Damaj, 2001; Sofuoglu et al. 2001). However, much of this research is inconsistent or shows only modest effects of cycle phase or hormone manipulations (Terner & de Wit, 2006). Moreover, research indicating that sex differences in response to nicotine may depend on the NRT formulation or interaction involving other genes suggests that simple hormonal levels are unlikely to fully explain reduced nicotine reinforcement in women. Laboratory studies examining more complex interactions may provide a clearer understanding of these mechanisms. For example, Ray and colleagues (Ray et al., 2006) found slightly lower levels of nicotine cigarette choice in women versus men, but the main finding was an interaction of sex by OPRM1 (mu opioid receptor) genotype. Nicotine choice among women was much greater for those homozygous for the A allele compared to those with one or two G alleles, while OPRM1 genotype had no effect on nicotine choice in men.

Other directions for the study of mechanisms for these sex differences include possible differences in neurotransmitter activity in response to nicotine or smoking. For example, in one study, women responded to amphetamine with less striatal dopamine release (via positron emission tomography) and blunted drug reward and other subjective responses, compared to men (Munro et al., 2006). (Menstrual cycle phase had no effect on responses to amphetamine.) Similar neuroimaging research may show comparable sex differences in response to nicotine and/or non-nicotine factors in smoking.

Finally, clinical research should take advantage of these non-nicotine factors that influence smoking reinforcement and reward in women to improve interventions for cessation. The fact that women do at least as well when quitting with non-nicotine medications suggests that further development of such medications is likely to improve cessation rates in women. Development of substitutes that mimic the sensory effects of smoking, such as the taste and olfactory stimuli of tobacco smoke inhalation, may effectively replace cigarette smoking in women early in quitting and help foster smoking abstinence. Use of counseling approaches that reduce control over the pattern of smoking leading up to the quit day may also aid long-term abstinence in women.

Acknowledgments The preparation of this chapter was supported by Grants DA12655, DA16483, and DA19478, and by University of Pennsylvania Transdisciplinary Tobacco Research Center (TTURC) Grant P50 DA/CA84718.

References

Benowitz, N. L., & Hatsukami, D. K. (1998). Gender differences in the pharmacology of nicotine addiction. *Addiction Biology, 3*, 383–404.

Benowitz, N. L., Lessov-Schlaggar, C. N., Swan, G. E., & Jacob, P. (2006). Female sex and oral contraceptive use accelerate nicotine metabolism. *Clinical Pharmacology and Therapeutics, 79*, 480–488.

Borrelli, B., Papandonatos, G., Spring, B., Hitsman, B., & Niaura, R. (2004). Experimenter-defined quit rates for smoking cessation: Adherence improves outcomes for women but not for men. *Addiction, 99*, 378–385.

Buka, S. L., Shenassa, E. D., & Niaura, R. (2003). Elevated risk of tobacco dependence among offspring of mothers who smoked during pregnancy: A 30-year prospective study. *American Journal of Psychiatry, 160*, 1978–1984.

Carpenter, M. J., Upadhyaya, H. P., LaRowe, S. D., Saladin, M. E., & Brady, K. T. (2006). Menstrual cycle phase effects on nicotine withdrawal and cigarette craving: A review. *Nicotine & Tobacco Research, 8*, 627–638.

Carter, B. L., & Tiffany, S. T. (2001). The cue-availability paradigm: The effects of cigarette availability on cue reactivity in smokers. *Experimental and Clinical Psychopharmacology, 9*, 183–190.

Centers for Disease Control and Prevention (2005). Cigarette smoking among adults—United States, 2004. *Morbidity and Mortality Weekly Report, 54*, 1121–1123.

Cepeda-Benito, A., Reynoso, J. T., & Erath, S. (2004). Meta-analysis of the efficacy of nicotine replacement therapy for smoking cessation: Differences between men and women. *Journal of Consulting and Clinical Psychology, 72*, 712–722.

Chaudhri, N., Caggiula, A. R., Donny, E. C., Booth, S., Gharib, M. A., Craven, L. A., et al. (2005). Sex differences in the contribution of nicotine and nonpharmacological stimuli to nicotine self-administration in rats. *Psychopharmacology, 180*, 258–266.

Cheeta S, Irvine, E. E., Tucci, S., Sandhu, J., & File, S. E. (2001). In adolescence, female rats are more sensitive to the anxiolytic effect of nicotine than are male rats. *Neuropsychopharmacology, 25*, 601–607.

Cinciripini, P. M., Lapitsky, L., Seay, S., Wallfisch, A., Kitchens, K., & Van Vunakis, H. (1995). The effects of smoking schedules on cessation outcome: Can we improve on common methods of gradual and abrupt nicotine withdrawal? *Journal of Consulting and Clinical Psychology, 63*, 388–399.

Conklin, C. A. (2006). Environments as cues to smoke: Implication for human extinction-based research and treatment. *Experimental & Clinical Psychopharmacology, 14*, 12–19.

Cooper, T. V., DeBon, M. W., Stockton, M., Klesges, R. C., Steenbergh, T. A., Sherrill-Mittleman, D., et al. (2004). Correlates of adherence with transdermal nicotine. *Addictive Behaviors, 29*, 1565–1578.

Damaj, M. I. (2001). Influence of gender and sex hormones on nicotine acute pharmacological effects in mice. *Journal of Pharmacology and Experimental Therapeutics, 296*, 132–140.

DiFranza, J. R., Aligne, C. A., & Weitzman, M. (2004). Prenatal and postnatal environmental tobacco smoke exposure and children's health. *Pediatrics, 113* (Supplement), 1007–1015.

Donny, E. C., Bigelow, G. E., & Walsh, S. L. (2006). Comparing the physiological and subjective effects of self-administered vs yoked cocaine in humans. *Psychopharmacology, 186*, 544–552.

Dransfield, M. T., Davis, J. J., Gerald, L. B., & Bailey, W. C. (2006). Racial and gender differences in susceptibility to tobacco smoke among patients with chronic obstructive pulmonary disease. *Respiratory Medicine, 100*, 1110–1116.

Dworkin, S. I., Mirkis, S., & Smith, J. E. (1995). Response-dependent versus response-independent presentation of cocaine: Differences in the lethal effects of the drug. *Psychopharmacology, 117*, 262–266.

Everitt, B. J., & Robbins, T. W. (2005). Neural systems of reinforcement for drug addiction: From actions to habits to compulsion. *Nature Neuroscience, 8*, 1481–1489.

Fortmann, S. P., & Killen, J. D. (1994). Who shall quit? Comparison of volunteer and population-based recruitment in two minimal-contact smoking cessation studies. *American Journal of Epidemiology, 140*, 39–51.

Grobe, J. E. (1999). *The importance of controllability over drug intake in moderating the effects of tobacco smoking.* Unpublished Ph.D. dissertation, University of Pittsburgh.

Grunberg, N. E., Winders, S. E., & Wewers, M. E. (1991). Gender differences in tobacco use. *Health Psychology, 10*, 143–153.

Henningfield, J. E., & Goldberg, S. R. (1983). Control of behavior by intravenous nicotine injections in human subjects. *Pharmacology, Biochemistry, & Behavior, 19*, 1021–1026.

International Early Lung Cancer Action Program Investigators (2006). Women's susceptibility to tobacco carcinogens and survival after diagnosis of lung cancer. *Journal of the American Medical Association, 296*, 180–184.

Killen, J. D., Fortmann, S. P., Newman, B., & Varady, A. (1990). Evaluation of a treatment approach combining nicotine gum with self-guided behavioral treatments for smoking relapse prevention. *Journal of Consulting and Clinical Psychology, 58*, 85–92.

Lerman, C., Perkins, K. A., & Gould, T. (in press). Nicotine dependence endophenotypes in chronic smokers. *NCI Smoking and Tobacco Control Monograph 22: Phenotypes, Endophenotypes, and Genetic Studies of Nicotine Dependence* (Chapter 8). Washington DC: US Public Health Service.

Lopez A. D., Collishaw N. E., & Piha T. (1994). A descriptive model of the cigarette epidemic in developed countries. *Tobacco Control, 3*, 242–247.

Munafo, M., Bradburn, M., Bowes, L., & David, S. (2004). Are there sex differences in transdermal nicotine replacement therapy patch efficacy? A meta-analysis. *Nicotine & Tobacco Research, 6*, 769–776.

Munafo, M. R., Shields, A. E., Berrettini, W., Patterson, F., & Lerman, C. (2005). Pharmacogenetics and nicotine addiction treatment. *Pharmacogenomics, 6*, 211–223.

Munro, C. A., McCaul, M. E., Wong, D. F., Oswald, L. M., Zhou, Y., Brasic, J., et al. (2006). Sex differences in striatal dopamine release in healthy adults. *Biological Psychiatry, 59*, 966–974.

Perkins, K. A. (1993). Weight gain following smoking cessation. *Journal of Consulting and Clinical Psychology, 61*, 768–777.

Perkins, K. A. (1999). Nicotine discrimination in men and women. *Pharmacology, Biochemistry & Behavior, 64*, 295–299.

Perkins, K. A. (2001). Smoking cessation in women: Special considerations. *CNS Drugs, 15*, 391–411.

Perkins, K. A. (2004). Response to Dar and Frenk: "Do smokers self-administer pure nicotine? A review of the evidence." *Psychopharmacology, 175*, 256–258.

Perkins, K. A., Ciccocioppo, M., Conklin, C., Milanak, M., Grottenthaler, A. & Sayette, M. (2008). Mood influences on acute smoking responses are independent of nicotine intake and dose expectancy. *Journal of Abnormal Psychology, 117*, 79–93.

Perkins, K. A., Conklin, C. A., & Levine, M. D. (2008). *Cognitive-behavioral treatment of smoking cessation.* New York: Routledge.

Perkins, K. A., Doyle, T., Ciccocioppo, M., Conklin, C., Sayette, M., & Caggiula, A. R. (2006). Sex differences in the influence of nicotine and dose instructions on subjective and reinforcing effects of smoking. *Psychopharmacology, 184*, 600–607.

Perkins, K. A., Epstein, L. H., Grobe, J. E., & Fonte, C. (1994). Tobacco abstinence, smoking cues, and the reinforcing value of smoking. *Pharmacology, Biochemistry, & Behavior, 47*, 107–112.

Perkins, K. A., Fonte, C., Meeker, J., White, W., & Wilson, A. (2001). The discriminative stimulus and reinforcing effects of nicotine in humans following nicotine pre-treatment. *Behavioural Pharmacology, 12*, 35–44.

Perkins, K. A., Gerlach, D., Broge, M., Grobe, J. E., Sanders, M., Fonte, C., et al. (2001). Dissociation of nicotine tolerance from tobacco dependence. *Journal of Pharmacology and Experimental Therapeutics, 296*, 849–856.

Perkins, K. A., Gerlach, D., Vender, J., Grobe, J. E., Meeker, J., & Hutchison, S. (2001). Sex differences in the subjective and reinforcing effects of visual and olfactory cigarette smoke stimuli. *Nicotine & Tobacco Research, 3*, 141–150.

Perkins, K. A., Grobe, J. E., Stiller, R. L., Fonte, C., & Goettler, J. E. (1992). Nasal spray nicotine replacement suppresses cigarette smoking desire and behavior. *Clinical Pharmacology & Therapeutics, 52*, 627–634.

Perkins, K. A., Grobe, J. E., D'Amico, D., Fonte, C., Wilson, A., & Stiller, R. L. (1996). Low-dose nicotine nasal spray use and effects during initial smoking cessation. *Experimental and Clinical Psychopharmacology, 4*, 157–165.

Perkins, K. A., Grobe, J. E., Weiss, D., Fonte, C., & Caggiula, A. (1996). Nicotine preference in smokers as a function of smoking abstinence. *Pharmacology, Biochemistry, & Behavior, 55*, 257–263.

Perkins, K. A., Jacobs, L., Ciccocioppo, M., Conklin, C. A., Sayette, M., & Caggiula, A. (2004). The influence of instructions and nicotine dose on the subjective and reinforcing effects of smoking. *Experimental and Clinical Psychopharmacology, 12*, 91–101.

Perkins, K. A., Jacobs, L., Sanders, M., & Caggiula, A. R. (2002). Sex differences in the subjective and reinforcing effects of cigarette nicotine dose. *Psychopharmacology, 163*, 194–201.

Perkins, K. A., Levine, M., Marcus, M., Shiffman, S., D'Amico, D., Miller, A., et al. (2000). Tobacco withdrawal in women and menstrual cycle phase. *Journal of Consulting and Clinical Psychology, 68*, 176–180.

Perkins, K. A., Sanders, M., D'Amico, D., & Wilson, A. (1997). Nicotine discrimination and self-administration as a function of smoking status. *Psychopharmacology, 131*, 361–370.

Perkins, K. A., Sayette, M., Conklin, C. A., & Caggiula, A. R. (2003). Placebo effects of tobacco smoking and other nicotine intake. *Nicotine & Tobacco Research, 5*, 695–709.

Perkins, K. A., & Scott, J. (in press). Sex differences in long-term smoking cessation rates due to nicotine patch. *Nicotine & Tobacco Research*.

Piasecki, T. M., & Baker, T. B. (2001). Any further progress in smoking cessation treatment? *Nicotine & Tobacco Research, 3*, 311–323.

Pickworth, W. B., Fant, R. V., Nelson, R. A., Rohrer, M. S., & Henningfield, J. E. (1999). Pharmacodynamic effects of new de-nicotinized cigarettes. *Nicotine & Tobacco Research, 1*, 357–364.

Prescott, E., Hippe, M., Schnohr, P., Ole Hein, H., & Vestbo, J. (1998). Smoking and risk of myocardial infarction in women and men: Longitudinal population study. *British Medical Journal, 316*, 1043–1047.

Ray, R., Jepson, C., Patterson, F., Strasser, A., Rukstalis, M., Perkins, K., et al. (2006). Association of OPRM1 Asn40Asp variant with the relative reinforcing value of nicotine in female smokers. *Psychopharmacology, 188*, 355–363.

Rodu, B., & Cole, P. (2007). Declining mortality from smoking in the United States. *Nicotine & Tobacco Research, 9*, 781–789.

Rose, J. E., & Hickman, C. S. (1987). Citric acid aerosol as a potential smoking cessation aid. *Chest, 92*, 1005–1008.

Scharf, D., & Shiffman, S. (2004). Are there gender differences in smoking cessation, with and without bupropion? Pooled- and meta-analyses of clinical trials of Bupropion SR. *Addiction, 99*, 1462–1469.

Silverstein, B., Feld, S., & Kozlowski, L. T. (1980). The availability of low-nicotine cigarettes as a cause of cigarette smoking among teenage females. *Journal of Health and Social Behavior, 21*, 383–388.

Sofuoglu, M., Babb, D. A., & Hatsukami, D. K. (2001). Progesterone treatment during the early follicular phase of the menstrual cycle: Effects on smoking behavior in women. *Pharmacology, Biochemistry, & Behavior, 69*, 299–304.

Steinberg, M. B., Akincigil, A., Delnevo, C. D., Crystal, S., & Carson, J. L. (2006). Gender and age disparities for smoking cessation treatment. *American Journal of Preventive Medicine, 30*, 405–412.

Terner, J. M., & de Wit, H. (2006). Menstrual cycle phase and responses to drugs of abuse in humans. *Drug and Alcohol Dependence, 84*, 1–13.

USDHHS (1988). *The Health Consequences of Smoking: Nicotine Addiction. A Report of the U.S. Surgeon General.* Washington DC: U.S. Public Health Service.

West, R., Hajek, P., Nilsson, F., Foulds, J., May, S., & Meadows, A. (2001). Individual differences in preferences for and responses to four nicotine replacement products. *Psychopharmacology, 153*, 225–230.

Wetter, D., Kenford, S. L., Smith, S. S., Fiore, M. C., Jorenby, D. E., & Baker, T. B. (1999). Gender differences in smoking cessation. *Journal of Consulting and Clinical Psychology, 67*, 555–562.

Yudkin, P., Munafo, M., Hey, K., Roberts, S., Welch, S., Johnstone, E., et al. (2004). Effectiveness of nicotine patches in relation to genotype in women versus men: Randomized controlled trial. *British Medical Journal, 328*, 989–990.

Chapter 10
The Functional Significance of Craving in Nicotine Dependence

Stephen T. Tiffany, Mathew W. Warthen, and Katherine C. Goedeker

Introduction

In 1954, craving was given a death sentence. A panel of experts convened by the World Health Organization advised that the term *craving* be abandoned because "a term such as 'craving' with its everyday connotations should not be used in the scientific literature ... if confusion is to be avoided" (Who Expert Committees on Mental Health and on Alcohol, 1955, p. 63). In the ensuing half century, craving has persisted in bedeviling scientists, but the term, and the variety of concepts it represents, simply refuses to die.

Unquestionably, craving remains an everyday word – a Google™ search of the terms *craving* or *crave* appearing in web pages updated over the past year (April 2006–March 2007) yielded approximately 10,000,000 hits. Craving has been addressed by scientists with escalating frequency. A search of the terms *craving* or *crave* in abstracts indexed by Medline or PsycINFO since 1960 (Fig. 10.1) shows that craving research was fairly limited in the 1960 s and 1970 s, began to proliferate in the 1980 s, and exploded in the 1990 s. This pace has continued to accelerate during the first half of the present decade with more than 2,100 abstracts containing the words *craving* or *crave* published over that period. Clearly, scientists have not abandoned their use of the term nor their interest in the processes it represents.

That is not to say that all disputes about craving have been resolved – craving remains a controversial topic. Nonetheless, research on craving has come a long way over the past 50 years and we now know much more about the measurement, manipulation, and functional significance of craving. However, our modern scientific understanding of craving is not universally appreciated by all drug-abuse researchers, and there remain fundamental questions about the functions of craving in addictive processes. A considerable portion of craving research has been conducted in the context of cigarette smoking and nicotine dependence and the focus of this chapter is on that research. As will be seen, craving is a robust and ubiquitous

S.T. Tiffany
Department of Psychology, University at Buffalo, the State University of New York, 368 Park Hall, Buffalo, NY 14260-4110, USA
e-mail: stiffany@buffalo.edu

R.A. Bevins, A.R. Caggiula (eds.), *The Motivational Impact of Nicotine and its Role in Tobacco Use*, DOI: 10.1007/978-0-387-78748-0_10, © Springer Science+Business Media, LLC 2009

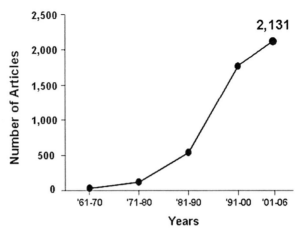

Fig. 10.1 The appearance of the terms *crave* or *craving* in abstracts since 1961 as compiled from MedLine and PsychInfo

phenomenon among cigarette smokers, so smoking represents an excellent vehicle for exposing and untangling the complexities of craving processes. Further, answers about craving generated through smoking research are likely to have considerable applicability to craving observed in other drug-abuse disorders.

Conventional Craving Assumptions

The customary conception of craving, one that has endured for at least the past 50 years, is that craving indexes the core motivation for drug addiction (Tiffany, 1990). For example, in a major review of the neurobiology of relapse, Weiss (2005) concluded, "Current conceptualizations of addiction recognize craving as a central driving force for ongoing drug use, as well as for relapse following abstinence." Over the years, other prominent researchers have made similar assertions about the role of craving in drug-abuse disorders (e.g., Anton, 1999; Baker, Morse, & Sherman, 1987; Ludwig, Wikler & Stark, 1974; Robinson & Berridge, 1993; Wise, 1988). The proposal that craving is at the motivational core of addiction has been assumed, explicitly and implicitly, by most models of craving proposed over the past 50 years.

A distinct implication of this formulation is that measures of craving and drug use should be strongly associated, and that relapse should be preceded by craving. Moreover, as drug-abuse motivation is typically presumed to represent the co-opting of naturally occurring motivational systems by drug-appetitive processes, the mechanisms subserving craving are presumed to be somewhat biologically and psychologically primal, reflecting the operation of fundamental brain reward pathways. The neural pathway most commonly implicated in addictive motivation involves the mesolimbic dopamine system, projecting from the ventral tegmental area (located in the midbrain at the top of the brainstem) and terminating in the nucleus accumbens (located in the base of the forebrain just ventral and medial to the head of the caudate and the putamen) Finally, craving is generally regarded as the subjective manifestation of the core motivational processes mediating addictive behavior – that is, craving is conscious (cf., Berridge & Robinson, 1995).

How Do We Study Craving?

Craving research has benefited greatly by the widespread implementation of two methodological advances. First, modern approaches to the measurement of craving rely on multi-item questionnaires that display considerable reliability and sensitivity to the dynamics of changes in craving over time (e.g., Bohn, Krahn, & Staehler 1995; Heishman, Singelton, & Liguori, 2001; Singleton, Tiffany, & Henningfield, 1994; Tiffany & Drobes, 1991; Tiffany, Singleton, Haertzen, & Henningfield, 1993, Tiffany, Fields, Singleton, Haertzen, & Henningfield, 1995). Second, craving processes can be examined under controlled laboratory conditions through the use of cue-reactivity (CR) procedures (Drummond, Tiffany, Glautier, & Remington, 1995). The CR paradigm draws on the common observation that craving can be reliably triggered when addicts are confronted with cues and situations that are strongly associated with previous episodes of drug use (Drummond et al., 1995). Most smokers, for example, will say that encounters with particular cues and situations, such as a pack of cigarettes, a friend smoking, or remembering past smoking episodes, will readily induce craving. Cue-induced craving is so widespread across addictive disorders that nearly all modern theories of drug dependence invoke cue-specific processes to explain craving and drug use.

Craving Assessment

Most research prior to 1990 evaluated craving with single-item scales of unknown psychometric properties. Over the past several years we have developed several multi-item craving instruments that allow for more precise, psychometrically sophisticated measurements of craving. Our first instrument was the Questionnaire on Smoking Urges (QSU; Tiffany & Drobes, 1991). Validation studies have provided considerable support for the reliability and stability of the latent structure of the questionnaire (e.g., Davies, Willner, & Morgan, 2000; Willner, Hardman, & Eaton, 1995). The QSU served as the prototype for subsequent alcohol, cocaine, heroin, and marijuana craving scales (Bohn et al., 1995; Heishman et al., 2001; Singelton et al., 1994; Tiffany et al., 1993, 1995). We have also developed a 10-item brief form of the QSU that yields a highly reliable estimate of craving in both laboratory and clinical settings (QSU-Brief; Cox, Tiffany, & Christen, 2001). This brief version of the QSU, which has been widely adopted in the nicotine field, has been translated into multiple languages. More recently, we have created a 4-item craving rating derived from the QSU-brief that provides a general craving measure suitable for multiple assessments of craving over a relatively short period. This craving assessment is highly reliable ($\alpha = .95$) and extremely sensitive to craving manipulations (e.g., Carter & Tiffany, 2001).

Factors that Affect Cigarette Craving

Cigarette craving can vary as function of several factors, but those that have been most clearly documented include cigarette abstinence, time of day, alcohol intoxication, stress/negative emotional states, environmental cues, and availability of cigarettes.

Cigarette Abstinence

A robust finding in the smoking literature is that cigarette craving increases dramatically when smokers are instructed to remain abstinent from cigarettes (Schuh & Stitzer, 1995; Tiffany & Drobes, 1991). As shown in Fig. 10.2, abstinence-induced craving is very common among daily smokers. This figure depicts data from daily smokers surveyed in the 2005 National Survey on Drug Use and Health (NSDUH; U.S. Department of Health and Human Services, 2006). The NSDUH is an annual survey of the use of licit and illicit drugs by the civilian, noninstitutionalized population of the United States aged 12 and older. The 2005 survey identified 8,017 daily smokers with a projected estimate of over 38 million daily smokers for the entire United States. Across all age groups, the vast majority of daily smokers, an average of nearly 93%, reported experiencing at least some craving when they had not smoked for a few hours.

In early research conducted in our laboratory, daily cigarette smokers reported significant increases in craving after only one hour of abstinence (Tiffany & Drobes,

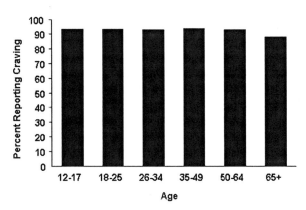

Fig. 10.2 Percentage of daily smokers reporting as experiencing at least some craving when not smoking for a few hours as a function of age group. Data Source: National Survey on Drug Use and Health (2005)

1991). Subsequent research by Schuh and Stitzer (1995) revealed that craving levels can rise within minutes of smoking a cigarette. Although the exact time course of abstinence-induced craving has not been fully mapped, abstinence-induced craving reaches peak levels within three to six hours of cigarette deprivation among daily smokers. Generalized increases in craving following cigarette abstinence appear to be controlled by nicotine deprivation, as this effect is reversed by nicotine delivered via a nicotine patch (Teneggi et al., 2002; Tiffany, Cox, & Elash, 2000).

Time of Day

The impact of time of day and abstinence on craving are clearly illustrated in research by Teneggi and his colleagues (Teneggi et al., 2002). In this study, regular cigarette smokers residing in a clinical research unit were asked to go three days without smoking or they were allowed to continue smoking at their regular rate. Over this period, they rated their craving for cigarettes at several points of each day. Fig. 10.3 shows the craving reports from these two conditions. During the ad lib smoking period, there was no systematic change in craving levels over time. In contrast, when the smokers were abstinent, there were two clear effects evident in the results. First, when abstinent, the smokers reported stronger craving than when smoking. Second, there was a strong daily patterning in craving levels, with craving lowest at the morning assessments and highest in the evening. This diurnal pattern was evident across all three assessment days. This is not the first study to show that craving levels can fluctuate over time; other researchers have reported that craving levels appear to peak in the evening hours for abstinent smokers (Fagerström, Schneider, & Lunnel, 1993; Glassman, Jackson, Walsh, Roose, & Rosenfield, 1984).

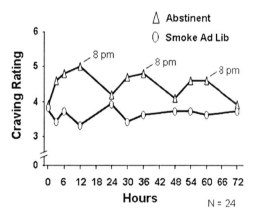

Fig. 10.3 Craving levels over a 72-hour period of cigarette abstinence or ad lib smoking. Data are from Teneggi, Tiffany, Squassante, Milleri, Luigi, & Bye (2002)

Alcohol Intoxication

Smoking and alcohol use have been reciprocally associated with future abuse and dependence (Lewinsohn, Rohde, & Brown, 1999; Werner, Walker, & Greene, 1996; Sher, Gotham, Erickson, & Wood 1996), and the probability of smoking and drinking increases based on the quantities of cigarettes or alcohol consumed (Resnicow, Smith, Harrison, & Drucker, 1999; Sutherland & Willner, 1998; Tucker, Ellickson, & Klein, 2002). Aside from these more distal associations, cigarettes and alcohol are often consumed simultaneously (Shiffman, Fischer, Paty, Gnys, Hickcox, & Kassel, 1994), suggesting possible causal links that are more proximal in nature. Burton & Tiffany (1997) found that alcohol intoxication produced a generalized increase in craving to smoke among daily cigarette smokers who were also social drinkers. The alcohol condition was compared against an alcohol-placebo condition, such that all participants believed that they were receiving alcohol, whether or not they actually did. Consequently, this result was due to the pharmacological effects of alcohol, not alcohol expectancy effects. The effect of alcohol intoxication on craving to smoke has been shown in other placebo-controlled studies with both daily and low-level smokers (Epstein, Sher, Young, & King, 2007; Glautier, Clements, White, Taylor, & Stolerman, 1996; Sayette, Martin, Wertz, Perrott, & Peters, 2005).

Stress and Negative Affect

Links between stress and smoking are abundant in clinical lore as well as experimental paradigms. Smokers report that they smoke more under stress and perceive themselves as under generally greater stress than nonsmokers (Parrott, 1999; Pomerleau & Pomerleau, 1990). Human and animal studies show strong between-subject associations between stress/negative affect (NA) and the initiation and maintenance of smoking/nicotine self-administration and good evidence for within-person effects of stress/NA cueing on relapse to smoking/nicotine self-administration (Kassel, Stroud & Paronis, 2003). Research from our laboratory revealed that induction of negative mood through imagery manipulations increases craving to smoke (Maude-Griffin & Tiffany, 1996; Tiffany & Drobes, 1990), an effect that has been replicated by other researchers (Erblich, Boyarsky, Spring, Niaura & Bovbjerg, 2003). A number of researchers have reported that exposure to acute laboratory stressors (Perkins & Grobe, 1992), or negative mood induction procedures (Conklin & Perkins, 2005; Willner & Jones, 1996) increases craving to smoke.

Smoking-Related Cues

The CR paradigm has been widely used to assess addicts' verbal and physiological responses to drug-related stimuli (Drummond et al., 1995). A meta-analysis of over 40 CR studies with cigarette smokers, alcoholics, heroin addicts and cocaine addicts showed that craving and autonomic reactions can display a great deal of cue-specificity (Carter & Tiffany, 1999). In this study, effect sizes for craving and autonomic measures were calculated as the difference between addicts' responses to drug cues and neutral cues. On average, drug-cue presentations produced significant increases in heart rate and sweat gland activity, and significant declines in skin temperature. With the exception of studies on alcoholics, cue-specific craving across groups was extremely robust, producing average effect sizes in excess of 1.20. Overall, the craving effects were substantially larger than effects observed with the autonomic measures; these latter effects, on average, were small.

This meta-analysis showed that the CR paradigm can produce robust craving and reliable physiological effects in addicts exposed to drug-related stimuli. We have developed several different procedures for presenting smoking related cues to cigarette smokers. As one example, we pioneered the use of imagery procedures to present drug-related cues to cigarette smokers (Tiffany & Hakenewerth, 1991). The results of that experiment and multiple subsequent studies have found that vividly imagining smoking-related scenarios produces robust, cue-specific craving (Burton & Tiffany, 1997; Cepeda-Benito & Tiffany, 1996; Conklin & Tiffany, 2001; Conklin, Tiffany & Vrana, 2000; Drobes & Tiffany, 1997; Elash, Tiffany & Vrana, 1995; Maude-Griffin & Tiffany, 1996; Tiffany et al., 2000; Tiffany & Drobes, 1990). We have also directly compared the impact of imaginal with in vivo (e.g., watching an experimenter smoke a cigarette) presentation of smoking cues, and found that the magnitude of cue-specific craving effects was the same across these two modes of stimulus presentation (Burton & Tiffany, 1997; Drobes & Tiffany, 1997; Tiffany et al., 2000).

In our imagery studies, we typically employ standardized sets of imagery materials consisting of both smoking-related scenarios, designed to evoke strong craving, and smoking-neutral scenarios. Conklin and Tiffany (2001) compared these standard imagery materials with personalized imagery scenarios developed from structured interviews with smokers about situations that they strongly associated with smoking and craving or in which they would not crave cigarettes. Imagery of the personalized material generated substantially higher ratings of image vividness and relevance than imagery of the standard imagery scenes. But, interestingly, personalized craving material did not trigger stronger craving than the standard material. Rather, personalization influenced the difference in craving effects between craving and non-craving imagery material: smokers reported substantially less craving to the personalized than to the standardized non-craving material. In essence, personalization cleaned up our non-craving control stimuli such that these imagery scenarios generated relatively low levels of craving. The net result across the two types of scenarios (craving and non-craving) was a substantially stronger cue-specific craving effect. The average cue-specific craving effect size (Cohen's d) for standardized imagery material was 1.19, an effect size nearly identical to that reported in the meta-analysis by Carter & Tiffany (1999) for CR studies with smokers. The effect size for the personalized material was 1.75, an increase of almost 50% over that obtained with standardized material.

We have used CR procedures across a series of studies to examine the impact of factors that may moderate the magnitude of craving responses to smoking cues. Our research has shown that, although cigarette abstinence produces generalized increases in craving, it does not selectively increase craving reactivity to smoking cues (Drobes & Tiffany, 1997; Maude-Griffin & Tiffany, 1996; Tiffany et al., 2000). Furthermore, the nicotine patch reduces the elevation in craving brought about by abstinence; it does not selectively dampen craving responses to smoking-related cues (Tiffany et al., 2000). The observation that cigarette abstinence does not enhance craving reactions to smoking cues is not unique to our laboratory – a similar pattern has been reported by numerous other researchers (Dawkins, Powell, West, Powell, & Pickering, 2006; McClernon, Hiott, Huettel, & Rose, 2005; McDonough & Warren, 2001; Payne, Smith, Sturges, & Holleran, 1996; Powell, Dawkins & Davis, 2002). We have also found that, although alcohol consumption increases craving in smokers, it does not sensitize smokers to smoking stimuli (Burton & Tiffany, 1997; see also Field, Mogg, & Bradley, 2005, cf., Sayette et al., 2005).

Cigarette Availability and Craving

In nearly all CR research, participants are not allowed to consume their drug during the experimental session. Many researchers have speculated that drug availability should moderate the magnitude of CR (e.g., Baker et al., 1987; Childress, McLellan, & O'Brien, 1986; Ehrman, Robbins, Childress, & O'Brien, 1992; Meyer, 1998). But findings regarding the effect of availability on CR have been mixed, and, when there has been an effect, the magnitude has been extremely modest (see review by Carter & Tiffany, 2001).

Research from our laboratory indicates that the extent to which drug availability influences CR depends on the immediacy of the drug-use opportunity. Past studies on availability may be limited in their use of a CR procedure that only manipulated the expected availability of post-session drug use. That is, in most availability research, participants were informed that they would or would not be able to use their drug at the completion of the experimental session (Juliano & Brandon, 1998; Droungas, Ehrman, Childress, & O'Brien, 1995; Childress et al., 1986). With this procedure, an addict is given the expectation of remote or distal drug availability but not allowed access to the drug in the presence of drug cues during the session. In contrast, availability might be manipulated by informing the addict that he or she would have immediate access to drug use in the presence of drug cues. One may suppose that the extent to which the participant has immediate access to a drug (local availability) might have a different impact on cue reactions than the situation in which access was permitted at the end of a session (distal availability).

Carter and Tiffany (2001) examined the impact of local availability on responses to drug cues by modifying the conventional CR paradigm. This procedure, the Cue-Availability Paradigm (CAP), allowed a trial-by-trial manipulation of cue availability. Local availability was manipulated by presenting smokers with either a glass of water or a lit cigarette behind a clear glass door and informing them of the probability (0%, 50%, or 100%) that they would be able to open the door at the end of the exposure trial and sample the cue. The door was locked or unlocked depending on the probability given to the participant at the beginning of the trial. If the door was unlocked, the smoker could take one puff of the cigarette on cigarette trials and one sip of water on the water trials. Craving ratings and physiological measures were collected in the presence of the target cues.

Carter and Tiffany (2001) found that participants reported higher craving on cigarette trials than on water trials and this difference in craving cues increased with the probability of gaining access to the cigarette (Fig. 10.4). The smokers also had higher levels of skin conductance on cigarette trials and this difference was most pronounced when they knew there was a 100% chance that the door was unlocked and they would be able to smoke the cigarette. Smokers also attempted to open the door more quickly on cigarette trials than water trials, but this effect was significant on only those trials on which they had some chance to sample the cigarette (50 and 100% trials). We have conducted a series of studies replicating these results showing that the opportunity to smoke a cigarette shortly after the presentation of a smoking cue increases the level of craving to the cue presentation (Bailey, Goedeker & Tiffany, 2007; Goedeker, Bailey & Tiffany, 2007; Tiffany, Goedeker & Bailey, 2007; see also Sayette, Wertz, Martin, Cohn, Perrott, & Hobel, 2003). Collectively, these findings show that, in a laboratory setting, the immediate availability of a cigarette has a pronounced impact on CR.

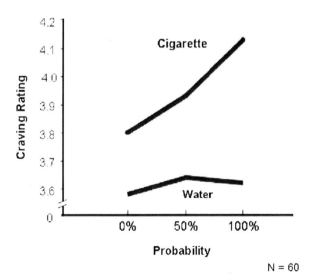

Fig. 10.4 Craving report by cue type and probability of accessing the cue on the trial. Data are from Carter & Tiffany (2001)

Tonic – Phasic Distinction in Cigarette Craving

Several researchers have suggested that craving might be decomposed into two or more components with each reflecting the operation of distinct craving processes (e.g., Drummond, 2000; Isbell, 1955; Tiffany, 2003). A continuous monitoring of craving levels within individuals would likely reveal that craving is relatively variable, displaying peaks, valleys, and brief-duration spikes over the course of a day. Such complex waveforms may comprise two fundamental components. The first component, tonic craving (Tiffany, 2003), is expressed as a slowly changing signal that may reflect abstinence or withdrawal-related craving. This pattern may also index biological processes with a relatively long time constant (e.g., withdrawal effects) and may also track diurnal variations in biological processes (Teneggi et al., 2002). The second component, superimposed on the first, captures fast onset but relatively short duration spikes in craving levels. This phasic craving (e.g., Tiffany, 2003) would presumably reflect cue-specific craving, which would only occur when addicts were confronted with environmental cues or emotionally charged stimuli that remind the addict of previous episodes of use or signal an impending occasion for drug use. Processes controlling tonic and phasic craving may operate somewhat independently. For example, as noted above, research from our laboratory suggests that abstinence-induced phasic craving and cue-specific cigarette craving appear to contribute additively to the total level of craving observed in a smoker at any given time (Bailey et al., 2007; Drobes & Tiffany, 1997; Maude-Griffin & Tiffany, 1996; Tiffany et al., 2000). Similarly, alcohol intoxication, which, like cigarette abstinence, produces a generalized increase in cigarette craving, also does not sensitize smokers to cigarette-related cues (Burton & Tiffany, 1997). We do not know the extent to which cue-reactive craving is constrained or magnified by other changes in tonic craving. In any case, the magnitude of cue-specific craving at any given point of time is best considered within the context of general levels of craving as assessed via reactions to neutral cues and/or baseline assessments of craving (Sayette, Shiffman, Tiffany, Niaura, Martin, & Shadel, 2000).

Craving and Drug Use

As noted earlier, most models of craving assume that craving represents the motivational process responsible for all drug use in the ongoing addict and all instances of relapse in the addict attempting abstinence (Tiffany, 1990). Evidence regarding the validity of this assumption is mixed, with many studies finding little or no relationship between craving and various measures of drug use including relapse (Tiffany, 1990; Tiffany & Conklin, 2000). On the other hand, there are some studies in which craving and drug use or craving and relapse are more strongly associated (e.g., Killen & Fortman, 1997; Ludwig et al., 1974; Shiffman et al., 1997). The factors that moderate the magnitude of the relationship between craving and drug use have not been identified. We hypothesize that, to the extent those relationships exist, they will be strongest when: (a) the measures of craving and drug use are highly reliable,

(b) the conditions of craving assessment and/or induction are maximally representative of the natural expression of craving, (c) neither craving nor drug-use measures are restricted in range, (d) multiple aspects of drug use are evaluated including measures of both drug seeking and drug consumption, and (e) assessments of craving and drug use are conducted in close temporal proximity. These conditions have rarely, if ever, been met in a single study. For example, few CR studies even include measures of smoking as one of the variables potentially affected by cue manipulations.

Our research with the cue-availability paradigm offers the possibility of examining craving–smoking relationships in some detail, as the procedure has multiple trials in which craving in the presence of cigarette cues is measured in conjunction with measures of latency to open the door and access the lit cigarette (drug seeking). As an example, we have looked at results from all four studies in which we used the cue-availability paradigm to calculate the correlation between craving report on trial when there is a 100% probability that the door to the cigarette is unlocked and the latency to open the door on that trial (Bailey et al., 2007; Carter & Tiffany, 2001; Goedeker, Bailey & Tiffany, 2007; Tiffany, Goedeker & Bailey, 2007). In this paradigm, craving report is at its highest level on these trials. The average correlation across studies was 0.24, which, overall, was significant with an aggregated sample size of 360 across experiments. Though significant, this association was not particularly impressive given that the coefficient of determination (r^2) represented less than 6% shared variance between craving and drug seeking. Certainly, in these data, this relationship was much weaker than suggested by the common assumption that craving drives all drug use.

Addressing the Craving– Drug Use Conundrum

Results from the past 50 years of research strongly suggest that the supposition that craving and drug use are tightly coupled presents a grossly distorted picture of the role of craving in addictive processes (Drummond, 2001). This conclusion has profound implications for research on nicotine dependence and, more broadly, all addictive disorders. First, given there is not a one-to-one relationship between craving and measures of drug seeking or drug consumption, craving cannot be used as a proxy for drug use. For example, a treatment that reduces cigarette craving will not necessarily attenuate smoking. Similarly, a treatment that does not affect cigarette craving might still reduce smoking.

Second, drug-use behaviors (seeking and consumption) cannot be used as surrogates for craving. This issue is most critical for those conducting animal research as these researchers do not have access to behaviors in their subjects that map readily on to human expressions of craving. Though many non-human animal investigators are acutely aware of the complexities of modern craving research, there continue to be studies that assert unreservedly that the results are directly indicative of the operation of craving mechanisms, with the primary dependent measure being lever pressing for drug infusions in rodents. The data generated from such studies may be ultimately relevant to behavioral and biological mechanisms of drug-motivation and might inform us about processes that are implicated in craving. However, human research shows that craving and drug seeking (or self-administration) are not isomorphic, and the network of connections between the processes that modulate these two domains of addictive behaviors is substantially more intricate than implied by these simple interpretations. Continued misapprehension of the relevant human research on craving impedes the development of meaningful animal models that might generate crucial insights into the biological and psychological substrates of craving.

Third, data on relationships between craving and drug use require theories that can accommodate the frequent finding that these two behavioral domains are somewhat dissociated. Several years ago, one of us (Tiffany, 1990; see also Tiffany, 1992; Tiffany & Carter, 1998; Tiffany & Conklin, 2000) presented such a theory proposing that the processes that control drug seeking and drug taking can operate independently from the processes that modulate craving. According to this theory, drug use in the experienced addict takes on the characteristics of automatized behavior. That is, over the course of a history of drug use, drug seeking and drug consumption becomes rapid, highly stimulus bound, coordinated, difficult to inhibit in the presence of enabling stimuli, cognitively non-demanding, and organized outside of conscious awareness. The following anecdote from Guthrie (1935) clearly captures the automatic nature of smoking:

> I once had a caller to whom I was explaining that the apple I had just finished was a splendid device for avoiding a smoke. The caller pointed out that I was smoking at the moment. The habit of lighting a cigarette was so attached to the finish of eating that smoking had been started automatically. (p. 116)

The concept of automaticity has a long history in psychological research (e.g., James, 1890) and has been fruitfully applied to areas as broad as attention, emotion, perception, learning, memory, motivation, skill acquisition, and social cognition (see Moors & De Houwer, 2006, for review). A theme that permeates this literature is that behaviors repeated under fixed stimulus conditions become increasingly controlled by cognitive processes that differ from those that are responsible for performance when the behavior is initiated. A hallmark of addictive behavior is that addicts seek and consume their drug frequently. Consequently, if the concept of automaticity is relevant for any domain of highly practiced behavior, it certainly should apply to addictive behavior. Consider regular smokers who, during the course of any given year, smoke thousands of cigarettes and, over their lifetime, smoke hundreds of thousands of cigarettes. With the opportunity for so much practice, it is hard to imagine anything other than the automatization of much of the behavior necessary for getting and consuming cigarettes. The cognitive processing model proposes that, over a history of repeated practice, the cognitive systems controlling cigarette procurement and consumption will become automatized. Tiffany (1990) hypothesized that the procedures for carrying out these automatized skills are stored in the form of action schemata (Fig. 10.5). These are memory structures that contain adequate information for the initiation and coordination of complex sequences of

Drug-Use Action Schemata

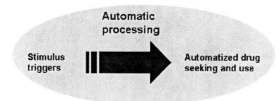

Encoded Information

Stimulus configurations for eliciting component actions

Procedures for enactment of specific actions

Coordination of specific actions into action sequences

Alternative action sequences in event of *minor* obstacles

Fig. 10.5 Proposed components of drug-use action schemata

drug-use behavior. In the experienced smoker, some stimulus conditions activate drug-use action schemata that, in turn, control smoking behavior. Notice that craving is nowhere invoked in this proposed sequence of cigarette seeking and smoking.

Although automaticity has been investigated thoroughly in human studies, this concept has also been addressed in animal research. For example, Dickinson (1985, 1989) proposed that instrumental behavior in animals might be controlled by two types of processes, stimulus–response (S–R) associations (habits) in which reinforcing a response leads to the strengthening of an association between contextual cues and the response, and response–outcome (R–O) associations, which control goal-directed actions. According to this perspective, the "S–R process is analogous to the cue-elicited automatic action schemata within Tiffany's (1990) theory in that both mediate involuntary and habitual responding" (Miles, Everitt, & Dickinson, 2003; page 927). Miles et al., (2003) demonstrated that rats given extended instrumental training for a cocaine–sucrose reinforcer were relatively immune to a devaluation procedure in which the cocaine–sucrose solution was paired with an aversive outcome. These authors interpreted the results as consistent with the hypothesis that components of drug seeking and taking are automatic and habitual. Beyond these implications for the cognitive processing account of drug use, the results demonstrate that elements of a theory derived from human–information processing models can be investigated in animal preparations. (See Dickinson, Wood, & Smith, 2002, and Miles, Everitt, Dally, & Dickinson, 2004, for similar research on automaticity and drug taking.)

Typically, automatic processing is contrasted with nonautomatic cognitive processing, which is generally described as limited by fixed-capacity cognitive functioning, situationally flexible, dependent on attention and intention, relatively slow, and cognitively effortful (e.g., Logan, 1991; Moors & De Houwer, 2006). Nonautomatic processing is required in new tasks or situations in which automatic

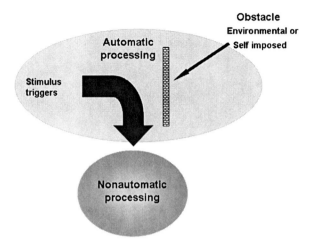

Fig. 10.6 The activation of nonautomatic processing

processing cannot adequately control responding and is also required to impede the initiation or completion of automatic processing. The cognitive processing theory associates craving with responses supported by nonautomatic cognitive processes activated in parallel with drug-use action schemata (Fig. 10.6). These are invoked when there is some obstacle that blocks the successful completion of an activated drug-use schema. This obstacle can arise from two sources: (1) Some environmental condition impedes the action schema in an addict not attempting to avoid drug use, or (2) An addict attempting to remain abstinent tries to block or impede a drug-use action schema. As an example of an environmental obstacle, what happens when a smoker, not trying to quit smoking, reaches for a pack of cigarettes only to discover that her cigarettes are gone? This situation will demand the invocation of nonautomatic processing to solve the problem.

The manifestations of this processing can be indexed across three broad classes of behavior. Motor behavior should be characterized by actions to overcome or neutralize the obstacle. Verbal responses should include reports of desire to use, a stated intention to use the drug, reports of frustration and annoyance (this is classic frustration paradigm), and, if prompted, descriptions of problem solving and planning to overcome the obstacle. Finally, there should be indices of somatovisceral activation linked both to the cognitive effort generated by the nonautomatic processing as well as responses that would support physical effort to overcome the obstacle.

Among the many implications of the cognitive processing model of drug craving and use are the following: (1) Smoking behavior, including actions to obtain and consume cigarettes, should have the hallmarks of automatic behaviors. (2) The level of automaticity represented by any single component of smoking behavior and the coordination and coherence of components across behavioral sequences will be determined by the extent to which the individual has engaged in those behaviors under fixed stimulus conditions. (3) Craving is not necessary for either smoking or smoking relapse. (4) Craving can occur among smokers not intending to quit as well as among those who are attempting abstinence. (5) Craving will be generated under circumstances strongly associated with past episodes of smoking, including all of the conditions outlined earlier as factors that influence craving. (6) Craving is activated when habitual, automatic smoking routines are interrupted, either by environmentally imposed obstacles in those not intending to quit or by self-generated obstacles to smoking in those attempting to abstain. (7) Craving is experienced as an aversive, distracting, cognitively demanding condition that can, either acutely or cumulatively, undermine a smoker's commitment to abstinence.

If Craving and Smoking Are Not Tightly Coupled, Why Study Craving?

A question we encounter during discussions about the generally weak associations between measures of craving and drug use is "Why do research on craving if it is not strongly linked to drug use?" We believe that abandoning craving research in light of the ambiguous relationship between craving and drug use would be a counterproductive response. Indeed, there are multiple compelling reasons for programmatic research on craving. These include:

Ubiquity of Craving Among Smokers

As noted earlier in this chapter, craving is extraordinarily common among regular smokers. But craving is not restricted to chronic, heavy smokers. It is even relatively widespread among relatively inexperienced, neophyte smokers (Colby, Tiffany, Shiffman, & Niaura, 2000). Craving is also highly persistent – former smokers can experience craving years after their last cigarette (Fletcher & Doll, 1969). The intensity of craving associated with cigarette smoking may be as strong as or stronger than craving associated with other addictive disorders (Kozlowski et al., 1989). The ubiquity and persistence of craving suggests that any comprehensive model of smoking must account for this prominent feature of nicotine dependence.

Prominence of Craving Among Abstinent Smokers

Although craving is not listed as a diagnostic feature of nicotine withdrawal (or dependence) in DSM-IV (American Psychiatric Association, 2000), it is a component of the ICD-10 (World Health Organization, 1992) diagnosis of tobacco withdrawal (as well as tobacco dependence). Abstinent smokers report that craving is the most salient (Shiffman & Jarvik, 1976) and frequent (Gritz, Carr, & Marcus, 1991) symptom they experience when they quit smoking. For example, in a recent laboratory-based study, withdrawal symptoms and craving were assessed with multiple instruments at several time points across a 72-hour period when smokers were abstinent or smoking ad lib (Teneggi et al., 2005). Abstinence produced significant increases in craving and withdrawal symptoms, but the average effect sizes for the craving differences were substantially larger (d = 1.33) than those seen in the withdrawal symptoms that did not assess craving (d = 0.43).

Aversive Nature of Craving

Tiffany (1997) described craving as the psychic pain of addiction. Abstinent smokers say that craving is the most troublesome symptom they experience when they quit smoking (Richter, McCool, Okuyemi, Mayo, & Ahluwalia, 2002; Seidman & Covey, 1999; West, Hajek, & Belcher, 1989), and concerns about craving appear to be a formidable obstacle preventing many smokers from even attempting to quit (Orleans, Rimer, Cristinzio, Keintz, & Fleisher, 1991). Craving is generally viewed as a major impediment to smokers' attempts to quit smoking, and advertisements for pharmacological smoking treatments (e.g., nicotine patches, gum, lozenges) typically emphasize the craving-relieving effects of these products. The following description of the difficulties of quitting smoking depicts the aversive, intrusive feature of craving:

> One of the more difficult aspects of quitting is an intense craving that overwhelms your ability to think about much of anything besides cigarettes, and the fear that not only are you going to suffer more, but that if you don't do something about this craving right now, it's going to get worse, and you're not going to get anything accomplished (posted by Chris on Tuesday, May 02, 2006 on Mixing Memory: http://scienceblogs.com/mixingmemory)

The aversive, cognitively demanding aspects of craving have been captured in laboratory studies. Research from our laboratory has shown that elicitation of craving through CR procedures also produces a decrement in cognitive performance on a parallel reaction-time task (Cepeda-Benito & Tiffany, 1996; see also Gross, Jarvik, & Rosenblatt, 1993; Sayette & Hufford, 1994). Similarly, in nearly all of our CR research, stimulus conditions that trigger craving also increase negative mood ratings and/or decrease positive mood ratings. The only exception to this pattern has been in our cue-availability research. Here, positive mood increases and negative mood decreases on trials in which there is a 100% probability of being able to access a lit cigarette (Bailey et al., 2007; Carter & Tiffany, 2001; Goedeker et al., 2007; Tiffany et al., 2007). At first blush, those findings might suggest that craving can be a pleasant, positive-affective experience, but a closer inspection of the data from those studies reveals a more complex story. Importantly, the level of positive mood on 100% cigarette available trials is not significantly correlated with the craving level reported on those same trials. Interestingly, the strongest affective correlate of craving on those trials is the level of negative mood on other trials in which access to the lit cigarette is completely restricted. That is, the negative mood that people experience when they are forced to look at a lit cigarette they cannot smoke is the best predictor of craving on trials when they look at a cigarette they know they will be able to access in a few seconds. Our interpretation of this pattern is that smokers are relieved when they know they can soon smoke a cigarette and are frustrated when they are told they cannot smoke. The level of frustration, and not positive affect (or even relief), is more tightly linked to the craving generated when they are allowed to smoke.

Craving as a Predictor of Relapse

Although any single instance of craving may not be strongly associated with immediate smoking behavior, research has shown that general levels of craving expressed during or after treatment can be significantly associated with the probability of subsequent smoking relapse (al'Absi, Hatsukami, Davis, & Wittmers, 2004; Baer, Kamark, Lichtenstein, & Ransom, 1989; Brandon, Tiffany, & Baker,1987; Catley, O'Connell, & Shiffman, 2000; Doherty, Kinnunen, Militello, & Garvey, 1995; Killen & Fortmann, 1997). Thus, craving assessments might identify smokers at greatest risk for relapse and could be used to formulate relapse-prevention interventions that target high-risk smokers.

Perhaps the largest study to examine relationships between cravings expressed during treatment and subsequent relapse was by Killen and Fortmann (1997). This report summarized the results of three treatment studies involving nearly 2,700 smokers. The results across all three studies were interpreted as showing that levels of craving over the first 24–48 hours of abstinence were negatively associated with time to relapse. Interestingly, subjects across these studies were *not* asked about their level of craving – they were asked to rate "how upsetting cravings and urges had been since quitting smoking." Smokers more *upset* about craving were more likely to relapse. This finding suggests that the extent to which craving is aversive or disruptive to functioning may be a better predictor of relapse than craving levels per se (see also Brandon et al., 1987; Tiffany & Carter, 1998).

Craving as a Core Attribute of Nicotine Dependence

As noted earlier, DSM-IV does not include craving as a diagnostic feature of either nicotine dependence or nicotine withdrawal. Nonetheless, a persuasive argument could be made that, given its ubiquity, salience and intensity, craving should be recognized as a core attribute of nicotine dependence in future iterations of DSM (e.g., Colby et al., 2000). This proposal, however, begs the question of the diagnostic utility of craving in diagnosis of dependence – a question that, in turn, raises a larger matter. What are the essential diagnostic features of nicotine dependence And that question is embedded in an even more general issue – what is the fundamental latent structure of dependence?

Modern diagnostic systems (i.e., DSM and ICD) define nicotine dependence as an entity somehow qualitatively or categorically distinct from non-dependent smoking. That is, they make the assumption that there is a natural boundary between dependent and nondependent smoking, a boundary defined by the collective presence of certain behavioral characteristics such as compulsive use, high levels of use, smoking despite knowledge of harm, tolerance, and withdrawal. In short, from this perspective, dependence represents a taxon, a conceptualization of smoking distinct from a dimensional or quantitative view of nicotine dependence (Tiffany Conklin, Shiffman & Clayton, 2004). The latter perspective, which is implicit or explicit in nearly all contemporary theoretical accounts of dependence (Tiffany et al., 2004), assumes that dependence varies along a continuum such that even very inexperienced smokers have some degree of nicotine dependence. These theories hold a dimensional perspective of dependence that does not "assume any functional discontinuity between light and heavy smokers" (Tiffany et al., 2004, p. 80). The issue – whether nicotine dependence is best conceived of as a dimension or a taxon – has not been systematically addressed by previous research.

The question of whether multiple indicators presumably indexing a single construct have a taxonic (categorical) or dimensional latent structure can be addressed by a group of statistical procedures known as taxometric analyses (Meehl, 1973; Meehl & Golden, 1982; Meehl & Yonce, 1994; Waller & Meehl, 1998). Taxometric analyses offer an empirical approach to discerning the presence (or absence) of a taxon among sets of indicators putatively representative of a construct (Ruscio, Haslam, & Ruscio, 2006; Waller & Meehl, 1998). Further, if a taxon is present in the data, these analyses will identify the indicators best suited to identifying that taxon and will estimate the base rate of the taxon in the data set.

We recently completed a taxometric analysis of smoking related data from the 2003 and 2002 National Surveys on Drug Use and Health (NSDUH; Goedeker & Tiffany, 2007). Results from MAMBAC, MAXEIG, and LMODE taxometric analyses on five indicator measures administered to adults who reported any smoking within the previous 30 days produced strong and consistent evidence of a nicotine dependence taxon across all analyses. The valid indicators included three multi-item subscales of the Nicotine Dependence Symptom Scale (NDSS; Shiffman, Waters, & Hickcox, 2004): Drive, Tolerance, and Continuity. The two additional indicators were each single items assessing the latency to smoke the first cigarette after waking and the number of cigarettes smoked per day. The dependence taxon, which had a base rate of 48% among past 30-day smokers, was highly replicable across both years of the survey (with over 11,000 smokers assessed at each year) and within male and female subgroups.

The NSDSS Drive subscale, a core component of the dependence taxon as identified by the taxometric analyses is, according to Shiffman et al. (2004), represented primarily by craving-related items. For example, the Drive item that correlates most strongly with the subscale total score is worded "When you don't smoke for a few hours, you start to crave cigarettes." Thus, members of the dependent taxon had stronger craving to smoke, higher levels of tolerance to nicotine, more rigid smoking patterns, shorter latencies to smoke their first cigarette upon waking, and smoked more cigarettes per day compared to nontaxon members. Beyond the importance of these findings for our understanding of the fundamental nature of nicotine dependence, the results also support the diagnostic utility of caving as a critical feature of the nicotine dependence taxon.

Future of Craving Research

We have no doubt that research on craving will continue to be an important focus of smoking research over the foreseeable future. There are many paths that research can follow including more penetrating investigations of the neurobiology of craving, fuller descriptions of the natural history of craving, greater exploration of genetic contributions to craving processes, further mapping of the conditions under which craving processes and smoking behaviors are linked, refined treatments (pharmacological and behavioral) for craving, and continued development of the CR paradigm. With regard to this last point, we believe that we have not pushed CR research as far as we could. Often, tobacco seeking and tobacco consumption have been neglected as central components of CR . Further, the key parameters of cues that control reactivity have not been systematically investigated, and there has been scant work on the psychometrics of the stimuli used in this research. Relationships between reactivity measures are rarely addressed, and we know virtually nothing about the natural history of CR. By and large, reactivity measures other than craving have been selected more on the basis of convenience than theory, and the generalizability of CR over time, situation, and person has not been systematically explored.

We also believe that CR research has been needlessly constrained in one additional way: We have caged CR in the laboratory and not examined it in free-ranging smokers. The CR phenomena are not restricted to the laboratory. Addicts readily describe situations and cues that trigger craving in their everyday lives (e.g., Childress et al., 1986; Ludwig, 1986; Tiffany & Baker, 1988). However, to the best of our knowledge, all of the experimental research on CR has been conducted in the laboratory; there has been no CR research in real-world settings. The absence of such research is surprising, as there are many reasons to expect that patterns of CR are affected by factors not readily captured in the laboratory:

First, the effect of a cue on craving may be moderated by the environmental setting or meta-context of the cue exposure (Dols, van den Hout, Kindt, & Willems, 2002). For example, an environmental context replete with other reminders of smoking, such as a familiar, smoke-filled bar or a frequented smoking area outside of a smoke-free building, could easily alter the magnitude of CR in that setting. Certainly, bars or smoking areas could be recreated in the laboratory, though the verisimilitude of the same simulation for all subjects in a study will be limited. Other critical situations may involve particularly idiosyncratic social features, such as smoking with close friends, which would not be readily reproducible in the laboratory.

Second, there are numerous moderating conditions, such as current emotional state, which may influence CR but are difficult to assess thoroughly in a laboratory setting. The relationships between affect and craving are complex as are the relationships between affective state and smoking (Kassel et al., 2003; Shiffman et al., 2002). Levels of negative affect are often positively correlated with both general levels of craving and cue-induced craving (e.g., Carter & Tiffany, 2001; Drobes & Tiffany, 1997), and, as described earlier, induction of negative affect and exposure to stress situations can, in their own right, trigger craving (e.g., Tiffany & Drobes, 1990; Maude-Griffin & Tiffany, 1996; Sinha, Catapano, & O'Malley 1999;

Sinha, Fuse, & Aubin, 2000; Sinha, Talih, Malison, Cooney, Anderson, & Kreek, 2003). However, all of these relationships were established in laboratory settings. The extent to which CR varies as a function of background emotional state in the natural environment has not been examined.

Third, CR studies are typically conducted without reference to recurrent cyclical patterns such as time of day or day of the week. Earlier in this chapter, we described research suggesting that time of day is correlated with cigarette craving, with craving in abstinent smokers often lowest in the morning hours and peaking in the evening hours (Teneggi et al., 2002). Moreover, Shiffman and his colleagues found that, of all the time periods assessed in abstinent smokers, craving in the morning was the best predictor of subsequent relapse (Shiffman et al., 1997). Research conducted by Tiffany and his associates have found that smoking rates in college student smokers are strongly influenced by the day of the week, with much more smoking occurring on Fridays and Saturdays than on any other days (Tiffany et al., in press). Time of day or day of week can be addressed as moderating factors in laboratory studies, though it would be logistically prohibitive to construct complete profiles of either of these factors in a single study.

Fourth, as detailed above, drug availability can influence,CR although the parameters and dimensions of availability that most affect reactivity are unknown. Availability is likely a complex concept (Carter & Tiffany, 2001; Sayette et al., 2003), but we have little guidance from naturalistic studies of craving and availability to direct our experimental manipulations. More generally, assessment of CR in the natural environment gives us the opportunity to identify new classes and configurations of variables as candidates for more intensive, controlled study in the laboratory environment.

Fifth, much of the non-supportive evidence regarding the presumed relationships between craving and measures of drug use comes from laboratory-based studies of CR. It is possible that the craving processes generated in these laboratory studies do not reflect CR in natural settings and are unsuited for a comprehensive evaluation of associations between craving and drug use. In contrast, assessment of craving and CR in the natural environment may expose forms or profiles of craving that might be more revealing of the factors that control the associations between craving and drug use.

Finally, since the first experiments in the 1970s, there have been over 150 studies utilizing the CRparadigm. This paradigm has become well established for studying psychological and neurobiological processes that motivate addictive drug use. Nevertheless, we know nothing about the generalizability of results from these laboratory studies to the real world, because CR has not been studied in the natural environment. That is, the external validity of the findings with regard to non-laboratory settings has not been investigated, and their relevance for the real world of the addicted person is unknown. There have been efforts to bring the real world into the laboratory through more detailed simulations of real-world cues or presentations of cues via virtual reality systems (Bordnick et al., 2004; Kuntze et al., 2001; Lee et al., 2003). These studies attempt to represent real world stimuli, but they do not demonstrate the extent to which the simulated conditions are representative of the addict's natural environment. Any study that endeavors to bring the real world into the laboratory in an effort to enhance ecological validity must establish the degree to which the supposed real-world stimuli are relevant and representative of the natural world (Scheidt, 1981).

These considerations have motivated us to begin examining CR effects under real-world conditions. To accomplish this, we have launched research to develop a procedure for assessing cigarette smokers' reactions to smoking-related cues when those cues are presented in the natural environment of the smokers. In this research, cues are presented via a Personal Digital Assistant (PDA) that smokers carry with them over multiple days. The PDA prompts smokers to complete CR trials several times throughout each day. Smokers also use the PDA to log each cigarette that they smoke. The use of the PDA to collect information about event-related behavior is an example of Ecological Momentary Assessment (EMA), which has been used successfully to monitor a variety of behaviors in real time (Stone & Shiffman, 2002). We call our new procedure, which combines CR procedures with EMA, CREMA. We anticipate that the data generated by this procedure will allow for estimation of the external validity of results produced by laboratory based CR procedures and, more importantly, create a new tool to explore cue-specific craving in the natural environment.

Final Note

Craving research has exploded over the past 20 years, increasing 50-fold compared to the preceding 20 years. The cumulative message of this burgeoning body of research is that craving continues to be an important topic in the addictions field, and for good reason. The desire to use drugs appears to be a hallmark of addictive disorders, an assertion that seems particularly characteristic of nicotine dependence. Many researchers and clinicians assume that the compulsive nicotine use in smokers is driven by a pathological level of desire. According to that popular view, craving is a direct manifestation of the motivational core of addictive behavior. Contrary to this perspective, craving is often not strongly and immediately linked to smoking. That observation suggests that any model of smoking motivation and craving that presumes that the latter is a direct index of the former, needs revision. We have summarized the potential significance of craving processes in characterizing, predicting, and diagnosing nicotine dependence. We believe that a full scientific explanation of nicotine dependence must account for cigarette craving, in all its complexity.

References

al'Absi, M., Hatsukami, D., Davis, G. L., & Wittmers, L. E. (2004). Prospective examination of effects of smoking abstinence on cortisol and withdrawal symptoms as predictors of early smoking relapse. *Drug and Alcohol Dependence, 73*, 267–278.

American Psychiatric Association (2000). *Diagnostic and Statistical Manual of Mental Disorders 4th Edition, Text Revision*. Washington, DC: Author.

Anton, R. F. (1999). What is craving? Models and implications for treatment. *Alcohol Research & Health: The Journal of the National Institute on Alcohol Abuse and Alcoholism, 23*, 165–73.

Baer, J. S., Kamark, T., Lichtenstein, E., Ransom, C. C. (1989). Prediction of smoking relapse: Analyses of temptations and transgressions after initial cessation. *Journal of Consulting and Clinical Psychology, 57*, 623–627.

Bailey, S., Goedeker, K. A., & Tiffany, S. T. (2007). *The impact of cigarette deprivation and cigarette availability on cue-reactivity in smokers*. Manuscript submitted for publication.

Baker, T. B., Morse, E., & Sherman, J. E. (1987). The motivation to use drugs: A psychobiological analysis of urges. In P. C. Rivers (Ed.), *The Nebraska symposium on motivation: Alcohol and addictive behavior* (pp. 257–323). Lincoln: University of Nebraska Press.

Berridge, K. C. & Robinson, T. E. (1995). The mind of an addicted brain: Neural sensitization of wanting versus liking. *Current Directions in Psychological Science, 4*, 71–76.

Bohn, M. J., Krahn, D. D. & Staehler, B. A. (1995). Development and initial validation of a measure of drinking urges in abstinent alcoholics. *Alcoholism: Clinical and Experimental Research, 19*, 600–606.

Bordnick, P. S., Graap, K. M., Copp, H., Brooks, J., Ferrer, M., & Logue, B. (2004). Utilizing virtual reality to standardize nicotine craving research: A pilot study. *Addictive Behaviors, 29*, 1889–1894.

Brandon, T. H., Tiffany, S. T., & Baker, T. B. (1987). Characterization of the process of smoking relapse. In F. Tims & C. Leukefeld (Eds.), *Relapse and Recovery in Drug Abuse* (NIDA Research Monograph, No. 72, pp. 104–107). Washington, DC: US Government Printing Office.

Burton, S. M., & Tiffany, S. T. (1997). The effect of alcohol consumption on imaginal and in vivo manipulations of smoking urges. *Addiction, 92*, 15–26.

Carter, B. L., & Tiffany, S. T. (1999). Meta analysis of cue reactivity in addiction research. *Addiction, 94*, 327–340.

Carter, B. L., & Tiffany, S. T. (2001). The cue availability paradigm: The effects of cigarette availability on cue reactivity in smokers. *Experimental and Clinical Psychopharmacology, 9*, 183–190.

Catley, D., O'Connell, K. A., Shiffman, S. (2000). Absentminded lapses during smoking cessation. *Psychology of Addictive Behaviors, 14*, 73–76.

Cepeda-Benito, A., & Tiffany, S. T. (1996). The use of a dual task procedure for the assessment of cognitive effort associated with cigarette craving. *Psychopharmacology, 127*, 155–163.

Childress, A. R., McLellan, A. T. & O'Brien, C. P. (1986). Conditioned responses in a methadone population: A comparison of laboratory, clinic and natural *settings*. *Journal of Substance Abuse Treatment, 3*, 173–179.

Colby, S. M., Tiffany, S., Shiffman, S., Niaura, R. S. (2000). Are adolescent smokers dependent on nicotine? A review of the evidence. *Drug and Alcohol Dependence, 59*, S83–S95.

Conklin, C. A. & Perkins, K. A. (2005). Subjective and reinforcing effects of smoking during negative mood induction. *Journal of Abnormal Psychology, 114*, 153–164.

Conklin, C. A., & Tiffany, S. T. (2001). The impact of imagining personalized versus standardized urge scenarios on cigarette craving and autonomic reactivity. *Experimental and Clinical Psychopharmacology, 9*, 399–408.

Conklin, C. A., Tiffany, S. T., & Vrana, S. R. (2000). Impact of imagining completed versus interrupted smoking on cigarette craving and secondary task performance. *Experimental and Clinical Psychopharmacology, 8*, 68–74.

Cox, L. S., Tiffany, S. T., & Christen, A. G. (2001). Evaluation of the brief questionnaire of smoking urges (QSU-Brief) in laboratory and clinical settings. *Nicotine and Tobacco Research, 3*, 7–16.

Davies, G. M., Willner, P., & Morgan M. J. (2000). Smoking-related cues elicit craving in tobacco "chippers": A replication and validation of the two-factor structure of the Questionnaire of Smoking Urges. *Psychopharmacology, 152*, 334–342.

Dawkins, L., Powell, J. H., West, R., Powell, J., & Pickering, A. (2006). A double-blind placebo controlled experimental study of nicotine: I - effects on incentive motivation. *Psychopharmacology, 189,* 355–367.

Dickinson, A. (1985). Actions and habits–The development of behavioural autonomy. *Philosophical Transactions of the Royal Society. Series B, Biological Sciences, 308,* 67–78.

Dickinson, A. (1989). Expectancy theory in animal conditioning. In S. B. Klein & R. R. Mowrer (Eds.), Contemporary learning theories: Pavlovian conditioning and the status of traditional learning theories (pp. 279–308). Hillsdale, NJ: Erlbaum.

Dickinson, A., Wood, N., & Smith, J. W. (2002). Alcohol seeking by rats: Action or habit? *Quarterly Journal of Experimental Psychology, 55,* 331–348.

Doherty, K., Kinnunen, T., Militello, F. S., & Garvey, A. J. (1995). Urges to smoke during the first month of abstinence: Relationship to relapse and predictors. *Psychopharmacology, 119,* 171–178.

Dols, M., van den Hout, M., Kindt, M. & Willems, B. (2002). The urge to smoke depends on the expectation of smoking. *Addiction, 97,* 87–93.

Drobes, D. J., & Tiffany, S. T. (1997). Induction of Smoking Urge Through Imaginal and In Vivo Procedures: Physiological and Self Report Manifestations. *Journal of Abnormal Psychology, 106,* 15–25.

Droungas, A., Ehrman, R., Childress, A. R., & O'Brien, C. (1995). Effect of smoking cues and cigarette availability on craving and smoking behavior. *Addictive Behaviors, 20,* 657–673.

Drummond, D. C. (2000). What does cue-reactivity have to offer clinical research? *Addiction, 95,* S129-S144.

Drummond D. C. (2001). Theories of drug craving, ancient and modern. *Addiction, 96,* 33–46.

Drummond, D. C., Tiffany, S. T., Glautier, S., & Remington, B. (1995). *Addictive Behaviour: Cue exposure, theory and practice.* London: John Wiley & Sons.

Ehrman, R. N., Robbins, S. J., Childress, A. R., & O'Brien, C. P. (1992). Conditioned responses to cocaine-related stimuli in cocaine abuse patients. *Psychopharmacology, 107,* 523–529.

Elash, C., Tiffany, S. & Vrana, S. (1995). The manipulation of smoking urges and affect through a brief imagery procedure: Self report, psychophysiological and startle probe responses. *Experimental and Clinical Psychopharmacology, 3,* 156–162.

Epstein, A. M., Sher, T. G., Young, M. A., & King, A. C. (2007). Tobacco chippers show robust increases in smoking urge after alcohol consumption. *Psychopharmacology, 190,* 321–329.

Erblich, J., Boyarsky, Y., Spring, B., Niaura, R., & Bovbjerg, D. H. (2003). A family history of smoking predicts heightened levels of stress-induced cigarette craving. *Addiction, 98,* 657–664.

Fagerström, K. O., Schneider, N. G. Lunnel, E. (1993). Effectiveness of nicotine patch and nicotine gum as individual versus combined treatments for tobacco withdrawal symptoms. *Psychopharmacology, 11,* 271–277.

Field, M., Mogg, K., & Bradley, B. P. (2005). Alcohol increases cognitive biases for smoking cues in smokers. *Psychopharmacology, 180,* 63–72.

Fletcher, C. & Doll, R. (1969). A survey of doctors' attitudes to smoking. *British Journal of Preventive and Social Medicine, 23,* 145–153.

Glassman, A. H., Jackson, W. K., Walsh, B. T., Roose, S. P., & Rosenfield, B. (1984). Cigarette craving, smoking withdrawal, and clonidine. *Science, 226,* 864–866.

Glautier, S., Clements, K., White, J. A. W., Taylor, C., & Stolerman, I. P. (1996). Alcohol and the reward value of cigarette smoking. *Behavioral Pharmacology, 7,* 144–154.

Goedeker, K. A., Bailey, S., & Tiffany, S. T. (2007). *The impact of local and distal cigarette availability on smokers' reactions to smoking stimuli.* Manuscript submitted for publication.

Goedeker, K. A. & Tiffany, S. T. (2007). *On the nature of nicotine addiction: A taxometric analysis.* Manuscript submitted for publication.

Gritz, E. R., Carr. C. R., & Marcus, A. C. (1991). The tobacco withdrawal syndrome in unaided quitters. *British Journal of Addiction, 86,* 57–69.

Gross, T. M., Jarvik, M. E., & Rosenblatt, M. R. (1993). Nicotine abstinence produces content-specific Stroop interference. *Psychopharmacology, 110,* 333–336.

Guthrie, E. R. (1935). *The psychology of learning.* New York: Harper & Brothers.

Heishman, S. J. Singelton, E. G., Liguori, A. (2001). Marijuana craving questionnaire: Development and initial validation of a self-report instrument. *Addiction, 96,* 1023–1034.

Isbell, H. (1955). Craving for alcohol. *Quarterly Journal of Studies on Alcohol, 16,* 38–42.

James, W. (1890). *The principles of psychology.* New York: Holt, Rinehart & Winston.

Juliano, L. M. & Brandon, T. H. (1998). Reactivity to perceived smoking availability and environmental cues: Evidence with urge and reaction time. *Experimental and Clinical Psychopharmacology, 6,* 45–53.

Kassel, J. D., Stroud, L. R., & Paronis, C. A. (2003). Smoking, stress, and negative affect: Correlation, causation, and context across stages of smoking. *Psychological Bulletin, 129,* 270–304.

Killen, J. D. & Fortmann, S. P. (1997). Craving is associated with smoking relapse: Findings from three prospective studies. *Experimental and Clinical Psychopharmacology, 5,* 137–142.

Kozlowski, L. T., Wilkinson, D. A., Skinner, W., Kent, C., Franklin, T., & Pope, M. (1989). Comparing tobacco cigarette dependence with other drug dependencies: Greater or equal 'difficulty quitting' and 'urges to use', but less 'pleasure' from cigarettes. *Journal of the American Medical Association, 261,* 898–901.

Kuntze, M. F., Stoermer, R., Mager, R., et al. (2001). Immersive virtual environments in cue exposure. *Cyber Psychology & Behavior, 4,* 497–501.

Lee, J. H., Ku, J., Kim, K., Kim, B., Kim, I. Y., Yang, B-H., et al. (2003). Experimental application of virtual reality for nicotine craving through cue exposure. *Cyber Psychology & Behavior, 6,* 275–280.

Lewinsohn, P. M., Rohde, P., & Brown, R. A. (1999). Level of current and past adolescent cigarette smoking as predictors of future substance use disorders in young adulthood. *Addiction, 94,* 913–921.

Logan, G. D. (1991). Automaticity and memory. In W. E. Hockley & S. Lewandowsky (Eds.), Relating theory and data: Essays on human memory in honor of Bennet B. Murdock (pp. 347–366). Hillsdale, NJ: Lawrence Erlbaum Associates, Inc.

Ludwig, A. M. (1986). Pavlov's "bells" and alcohol craving. *Addictive Behaviors, 11,* 87–91.

Ludwig, A. M., Wikler, A. & Stark, L. H. (1974). The first drink: Psychobiological aspects of craving. *Archives of General Psychiatry, 30,* 539–547.

Maude-Griffin, P. M., & Tiffany, S. T. (1996). Production of smoking urges through imagery: The impact of affect and smoking abstinence. *Experimental and Clinical Psychopharmacology, 4,* 198–208.

McClernon, F. J., Hiott, F. B., Huettel, S. A., & Rose, J. E. (2005). Abstinence-induced changes in self-report craving correlate with event-related FMRI responses to smoking cues. *Neuropsychopharmacology, 30,* 1940–1947.

McDonough, B. E., & Warren, C. A. (2001). Effects of 12-h tobacco deprivation on event-related potentials elicited by visual smoking cues. *Psychopharmacology, 154,* 282–291.

Meehl, P. (1973). MAXCOV-HITMAX: A taxometric search method for loose genetic syndromes. In P. Meehl (Ed.), *Psychodiagnosis: Selected papers* (pp. 200–224). Minneapolis, MN: University of Minnesota Press.

Meyer, R. E. (1988). Conditioning phenomena and the problem of relapse in opioid addicts and alcoholics. In R. B. Ray (Ed.), *Learning factors in substance abuse* (pp. 161–179). Washington, DC: U.S. Department of Health and Human Services.

Meehl, P., & Golden, R. (1982). Taxometric methods. In P. Kendall & J. Butcher (Eds.), *Handbook of research methods in clinical psychology* (pp. 127–181). New York: John Wiley.

Meehl, P., & Yonce, L. (1994). Taxometric analysis: Detecting taxonicity with two quantitative indicators using means above and below a sliding cut (MAMBAC procedure). *Psychological Reports, 74,* 1059–1274.

Miles, F. J., Everitt, B. J., Dally, J. D., & Dickinson, A. (2004). Conditioned activity and instrumental reinforcement following long-term oral consumption of cocaine by rats. *Behavioral Neuroscience, 118,* 1331–1339.

Miles, F. J., Everitt, B. J., & Dickinson, A. (2003). Oral Cocaine Seeking by Rats: Action or Habit? *Behavioral Neuroscience, 117,* 927–938.

Moors, A. & De Houwer, J. (2006). Automaticity: A Theoretical and Conceptual Analysis. *Psychological Bulletin, 132,* 297–326.

Orleans, C. T., Rimer, B. K., Cristinzio, S. Keintz, M. K., & Fleisher, L. (1991). A national survey of older smokers: Treatment needs for a growing population. *Health Psychology, 10,* 343–351.

Parrott, A. C. (1999). Paradoxical tranquilizing and emotion-reducing effects of nicotine. *Psychological Bulletin, 86,* 643–661.

Payne, T. J., Smith, P. O., Sturges, L. V., & Holleran, S. A. (1996). Reactivity to smoking cues: mediating roles of nicotine dependence and duration of deprivation. *Addictive Behaviors, 21,* 139–154.

Perkins, K. A. & Grobe, J. E. (1992). Increased desire to smoke during acute stress. *British Journal of Addiction, 87,* 1037–1040.

Pomerleau, O. F. & Pomerleau, C. S. (1990). Biobehavioral studies in humans: Anxiety, stress, and smoking. In Bock, G. & Marsh, J. (Eds.), The biology of nicotine dependence (CIBA Foundation Symposium No. 152, pp. 225–239). Chichester: John Wiley & Sons Ltd.

Powell, J., Dawkins, L., & Davis, R. E. (2002). Smoking, reward responsiveness, and response inhibition: tests of an incentive motivational model. *Biological Psychiatry, 51,* 151–163.

Resnicow, K., Smith, M., Harrison, L., & Drucker, E. (1999). Correlates of occasional cigarette and marijuana use: Are teens harm reducing? *Addictive Behaviors, 24,* 251–266.

Richter, K. P., McCool, R. M., Okuyemi, K. S., Mayo, M. S., & Ahluwalia, J. S. (2002). Patients views on smoking cessation and tobacco harm reduction during drug treatment. *Nicotine & Tobacco Research, 4,* S175-S182.

Robinson, T. E. & Berridge, K. C. (1993). The neural basis of drug craving: An incentive-sensitization theory of addiction. *Brain Research. Brain Research Reviews, 18,* 247–291.

Ruscio, J., Haslam, N., & Ruscio, A. M. (2006). *Introduction to the taxometric method.* Hillsdale, NJ: Lawrence Erlbaum Associates.

Sayette, M. A., & Hufford, M. R. (1994). Effects of cue exposure and deprivation on cognitive resources in smokers. *Journal of Abnormal Psychology, 103,* 812–818.

Sayette, M. A., Martin, C. S., Wertz, J. M., Perrott, M. A., & Peters, A. R. (2005). The effects of alcohol on cigarette craving in heavy smokers and tobacco chippers. *Psychology of Addictive Behaviors, 19,* 263–270.

Sayette, M. A., Shiffman, S., Tiffany, S. T., Niaura, R. S., Martin, C. S., Shadel, W. G. (2000). The measurement of drug craving. *Addiction, 95,* S189–S210.

Sayette, M. A., Wertz, J. M., Martin, C. S., Cohn, J. F., Perrott, M. A., & Hobel, J. (2003). Effects of smoking opportunity on cue-elicited urge: a facial coding analysis. *Experimental and Clinical Psychopharmacology, 11,* 218–227.

Scheidt, R. J., (1981). Ecologically-Valid Inquiry: Fait Accompli? *Human Development, 24,* 225–228.

Schuh, K. J. & Stitzer, M. L. (1995). Desire to smoke during spaced smoking intervals. *Psychopharmacology, 120,* 289–295.

Seidman, D. F. & Covey, L. S. (1999). *Helping the hard-core smoker: A clinician's guide.* Mahway, NJ: Erlbaum.

Sher, K. J., Gotham, H. J., Erickson, D. J., & Wood, P. K. (1996). A prospective, high-risk study of the relationship between tobacco dependence and alcohol use disorders. *Alcoholism: Clinical & Experimental Research, 20,* 485–492.

Shiffman, S., Gwaltney, C. J., Balabanis, M. H., Liu, D. S., Paty, J. A., Kassel, J. D. et al. (2002). Immediate antecedents of cigarette smoking: An analysis from ecological momentary assessment. *Journal of Abnormal Psychology, 111,* 531–545.

Shiffman, S, Engberg, J. B., Paty, J. A., Perz, W. G., Gnys, M., Kassel, J. D., et al. (1997). A day at a time: Predicting smoking lapse from daily urge. *Journal of Abnormal Psychology, 106,* 104–116.

Shiffman, S., Fischer, L., Paty, J., Gnys, M., Hickcox, M., & Kassel, J. (1994). Drinking and smoking: A field study of their association. *Annals of Behavioral Medicine, 16,* 203–209.

Shiffman, S. & Jarvik, M. E. (1976). Smoking withdrawal symptoms in two weeks of abstinence. *Psychopharmacology, 50,* 35–39.

Shiffman, S., Waters, A., & Hickcox, M. (2004.) The Nicotine Dependence Syndrome Scale: A multidimensional measure of nicotine dependence. *Nicotine & Tobacco Research, 6,* 327–348.

Singleton, E. G., Tiffany, S. T., & Henningfield, J. E. (1994, July). Development and validation of a new questionnaire to assess craving for alcohol. Paper presented at the 56th Annual Scientific Meeting, College on Problems in Drug Dependence, Palm Beach, FL.

Sinha, R., Catapano, D., & O'Malley, S. (1999). Stress-induced craving and stress response in cocaine individuals. *Psychopharmacology, 142,* 343–351.

Sinha, R., Fuse, T., & Aubin, L. R. (2000). Psychological stress, drug-related cues and cocaine craving. *Psychopharmacology, 152,* 140–148.

Sinha, R., Talih, M., Malison, R., Cooney, N., Anderson, G. M., & Kreek, M. J. (2003). Hypothalamic-pituitary-adrenal axis and sympatho-adreno-medullary responses during stress-induced and drug cue-induced cocaine craving states. *Psychopharmacology, 170,* 62–72

Stone, A. A., & Shiffman, S. (2002). Capturing momentary, self-report data: A proposal for reporting guidelines. *Annals of Behavioral Medicine, 24,* 236–243.

Sutherland, I., & Willner, P. (1998). Patterns of alcohol, cigarette and illicit drug use in English adolescents. *Addiction, 93,* 119–1208.

Teneggi, V., Tiffany, S. T., Squassante, L., Milleri, S., Luigi, Z., & Bye, A. (2002) Smokers deprived of cigarettes for 72 hours: Effect of nicotine patches on craving and withdrawal. *Psychopharmacology, 164,* 177–187.

Teneggi, V., Tiffany, S. T., Squassante, L., Milleri, S., Ziviani, L., & Bye, A. (2005). Effect of sustained-release (SR) bupropion on craving and withdrawal in smokers deprived of cigarettes for 72 h. *Psychopharmacology, 183,* 1–12.

Tiffany, S. T. (1990). A cognitive model of drug urges and drug use behavior: Role of automatic and nonautomatic processes. *Psychological Review, 97,* 147–168.

Tiffany, S. T. (1992). A critique of contemporary urge and craving research: Methodological, psychometric, and theoretical issues. *Advances in Behaviour Research and Therapy, 14,* 123–139.

Tiffany, S. T. (1997). New perspectives on the measurement, manipulation and meaning of drug craving. *Human Psychopharmacology: Clinical and Experimental, 12,* S103–S113.

Tiffany, S. T. (2003, December). Drug craving: What can we learn from rats? Paper presented at the annual meeting of the American College of Neuropsychopharmacology. San Juan, Puerto Rico.

Tiffany, S. T., Agnew, C., Maylath, N., Dierker, L., Flaherty, B. Richardson, E., Balster, R., Segress, M. H., Clayton, R., & and the Tobacco Etiology Research Network (TERN). (2007) The University Project of the Tobacco Etiology Research Network (UpTERN). *Nicotine & Tobacco Research, 9,* S611–S625.

Tiffany, S. T. & Baker, T. B. (1988). The role of aversion and counseling strategies in treatments for cigarette smoking. In T. B. Baker & D. S. Cannon (Eds.), *Assessment and treatment of addictive disorders* (pp. 238–289). New York: Praeger.

Tiffany, S. T., & Carter, B. L. (1998). Is craving the source of compulsive drug use? *Journal of Psychopharmacology, 12,* 23–30.

Tiffany, S. T., & Conklin, C. A. (2000). A cognitive processing model of alcohol craving and compulsive alcohol use. *Addiction, 95,* S145–S153.

Tiffany, S. T., Conklin, C. A., Shiffman, S., & Clayton, R. R. (2004). What can dependence theories tell us about assessing the emergence of tobacco dependence? *Addiction, 99,* S78–S86.

Tiffany, S. T., Cox, L. S., & Elash, C. A. (2000). Effects of transdermal nicotine patches on abstinence-induced and cue-elicited craving in cigarette smokers. *Journal of Consulting and Clinical Psychology, 68,* 233–240.

Tiffany, S. T., & Drobes, D. J. (1990). Imagery and Smoking Urges: The manipulation of affective content. *Addictive Behaviors, 15,* 531–539.

Tiffany, S. T., & Drobes, D. J. (1991). The development and initial validation of a questionnaire on smoking urges. *British Journal of Addiction, 86,* 1467–1476.

Tiffany, S. T., Fields, L., Singleton, E., Haertzen, C., & Henningfield, J. E. (1995). *The development of a heroin craving questionnaire.* Unpublished manuscript.

Tiffany, S. T., Goedecker, K. A., & Bailey, S. *Does cue-reactivity predict relapse? A laboratory-based evaluation.* Manuscript submitted for publication.

Tiffany, S. T., & Hakenewerth, D. M. (1991). The production of smoking urges through an imagery manipulation: Psychophysiological and verbal manifestations. *Addictive Behaviors, 16,* 389–400.

Tiffany, S. T., Singleton, E., Haertzen, C. & Henningfield, J. E. (1993). The development of a cocaine craving questionnaire. *Drug and Alcohol Dependence, 34,* 19–28.

Tucker, J. S., Ellickson, P. L., & Klein, D. J. (2002). Five-year prospective study of risk factors for daily smoking in adolescence among early nonsmokers and experimenters. *Journal of Applied Social Psychology, 32,* 1588–1603.

U.S. Department of Health and Human Services, Substance Abuse and Mental Health Services Administration (2006). Office of Applied Studies. NATIONAL SURVEY ON DRUG USE AND HEALTH, 2005 [Computer file]. ICPSR04596-v1. Research Triangle Park, NC: Research Triangle Institute [producer]. Ann Arbor, MI: Inter-university Consortium for Political and Social Research [distributor], 2006-11-16.

Waller, N., & Meehl, P. (1998). *Multivariate taxometric procedures: Distinguishing types from continua.* Thousand Oaks, CA: Sage.

Weiss, F. (2005). Neurobiology of craving, conditioned reward and relapse. *Current Opinion in Pharmacology, 5,* 9–19.

Werner, M. J., Walker, L. S., & Greene, J. W. (1996). Concurrent and prospective screening for problem drinking among college students. *Journal of Adolescent Health, 18,* 276–285.

West, R., Hajek, P., & Belcher, M. (1989). Time course of cigarette withdrawal symptoms while using nicotine gum. *Psychopharmacology, 99,* 143–145.

Willner, P., Hardman, S., & Eaton, G. (1995). Subjective and behavioral evaluation of cigarette cravings. *Psychopharmacology, 118,* 171–177.

Willner, P. & Jones, C. (1996). Effects of mood manipulation on subjective and behavioural measures of cigarette craving. *Behavioural Pharmacology, 7,* 355–363.

Wise, R. A. (1988). The neurobiology of craving: Implications for understanding and treatment of addiction. *Journal of Abnormal Psychology, 97,* 118–132.

Who Expert Committees on Mental Health and on Alcohol, (1955). The 'craving' for alcohol. *Quarterly Journal of Studies on Alcohol, 16,* 33–66.

World Health Organization (1992). *The ICD-10 classification of mental and behavioural disorders.* Geneva: Author.

Chapter 11
The Motivational Impact of Nicotine and Its Role in Tobacco Use: Final Comments and Priorities

Michael T. Bardo and Paul Schnur

Minimizing the incidence of tobacco use requires a broad spectrum approach across the lifespan. For adolescents who are at risk for initiation, changes in public policy in the United States have reduced access to cigarettes, and school-based prevention programs have been implemented with some success (Nabors, Iobst, & McGrady, 2007). Mass media campaigns targeting youth at risk have also shown some efficacy (Emery et al., 2005), although this may not generalize to televised campaigns that are sponsored specifically by tobacco companies (Wakefield et al., 2006). When prevention efforts fail and tobacco use ensues, intervention strategies tend to shift from universal campaigns that reach the general population to more intense behavioral and pharmacological interventions that target selected groups or individuals. Although there has been an increasing emphasis on tobacco cessation programs that target youths in school (Curry et al., 2007), the quit rate among youths is low. As a result, tobacco use often escalates into a pattern that may be characterized as dependent use, coupled with a high rate of relapse upon each quit attempt. Understanding the neurobehavioral motivational systems involved in tobacco use and dependence, which is the subject of this book, is important for improving treatment strategies. In this last chapter, we present a few final comments for emphasis and provide a perspective from the National Institutes of Health (NIH) for future research.

Some Final Comments

As a whole, the combination of chapters in this book highlights the multi-faceted nature of the work being conducted on the motivational aspects of tobacco use. The concepts and mechanisms covered range from molar to molecular, from "craving" to cyclic AMP responsive element binding protein (CREB). While there is little doubt that a multi-pronged approach to the problem of tobacco use will advance the field at a brisk pace, the ultimate answers from a health perspective rest at the level of human trials. Three chapters from this book concentrated on some of

M.T. Bardo
Department of Psychology, University of Kentucky, Lexington, KY 40536-0509 USA
e-mail: mbardo@uky.edu

R.A. Bevins, A.R. Caggiula (eds.), *The Motivational Impact of Nicotine and its Role in Tobacco Use*, DOI: 10.1007/978-0-387-78748-0_11, © Springer Science+Business Media, LLC 2009

the most relevant issues regarding tobacco smoking behavior in humans (Perkins, 2007; Rose, 2007; Tiffany, Warthen, & Goedeker, 2007). In the Perkins chapter, a strong case is made for sex differences in smoking cessation, with females being generally less responsive than males to nicotine replacement, which has obvious implications in treatment. However, since studies with laboratory animals indicate that female hormones tend to enhance, rather than blunt, the psychoactive effects of nicotine (Chaudhri et al., 2005; Faraday, Blakeman, & Grunberg, 2005; Harrod et al., 2004), it is possible that sex differences observed in humans may be associated more with socio-psychological factors than with neurohormonal status. The work of Perkins suggests that conditioning cues may be especially important, and the chapter by Tiffany and colleagues provides ample support for this notion. Given the role of environment cues, which are both discrete (e.g., image of a lit cigarette) and contextual (e.g., familiar tavern), the efficacy of various treatment strategies in blunting the impact of these cues needs direct experimental investigation. In the chapter by Rose, a comprehensive coverage of currently available pharmaco- and immunotherapies shows that multiple strategies can be effective in reducing the reinforcing effect of nicotine and tobacco use. However, since environmental cues may be critical triggers for relapse among smokers attempting to quit, a major challenge will be to determine to what extent these therapies, as well as future therapies, blunt the impact of smoking-related cues independent of nicotine. Indeed, since some conditioned responses to nicotine may involve neurobehavioral mechanisms independent from the unconditioned effects of nicotine (Forget, Hamon, & Thiébot, 2005; Papp, Gruca, & Willner, 2002), it might be useful to develop alternate therapies that specifically target the conditioning processes underlying tobacco use and relapse.

The importance of factors other than the direct primary and secondary reinforcing effects of nicotine in controlling the motivation to use tobacco is further highlighted in the chapters by Caggiula et al., (2007), Markou and Paterson (2007), and Bevins (2007). Caggiula's work points to a reward-enhancing effect of nicotine that is independent of its conditioned reinforcing effect. In essence, the notion is that nicotine is able to enhance the positive incentive value of environmental reinforcers. This is an important point that requires further investigation to determine to what extent it is specific to nicotine or generalized to other drugs of abuse within the stimulant class (e.g., cocaine, amphetamine), as well as outside the stimulant class (e.g., morphine, diazepam). The chapter by Markou and Paterson also stresses the importance of factors beyond the primary and secondary reinforcing effects of nicotine, specifically providing evidence that the cognitive enhancing effect of nicotine and the avoidance of negative withdrawal symptoms contribute to the motivational aspects of tobacco use. In the chapter by Bevins, the role of nicotine as a conditioned stimulus and occasion setter in a Pavlovian preparation is also outlined, adding further to the complex interplay of the various roles that nicotine may serve in controlling motivated behavior. However, since much of this work has been limited to the preclinical level, it will be important to determine to what extent these various conditioning factors are applicable to human smokers.

Regarding the molecular level of analysis, the remaining chapters by Brunzell and Picciotto (2007), Placzek and Dani (2007) and Dwoskin et al., (2007) represent some novel approaches for understanding the critical cellular targets that may inform novel medication development. The fact that three chapters are dedicated to molecular/neurochemical levels of analysis probably represents an accurate reflection of the general enthusiasm for this type of analysis for enhancing biomedical treatments for tobacco dependence. The chapter by Placzek and Dani characterizes the complex interplay of various neurotransmitter systems, including both monoamines and excitatory amino acids, in controlling reward-relevant midbrain dopamine systems. The chapters by Brunzell and Picciotto and by Dwoskin and colleagues present the most updated nomenclature for the nicotinic cholinergic receptor subtypes, implicating an important role for high affinity β2-containing receptors and their associated intracellular signaling cascades in the addiction process. Inhibition of the reward-relevant binding sites, as well as inhibition of the ion channel and/or the intracellular signaling cascades involved in synaptic plasticity, may all represent therapeutic targets for future research.

Future Priorities: The NIH Perspective

The NIH, and the National Institute on Drug Abuse (NIDA) in particular, has a long-standing commitment to research aimed at understanding nicotine addiction and in developing a variety of behavioral and pharmacological approaches to its amelioration. Indeed, NIDA has been at the forefront of efforts to recognize and publicize the addictive nature of nicotine. Research support has been provided for investigations of the direct effects of voluntary nicotine exposure (i.e., self-administration), as well as for studies of the consequences of involuntary exposure (gestational/prenatal).

NIDA supports a wide range of basic and clinical research; for example, the mechanisms of nicotine reward, the effects of nicotine on brain structure and function, the genetic, social and environmental antecedents of vulnerability to addiction, and the consequences of direct and indirect exposure to nicotine. Across all of these areas, NIDA supports research investigating the effects of sex or gender, and age or developmental stage. NIDA encourages research at multiple levels of analysis (from cells to social groups) and recognizes the value in a diversity of research paradigms and techniques. The extent of NIDA's interest in nicotine research is too broad to cover here, but some of NIDA's continuing and future research priorities for nicotine addiction are outlined below.

Long-Term Surveys of Tobacco Use

NIDA tracks patterns of drug use, including tobacco use, among adolescents and other populations through support of long-term epidemiological studies, such as the Monitoring the Future (MTF) survey (http://www.monitoringthefuture.org/). The

MTF has conducted drug use surveys among 12th grade students since the mid-1970s and began including 8th and 10th graders in 1990. In addition to monitoring drug use patterns, data from the MTF allow the identification of emerging trends that can guide the development of responsive prevention efforts.

Genetics/Epigenetics

Genetics clearly contribute to an individual's vulnerability to nicotine addiction (e.g., Mineur & Picciotto, 2007). Moreover, epigenetic research is beginning to identify environmental influences on gene expression that contribute to addiction vulnerability. Two efforts that demonstrate NIDA's commitment to understanding the genetic and epigenetic underpinnings of nicotine addiction are the Perlegen polymorphism contract and the NIDA Center for Genetics Studies. The Perlegen polymorphism contract supports a high throughput genome-wide search for single nucleotide polymorphisms (SNPs) that differentiate between individuals who are nicotine-dependent and those who smoked but never became dependent. The NIDA Center for Genetic Studies (http://zork.wustl.edu/nida/) is a resource that stores clinical data, diagnostic data, pedigree information, and biomaterials (including DNA, plasma, cryopreserved lymphocytes, and/or cell lines) from human subjects participating in studies from NIDA-supported Principal Investigators that form the NIDA Genetics Consortium (NGC). NGC data and resources can be made available to qualified investigators.

Nicotine Vaccine

As mentioned in the chapter by Rose (2007), the possibility of immunizing an individual against a specific drug, such as nicotine, relies on employing the body's own immune system to sequester nicotine molecules in the bloodstream, so as to prevent them from ever entering or affecting the brain. In 2000, NIDA embraced this concept and decided to support and guide a major nicotine vaccine effort in collaboration with Nabi, a Florida-based pharmaceutical company. Studies on NicVAX®, the nicotine conjugate vaccine that resulted from this joint research endeavor, show it to be safe and capable of generating antibodies that block nicotine's entry into the brain (Hatsukami et al. 2005). An effective nicotine vaccine would be an important addition to currently available treatment options, particularly as a treatment option to prevent relapse following abstinence, and would improve the likelihood of reducing adult tobacco use.

Drug Exposure and Development

The relationship between drug exposure and development is complex and wide-ranging. Of particular interest are the neurobiological and behavioral consequences of drug exposure during the in utero, perinatal, and adolescent periods. As a result of NIDA supported research, we are beginning to understand how genetic variability, learning, social influence, environmental cues, and neurobiological changes/adaptations, affect vulnerability and co-morbidity throughout development. We are using this knowledge to shape prevention and treatment strategies.

Co-morbidity

It is widely recognized that nicotine addiction is often found in association with addiction to alcohol and other drugs. Addiction to nicotine is also highly associated with several mental disorders, including schizophrenia and depression (e.g., Williams & Ziedonis, 2004). Since co-occurrence of smoking and mental disorders is an area that overlaps the missions of multiple NIH Institutes, NIDA works with the National Institute on Mental Health (NIMH) and the National Institute on Alcohol Abuse and Alcoholism (NIAAA) to promote research that investigates common neural substrates, genetic variability, and other factors that will allow a more complete understanding of these co-morbid disorders. By understanding the interaction among the host of important social, environmental, genetic, and biological factors, it is hoped that effective, tailored interventions may be developed for this complex population of smokers.

Neurobiological Substrates of Behavior

An area of continuing high priority for NIDA is to understand the neurobiological mechanisms of nicotine addiction. NIDA's support of basic research into the neurobiological substrates of behavior includes: (1) studies relating drugs of abuse to neural systems; (2) behavioral consequences of receptor subtype activation/inactivation; (3) function of endogenous systems (e.g., endorphins, anandamide, excitatory amino acids, etc., in health and disease); (4) neural mechanisms of drug-induced modification of cognitive processes (e.g., learning, memory, attention, associations, decision making); (5) models of addiction, including neural circuits underlying natural and drug reward, biobehavioral models of craving, relapse, compulsive behavior, and extinction; and (6) behavioral, physiological, or biochemical consequences of acute or chronic exposure to addictive drugs.

National Cooperative Drug Discovery Group (NCDDG)

Over the past decade or so, there have been major advances in our understanding of the protein targets, neural circuitry, and behavioral phenomena associated with addiction, and in the effects of drugs of abuse on CNS processes associated with addictive behavior; some of these advances have been covered in the chapters by Brunzell and Picciotto (2007), Placzek and Dani (2007) and Dwoskin et al., (2007).

The NCDDG is a ligand discovery and translational initiative in which the objective is the development of molecules with a particular profile of action as prototypes for medications to treat addiction or serve as tools to advance research in the treatment development domain. Components of NIDA-relevant NCDDG research projects can include, but are not limited to: (1) assessment of the behavioral profile of novel ligands in tests of reinforcement, relapse, and withdrawal; (2) tests of the ability of novel ligands to modulate cellular processes of plasticity in reward-relevant regions of the brain; (3) assessment of ligand efficacy on G-protein coupled receptors and ligand-gated ion channel activation; and (4) receptor activation effects on down-stream intracellular systems or in modulating the release of addiction-relevant neurotransmitters.

Finally, it should be mentioned that the highlights of NIDA's efforts and emerging priorities are regularly updated on www.smoking.drugabuse.gov. Information on Funding Opportunity Announcements (FOAs) in which NIDA participates can be found at: http://www.nida.nih.gov/funding/. Importantly, however, NIDA also depends upon extramural scientists to help shape the research agenda through regular communication at scientific meetings and symposia, as exemplified by the Nebraska Symposium on Motivation.

Acknowledgment The authors would like to thank Dr. Allison Chausmer for her contribution to the writing of this chapter. MTB supported by USPHS grant U19 DA17548.

References

Bevins, R. A. (2007). Altering the motivational function of nicotine through conditioning processes. In: R. A. Bevins and A. R. Caggiula (Eds.), *55th annual Nebraska symposium on motivation: The motivational impact of nicotine and its role in tobacco use* (pp. xx-xx). Lincoln NE: University of Nebraska Press.

Brunzell, D. H., & Picciotto, M. R. (2007). Molecular mechanisms underlying the motivational effects of nicotine. In: R. A. Bevins and A. R. Caggiula (Eds.), *55th annual Nebraska symposium on motivation: The motivational impact of nicotine and its role in tobacco use* (pp. xx-xx). Lincoln NE: University of Nebraska Press.

Caggiula, A. R., Donny, E. C., Palmatier, M. I., Liu, X., Chaudhri, N., & Sved, A. F. (2007). The role of nicotine in smoking: A dual-reinforcement model. In: R. A. Bevins and A. R. Caggiula (Eds.), *55th annual Nebraska symposium on motivation: The motivational impact of nicotine and its role in tobacco use* (pp. xx-xx). Lincoln NE: University of Nebraska Press.

Chaudhri, N., Caggiula, A. R., Donny, E. C., Booth, S., Gharib, M. A., & Craven, L. A., et al. (2005). Sex differences in the contribution of nicotine and nonpharmacological stimuli to nicotine self-administration in rats. *Psychopharmacology, 180*, 258–266.

Curry, S. J., Emery, S., Sporer, A. K., Mermelstein, R., Flay, B. R., Berbaum, M., et al. (2007). A national survey of tobacco cessation programs for youths. *American Journal of Public Health, 97*, 171–177.

Dwoskin, L. P., Pivavarchyk, M., Joyce, B. M., Neugebauer, N. M., Zheng, G., Zhang, Z., et al. (2007). Targeting reward-relevant nicotinic receptors in the discovery of novel pharmacotherapeutic agents to treat tobacco dependence. In: R. A. Bevins and A. R. Caggiula (Eds.), *55th annual Nebraska symposium on motivation: The motivational impact of nicotine and its role in tobacco use* (pp. xx-xx). Lincoln NE: University of Nebraska Press.

Emery, S., Wakefield, M. A., Terry- McElrath, Y., Saffer, H., Szczypka, G., O'Malley, P. M., et al. (2005). Televised state-sponsored antitobacco advertising and youth smoking beliefs and behavior in the United States, 1999–2000. *Archives of Pediatrics & Adolescent Medicine, 159*, 685–687.

Faraday, M. M., Blakeman, K. H., & Grunberg, N. E. (2005). Strain and sex alter effects of stress and nicotine on feeding, body weight, and HPA axis hormones. *Pharmacology, Biochemistry & Behavior, 80*, 577–589.

Forget, B., Hamon, M., & Thiébot, M. H. (2005). Cannabinoid CB1 receptors are involved in motivational effects of nicotine in rats. *Psychopharmacology, 181*, 722–734.

Harrod, S. B., Mactutus, Bennett, K., Hasselrot, U., Wu, G., Welch, M., et al. (2004). Sex differences and repeated intravenous nicotine: Behavioral sensitization and dopamine receptors. *Pharmacology, Biochemistry & Behavior, 78*, 581–592.

Hatsukami, D. K., Rennard, S., Jorenby, D., Fiore, M., Koopmeiners, J., de Vos, A., et al. (2005). Safety and immunogenicity of a nicotine conjugate vaccine in current smokers. *Clinical Pharmacology & Therapeutics, 78*, 456–467.

Markou, A., & Paterson, N. E. (2007). Multiple motivational forces contribute to nicotine dependence. In: R. A. Bevins and A. R. Caggiula (Eds.), *55th annual Nebraska symposium on motivation: The motivational impact of nicotine and its role in tobacco use* (pp. xx-xx). Lincoln NE: University of Nebraska Press.

Mineur, Y. S., & Picciotto, M. R. (2008). Genetics of nicotinic acetylcholine receptors: relevance to nicotine addiction. *Biochemical Pharmacology, 75*, 323–333.

Nabors, L., Iobst, E. A., & McGrady, M. E. (2007). Evaluation of school-based smoking prevention programs. *Journal of School Health, 77*, 331–333.

Papp, M., Gruca, P., & Willner, P. (2002). Selective blockade of drug-induced place preference conditioning by ACPC, a functional NDMA-receptor antagonist. *Neuropsychopharmacology, 27*, 727–743.

Perkins, K. A. (2007). Sex differences in nicotine reinforcement and reward: Influences on the persistence of tobacco smoking. In: R. A. Bevins and A. R. Caggiula (Eds.), *55th annual Nebraska symposium on motivation: The motivational impact of nicotine and its role in tobacco use* (pp. xx-xx). Lincoln NE: University of Nebraska Press.

Placzek, A. N., & Dani, J. A. (2007). Synaptic plasticity within midbrain dopamine centers contributes to nicotine addiction. In: R. A. Bevins and A. R. Caggiula (Eds.), *55th annual Nebraska symposium on motivation: The motivational impact of nicotine and its role in tobacco use* (pp. xx-xx). Lincoln NE: University of Nebraska Press.

Rose, J. E. (2007). New findings on nicotine addiction and treatment. In: R. A. Bevins and A. R. Caggiula (Eds.), *55th annual Nebraska symposium on motivation: The motivational impact of nicotine and its role in tobacco use* (pp. xx-xx). Lincoln NE: University of Nebraska Press.

Tiffany, S. T., Warthen, M. W., & Goedeker, K. C. (2007). The functional significance of craving in nicotine dependence. In: R. A. Bevins and A. R. Caggiula (Eds.), *55th annual Nebraska symposium on motivation: The motivational impact of nicotine and its role in tobacco use* (pp. xx-xx). Lincoln NE: University of Nebraska Press.

Wakefield, M., Terry-McElrath, Y., Emery, S., Saffer, H., Chaloupka, F. J., Szczypka, G., et al. (2006). Effect of televised, tobacco company-funded smoking prevention advertising on youth smoking-related beliefs, intentions, and behavior. *American Journal of Public Health, 96*, 2154–2160.

Williams, J. M., & Ziedonis, D. (2004). Addressing tobacco among individuals with a mental illness or an addiction. *Addictive Behaviors, 29*, 1067–1083.

Index

Note: The letters *t* and *f* in the index locators refer to *tables* and *figures* respectively

LaVergne, TN USA
16 September 2009
158118LV00005B/80/P